ARC OF THE VALLEY

ANTON COMMISSARIS

Copyright © 2021 by Anton T. Commissaris

All rights reserved. No part of this book may be reproduced or used in any manner without written permission of the copyright owner except for the use of quotations in a book review.

"Writing a book is an adventure. To begin with, it is a toy and an amusement. Then it becomes a mistress, then it becomes a master, then it becomes a tyrant. The last phase is that just as you are about to be reconciled to your servitude, you kill the monster and fling him to the public."

WINSTON CHURCHILL

PART I

CHAPTER 1

FAILING FAST

*"Be brave. Take risks.
Nothing can substitute experience."*
PAULO COELHO

My alarm disrupted the quiet of a Menlo Park morning in March 2006, and I struggled out of bed. I'd promised to meet my friend and former coworker, Rob Claassen, for a round of dawn golf at the Palo Alto municipal course. I knew an invigorating morning was in store, but I didn't know that what awaited me would be a transformative moment in my life and ultimately in the financial and tech world's makeup.

I dressed, jumped in my car, turned on the radio, and headed off in the darkness. As I arrived and waited for Rob by the golf clubhouse, I could hear the faint hum of traffic from the 101 freeway as the valley stirred. A light airplane buzzed overhead with red lights flashing at the end of its wingtips. It turned and began its landing approach to the nearby Palo Alto airstrip at the edge of the San Francisco Bay's southern tip. Was the pilot some young daredevil entrepreneur taking early morning flight lessons? Perhaps a billionaire venture capitalist or tech titan company leader commuting to work in Palo Alto from his vineyard estate in Napa Valley? Anything was possible. I was in Silicon Valley.

The Valley was the twenty-first century's answer to Florence during the Renaissance. Since the dot-com collapse of 2000-2001, the Valley had solidified its position as the global center for creativity in technology and business. It attracted entrepreneurs from all over the world who incubated new companies, created new products and services, and invented new business models. The region's entrepreneurial infrastructure was second to none, with an extensive network of financial, legal, business, and other startup expertise to complement and fortify all the innovation flowing from creative technologists. Cutting-edge academic and research institutions nourished the Valley and delivered driven graduates into the region's workforce each year, including two of the nation's leading universities: the University of California at Berkeley in the northeast and Stanford University down south in Palo Alto.

Silicon Valley's competitive advantage was its creative edge. Entrepreneurs who gathered here were permitted to think differently, dream big, and engage in risk-laden innovation ventures like no other place in the world. If they failed, so be it. They could learn from that. Failure was the inevitable companion of the stupendous risk required for breakout success. And it was the rare breakout successes that paid for the pile of other failures, and then some.

Rob arrived, and we began our round as dawn broke. A few holes in, we came together on a long, flat par five to chat as we waited for the group in front of us to play out.

Rob and I first met in early 1996 as young attorneys at Wilson Sonsini Goodrich & Rosati, the powerhouse Silicon Valley law firm located in the Stanford Industrial Park on Page Mill Road in Palo Alto. I left after four years there at the end of 1999 to chase the Valley entrepreneurial dream. As a Valley lawyer, I felt more like a game umpire than a player—and I wanted to play. I was also burned out and in need of an escape from the drudgery of legal life. I wanted to join a hot startup working in business development. I didn't know where this path would lead, but wherever it did, it seemed like a better alternative to more decades of time-based billing for services. I had to bet on myself to make something from it. I risked failure in leaving my lucrative legal career behind, but that was the Valley way. If you want to play, you have to be ready to swing for the fences. You can quickly strikeout, fly out, or be thrown out, but you'll never win if you're not in the game.

Shortly after I handed in my notice at Wilson Sonsini, on the cusp of the year 2000, Jeff Saper stepped into an elevator behind me. Saper was one of the firm's longest-serving and prominent corporate partners, and he surely raked in millions during the Valley's boom. He'd heard I was leaving, and instead of wishing me luck, he couldn't resist a snide send-off: "Commissaris, most folks who leave the law end up coming back to it, you know. They find that it's not quite what they thought it was out there."

I'm sure what Saper said was true enough. "We'll see," I replied with a dry smile as the doors slid open to let us out. I was still riding an adrenaline high from the fact that I'd done it. I pulled the trigger and was walking away from life as a lawyer. I didn't think I'd be coming back.

But in just a few short years since I'd left Wilson Sonsini, the Valley had gone from boom to bust as the dot-com era went into meltdown in 2001. I'd moved on from my first consumer-focused startup to a new business-focused venture. I thought this would be a more stable environment to soft-land my recent career change amidst the market turbulence. My second company raised funding on the back of some early major enterprise wins that showed tremendous potential. But somehow, more wins didn't come quickly or consistently enough, and it became a struggle to achieve growth. We weren't winning, but we weren't failing either, and it still felt like the company might make it out of the woods. I'd been there for nearly four years before I met up with Rob that fateful early morning in March.

Rob, on the other hand, had stayed at Wilson Sonsini and was reaping the benefits. After sensibly resisting the temptation to join the flock of attorneys who left the firm for greener pastures, he was now a partner at the preeminent law firm in Silicon Valley.

"So, how's it going with your company?" Rob asked.

"You know," I said, "I think this year's going to be the turning point—there are some solid signs that we're finally on track."

Rob countered skeptically, "Hey Anton, you've been saying that for the last couple of years. What makes you think it's any different at this point?"

I didn't have an answer for him, and I was puzzled by his skepticism and lack of encouragement. I might have expected more sympathy from a good friend. But a beautiful day was dawning, and the group ahead of us moved off the green. I left that skepticism behind me as we played our next shots and finished our round without any further mention of work. After a quick clubhouse breakfast, we parted ways to show up to work at a decent hour.

As the following days turned to weeks, Rob's words sank in. Had I left the lucrative legal profession to end up in a pool of startup mediocrity and career complacency? I'd endured and somehow survived the dot-com meltdown of the early 2000s, and I worked hard to stabilize my career transition. I was not about to admit that Jeff Saper was right—not yet. And Rob was still a lawyer, whereas I'd been out for a few years with real-world startup experience under my belt. I now realized that working in the legal profession was starkly different from working in a startup. Lawyers advise startups on ways to navigate Silicon Valley with a view towards regulatory compliance and deal transactions without ever understanding what it takes to build and grow a company from scratch. Only someone who's worked in a startup could appreciate the challenges of what goes on in the trenches. It was easy for him to say.

But it gnawed at me that he might be right. I thought about the Valley around me. We were living against a backdrop of massive opportunity and unprecedented success in the second wave of the internet economy, which came to be known as web 2.0. I interpreted the 2.0 moniker as both a reference to the revival of the internet economy and a more participatory and social web. The new era of websites emphasized user-generated content and interoperability (with other products, systems, and devices) for end-users. Two years earlier, Google—in only six years since its inception—had gone public and exploded toward a $27 billion valuation. Facebook, MySpace, YouTube, and many other web 2.0 companies emerged to stake their claims to a slice of the global internet pie. In 2005, News Corporation acquired MySpace for $580 million. In October 2006, not long after Rob delivered his sobering statement to me, Google would buy YouTube for $1.65 billion. The tech world had never seen anything of that magnitude so quickly—not even in the first dot-com boom. An internet renaissance was happening.

The surrounding success was intoxicating. The Valley mantra of "go big or go home" or "if you're going to fail, then fail fast" was confronting me. The reality was that my current company was mediocre, and the Valley is a place where that just doesn't cut it. In the early days, we won a couple of significant deals with US military contractors. We then raised a Series A investment of $5 million from Sequoia Capital, one of the Valley's most prestigious venture capital firms. They've successfully backed Apple, Oracle, PayPal, Google, YouTube, Instagram, and Stripe, among others, and created more than a trillion dollars in public market value. Yet, bringing in money from Sequoia does not guarantee success. The company must execute. And in four years, our company hadn't.

In Silicon Valley, where so much achievement is rapid, the value of time gets accentuated. The disruption of multi-billion dollar global companies and sometimes entire industries can happen in just a few short years. Someone once told me that "a day is a long time in the life of a startup," which rang true. The best startups led by the best founders leave no room for complacency. They maximize every available minute to find ways to march forward faster and relentlessly. The entire team must dedicate itself to generating results with a sense of perpetual urgency to achieve success against the odds. The company's survival is on the line day in and day out.

In this atmosphere, so much hard work, emotional energy, and time are sacrificed and poured into a company while knowing it might eventually die and pay zero dividends. There are no guarantees of success in life, but in the world of startups, it's odd to think that so many ventures launch when they're mostly guaranteed to fail. The constant question becomes, "Is this company on the verge of breaking out, or is it a waste of time?" It's a classic dilemma, particularly for founding team members who are emotionally and financially invested in the outcome. Often, one can point to milestones as signals of pending success. That big deal we closed last quarter, the new rockstar vice president of marketing we just hired, the next software release our customers have been clamoring for that will change everything. It's a similar dilemma for the venture capitalists who have plowed new money into a once-promising but now struggling startup. Do we give them more money to keep the lights on, or are we just throwing good money after bad? It's emotionally exhausting to walk away from all the future potential and previous effort invested. After all, the Valley is rife with legendary success stories where the company snatches victory from the jaws of defeat. Looking back from the perch of success, a founder may recount how they laid off dozens of employees and faced not making payroll several times. Yet, somehow, through a mix of personal heroics and good fortune, that founder was able to pull the company back from the brink to find eventual success.

But if a startup can't achieve growth combined with continuous learning that leads to improvement every day, then it's stagnating. All that frenetic energy might only mean that it's going sideways, wasting time in a slow death march.

No one wants to be part of a zombie company that's ranked among Silicon Valley's walking dead. Rob was right. If I didn't shake things up, I'd be telling him the same story in another year. I was still on the sidelines. I didn't leave Wilson Sonsini for this, and I wasn't going back because of this.

Rob's skepticism was a wake-up call. I now saw my situation in the context of the success around me and the nature of Valley life. So after more than four years with my second startup company, I decided it was time to break away. The risk of staying seemed higher than the risk of leaving. I was not going to waste any more time. Not in Silicon Valley.

CHAPTER 2

OBJECTIVIST VALLEY

"Wealth is the product of man's capacity to think."

AYN RAND

I began to network and reached out to an acquaintance, Relik Pri-Noy, to meet for coffee.

Relik was a recent Israeli immigrant who found his way in the Valley through his formidable financial analysis skills and tapping into the Israeli entrepreneurial community.

Over coffee, Relik mentioned a young entrepreneur he'd recently met who was working on a service like Quicken, and Relik spoke well of it. Quicken was the leading personal finance software package from Intuit, a public company headquartered in Mountain View, just a handful of exits down the 101 freeway from where I lived in Menlo Park.

Relik was a skeptic by trade and a successful one at that. Yet, he was impressed by this entrepreneur and what he was building. This piqued my interest, and I asked Relik how he met him.

I knew Relik was a devoted follower of Ayn Rand's brand of objectivism, and I knew enough about it to know that Rand's work resonated with a particular libertarian-meets-laissez-faire-capitalist crowd in the Valley. Relik said it was through one of these gatherings that he and his wife met another young couple, Poornima Vijayashankar and Aaron Patzer.

One weekend, some of the people from the objectivist group went on a hike in Big Sur. Out on the trail, with the vast, rugged range of the Santa Lucia Mountains stretching out before them and the crashing waves of the deep blue Pacific coast below, Aaron and Relik fell into dialogue. When Aaron learned that Relik was a startup business consultant, he shared his plans for his startup. He explained in just a few words that he planned to build a new management system for private finances. It didn't sound like something Relik would need or that anyone would, for that matter. Relik decided he was going to shoot this idea down. However, he felt he should sit down with Aaron and let him explain his project. He was a fellow objectivist, and that was the least he could do. But he would need to be honest.

Aaron set up an appointment to come over to Relik's house to discuss his venture. It wasn't a formal meeting, but the business purpose was clear. Aaron would pitch his new company, and Relik would listen and provide objective business feedback.

A few days later, Aaron arrived at Relik's place and calmly began his pitch. His idea was to create a free web service that would automatically scrape your financial records and categorize them to help manage your finances. Relik asked a few questions by which he sought to confirm his initial suspicion that it was an ill-conceived idea. However, as Aaron answered the questions, Relik realized that the reasoning was gradually swaying him. Aaron's designs for the service were well conceived. There was an economic model to it: Mint would also analyze a user's spending to recommend credit cards and other financial products and services designed to save the user money. Mint would earn commissions from these savings offers from its financial partners and deliver a new customer to them in the process. Mint would only take a few minutes to set up, and after that, a user's finances would be on autopilot. The service would be so easy and beneficial to use that consumers, who generally struggled with their finances and hated dealing with them, would indeed use it.

Relik paused to consider some other successful digital businesses that obtained vast data sets through a service. For example, Facebook would know your friends, family, and likes, and Google would identify your interests and needs from your search queries. Now, here's this guy with a model where he's creating an incentive for people to expose their consumption behavior through a personal finance monitoring service, providing insight into where and how they spend their money and where they might save money. This was the "aha" moment for Relik. Aaron was going to get all this data because it solved a definite problem for the user, but he also had a specific way to monetize it.

Aaron had just come up with the name for the service. He called it "Mint."

Relik's first impression of Aaron was that he was an excellent objectivist. There was a strong hint of Howard Roark, Rand's protagonist in her *Fountainhead* novel, about Aaron. He seemed to be a brilliant, young, individualistic, and visionary web architect who was determined to use his highest thinking to design a new personal finance service without compromise. Aaron possessed an unswerving devotion to his thinking and judgment that seemed justified. Yes, there was a touch of naiveté about him because he was young, but he was authentic. Relik thought of Aaron as a functional introvert. He didn't go out of his way to engage others, but he could interact with people when it suited him. There was also an air of confidence and integrity about him. He had a degree from Duke University and so came with a particular pedigree. Relik imagined that Aaron came from a supportive family, and, together with an excellent education, he was confident in his ability to succeed. The product idea was a complete one, and he could be a strong leader for it.

Relik told Aaron of his intention to shoot his idea down, but now he was convinced he should go ahead with this company. Relik thought that, as a young engineer, Aaron would benefit from a more mature chief executive officer (CEO) as a business partner. As they discussed this, Aaron was quick to assert that he wanted to be the CEO.

In the end, Relik accepted that Aaron had the mind and character to pull it off despite his youth. Aaron would be wise to get the right people around him to add experience and expertise to his raw edges. Relik would help by tapping his network to connect Aaron with the right people. That's where I entered, and that's why I was now captivated by Relik's description of Aaron and his service.

"But what about Quicken?" I asked. "How is this guy's software different and better?" Relik responded with a technical answer that didn't quite register with me, but I could see how impressed he was nonetheless.

"Alright," I said, "why don't you introduce me to him? I can take a look at what he's got and give you my thoughts. Who knows, perhaps I can help him out."

Relik knew I had broad Silicon Valley experience working at Wilson Sonsini, helping numerous startups navigate the Valley's networks and best business practices to grow their ventures. I'd worked on a range of corporate securities deals, assisting companies with their formation, venture financings, mergers and acquisitions, and initial public offerings (IPOs). I'd also worked on sophisticated technology licensing transactions that were critical to the way companies both protected and monetized their intellectual property. Relik thought that this experience and my robust network might prove useful to Aaron and his venture. It was enough for Relik to be comfortable making the introduction to Aaron, which he agreed to do as we parted ways.

I was left to ponder about Ayn Rand and objectivism since I was about to meet Aaron, who identified with this movement. Perhaps therein lay some clues to assessing Aaron's entrepreneurial character. The Valley was home to men and women who thought they were like Howard Roark, who, driven by his genius, had a single-minded determination to follow a personal vision. They intended to remake the world as they saw it and damn the consequences.

Would Aaron be of the same mold?

CHAPTER 3

AARON PATZER

"Spring is the time of plans and projects."
LEO TOLSTOY

Relik introduced me to Aaron by email, and we agreed to meet at Cafe Borrone in Menlo Park, a hub of Valley activity near where I lived.

In the early morning, Cafe Borrone is a breakfast networking scene. Mostly men swoop in to grab a coffee and make connections. Deal dating occurs later in the morning when venture capitalists (VCs) coast in to meet with fundraising entrepreneurs. Older gentlemen, and sometimes ladies, in more business-casual attire, listen intently to much younger brethren dressed in street-casual clothing. Laptops and tablets flip open, and the conversation turns from small talk to a pitch as the young entrepreneurs demonstrate why their startup will be the next industry disruptor.

Silicon Valley is perhaps unique as a place where more senior and experienced professionals look to their younger brethren for advice on which way the world is about to turn. It may be because technology evolves so rapidly that only those who grew up with it natively can genuinely appreciate its breakthrough direction and value to society. These aspiring entrepreneurs are often unencumbered by not having borne witness to the history of failures in the sector of their choosing. They focus more on improving software and services to solve problems rather than on what might go wrong in trying to do so. The VC's job is to spot the smartest and most driven among the bunch and support them on the way to either riches or ruin.

On my way to Borrone to meet Aaron for the first time in May 2006, I called Relik to ask how I would recognize him. I knew he was a young, caucasian guy in his early twenties, but that's all. "He looks like a normal guy," Relik said. "Oh, and he's very muscular. He works out a lot."

For a brief moment, this seemed odd. It wasn't in keeping with the image I had in my mind of an engineering nerd. Then again, there was a particular cerebral type in the Valley that takes a quantitative approach to every aspect of their lives in pursuit of wholesale optimization. This spans from their body to their finances to their social life. It's part of the culture of peak performance—they're the body hackers. Sometimes, since they were nerds growing up, they overcompensate for this with unconscious peacocking in an obsessive pursuit of excellence, craving the respect they never had when younger.

I knew Aaron was from the Midwest, somewhere in Indiana. I imagined this would make him more down-to-earth than cocksure. My wife and her family also hailed from that part of the country, and I thought this was something I could use to break the ice.

These thoughts were still swirling in my head as I came up from the underground parking to approach the cafe. Aaron spotted me first and strode over to greet me. We shook hands, relieved that we had not mistaken each other for someone else. Then, I ordered a coffee, and he had tea. Since the day was pleasant and warm, we sat al fresco under a red umbrella next to a bubbling fountain. El Camino Real's traffic noise was low enough for us to talk comfortably, apart from the occasional distraction of a truck rumbling through the traffic lights.

Aaron was young and clean-cut. He had hazel eyes, clear skin, and light brown, short, wavy hair. Aaron dressed in worn blue jeans with a wrinkled blue and gray striped shirt loosely unbuttoned at the neck and with the sleeves rolled up. He wore oxford-style, brown, lace-up shoes. Aaron was understatedly handsome, polite, and articulate if a little on the reserved side.

As we sat to chat, I noticed that Aaron rested both elbows on his chair with his hands clasped together in front of him as he hunched forward slightly, and his neck craned. He projected attentiveness and investment. We chatted about the Midwest as I mentioned my wife was from Indianapolis. He was from Evansville, a smaller town in southern Indiana, with about 120,000 people.

We turned to discuss Mint. He told me it was personal finance software for consumers to understand and manage their money better. All well and good, but I got right to the elephant in the room: "What about Quicken?"

Aaron explained that Quicken was too challenging to use; he thought that good software should be simple to start using. Quicken was anything but simple. It required users to go through dozens of screens to set it up properly, and it was also hard work to maintain. But its biggest problem was the categorization of downloaded transactions from a consumer's various bank accounts to the program. Categorization determines the merchant's location and identity, the area of spending (e.g., groceries), and the amount spent. Categorization needs to be accurate to generate correct spending, budgeting, and other reports.

Aaron explained he'd consistently tracked his money weekly, but something happened to interrupt his schedule after getting his first real job after college. He was so busy at work that he fell behind on managing his finances for several weeks. When Aaron finally came up for air on his first free weekend, he sat down, opened his laptop, and used Quicken to download all the bank transactions from those past weeks. Aaron spent the rest of the afternoon manually fixing the categorization errors that appeared in more than half of the transactions.

Quicken's categorization foibles hadn't bothered Aaron previously as he'd manually fixed the errors without too much effort, provided he kept up his weekly Quicken maintenance. But now, it dawned on him that most consumers wouldn't be like him. Few people would maintain their finances every week. This meant they were likely to hit the wall of categorization errors when they tried to get started or stay up to date and would quickly give up on the software.

Aaron hadn't understood before how poorly Quicken managed this process. Quicken was not quick. It was painful.

Aaron developed a new categorization algorithm for the Mint service to solve this problem. It would mean that most bank transactions would come into Mint cleanly, and consumers would not have to spend time and effort to fix categorization errors. I asked him to explain categorization to be sure I understood it correctly. He summarized it as automatically assigning the correct merchant name to a transaction—for example, "Shell gas station." That one was obvious, but with millions of merchants large and small across the country, the capacity for error was tremendous.

The second part of categorization was understanding how consumers spent their money. It was likely gas at a Shell service station, but it could also be a magazine and drinks from the station mini-mart. For any given transaction, categorization correctly determined who the merchant was and how the money gets spent on various goods and services.

This is where Aaron leaned back and held his hands up as if gently holding a chalice. His palms faced each other as he slightly bent his index fingers at the middle knuckle with his other three fingers curled softly under. It was as if Aaron was holding something out for me to examine. "Good software should do the work for you, not the other way round," he said.

I hadn't heard this before. It resonated. I detected a philosophical approach in Aaron's thinking, and I was ready to hear more from him.

He explained that part of the problem with Quicken and Microsoft Money stemmed from the business model they used. Intuit and Microsoft were both selling packaged desktop software, primarily through retail channels. This was software that users downloaded and installed on the hard drive of their personal computer (PC) instead of accessing the software as a service over the internet. Their goal was to get customers to upgrade to a new and better version every two to three years. That's how they'd continue to monetize their users. But the only way anyone would upgrade was if there were a slew of new features they could promote that customers didn't want to miss out on. So it was that for years, Intuit and Microsoft added more features to get consumers to upgrade and to one-up each other. This feature creep meant the software became bloated over time with more functionality that fewer consumers ever used. The bloat also made it difficult to access the standard features that most consumers bought the software for in the first place.

As an on-again, off-again Quicken user over the years, this made sense to me. I bought the software and wasn't able to use it effectively. When Intuit came out with its next version, stacked full of new features, I purchased it again, thinking I might finally see improvements. I didn't. More features meant less ease of use.

Aaron then zeroed in on the core problem with traditional personal finance software: it was designed more for accountants than for consumers. Indeed, only a tiny percentage of the population appreciated the level of sophistication Quicken offered. This cohort of bean counters was obsessed with precise financial tracking and reporting. For the rest of us, this represented complexity and annoyance. We'd rather do something else—anything else. Aaron believed that most people only wanted to spend a few minutes on their finances each week and would only do it if the software was simple. He'd designed the software so your finances could just about run on autopilot.

He paused and then explained how Quicken and Microsoft Money didn't help *improve* your finances. You could get a good picture of what's going on with enough work, but what does one do with all those excellent reports, charts, and graphs? For the bean counters, perhaps it meant analytical satisfaction and sleep at night. For the rest of us, it meant little.

Mint would break new ground and focus on helping people find where they were overspending and then finding ways to save more money. These savings offers would be quantified in dollar amounts so that the user would know from a reasonably accurate estimate how much money they'd save with the new product or service. This calculation was made possible from the spending data and other financial information Mint maintained for that user. When the customer acted on a Mint savings offer and signed up for a new service, Mint would get paid an affiliate commission from the financial partner's customer acquisition marketing budget.

It was a triple-win system. Mint's customers saved money, Mint's financial partners acquired new customers, and Mint generated revenue to offer a free service. It was elegant. I was beginning to see Aaron as a genuine entrepreneur with an incredible capacity for service design. That made him part of a rare breed. Sure, the Valley was full of wunderkinds running around starting companies, but many focused on audience growth and personal chutzpah. There was little point talking to them about how they'd make money—that would come later, somehow. Having lived through the dot-com meltdown just a few years earlier, I marveled at how short memories were about the need for a business model and how quickly entrepreneurs and their VC backers could slip back into bad habits.

I tried to get a sense from Aaron as to how far he'd developed the product. Was this merely an idea he would start pitching to venture capitalists, or had he built something? He told me he'd spent the last ten months in his apartment working seven days a week on the architecture, code, and algorithms for Mint and that the basic prototype was ready to show. He had a roommate in his Sunnyvale apartment whom he'd hired as his first engineer to help build the product, but he had no real money to pay him. He'd been living off his savings for the past year, and he'd drained them. He needed to do something quickly.

We discussed a few other things, including the need to access account aggregation technology to ingest consumer banking data into Mint and some of the legal and operational issues involved in starting and funding a company. He listened intently, absorbing information in areas where he had no expertise. My gut told me he had something about him that might make it happen against all the odds. Silicon Valley was a place where you were permitted to dream that the impossible could become possible. So why not Aaron? He was still young, to be sure, yet he radiated an aura of inner strength, calm, and confidence. I could see he had a beautiful mind. He also exhibited an unusual mix of technical rigor and user empathy. The same person who could lock himself away for months on end alone while indexing millions of merchants from the Yellow Pages for categorization could also relate to consumer anxiety when managing finances. He was different from some of the pseudo-entrepreneurs and wannabes I'd met in the Valley over the years.

I remembered one guy, in particular, Mike from Canada, who I'd also met for the first time at Cafe Borrone. He wowed and dazzled with his keen vision for a faster Internet powered by peer-to-peer file sharing. He was a fast-talking showman. At one point, he interrupted his pitch to me and asked me for a twenty-dollar bill. When I gave it to him, he tore it up into tiny pieces and then, with a sleight of hand, handed it back to me as a hundred dollar note. In a previous life, he'd been a master designer of magic tricks for the top magician shows in Las Vegas. As an entrepreneur, he fizzled. You need more than smoke and mirrors to start a real company. You need to be an authentic entrepreneur with a unique vision for the problem you're trying to fix, the core skill set to build a service solution, and an iron-clad determination to see it through. I felt Aaron had these traits.

As we finished our meeting, I leaned back and casually asked Aaron, "Well, how can I help?"

Aaron was receptive but wanted to go away and process the question before giving me an answer. No doubt, his engineering brain wanted to scan all the ways he could match my experience and skills to his needs to get his startup show on the road.

We both got up to leave. As we walked away from the cafe together, I sensed a genuine connection between us. I was confident our first conversation would not be our last. As we shook hands to say goodbye, Aaron stopped and abruptly blurted out the question, "What's your favorite book?"

It was a personal question and a departure in tone from our informal business discussion. I wasn't sure if it was Aaron's social awkwardness at play, whether he was trying in some way to bond, or whether this was some sort of personality test he needed to run before he'd consider working with me.

My instincts told me I should answer the question precisely, and as I scanned my mind, I came up with *Anna Karenina* by Leo Tolstoy.

No sooner had I answered his question did he follow it up with, "Why?" I scanned again and improvised:

"Because it's a story of human love in all its glory and tragedy. It portrays a mother's love for her child and romantic, but unrequited, love. It also examines the stupidity of the aristocracy's societal norms and institutions and the misery they can inflict."

I sensed I was on a roll, so I decided to continue.

"It contrasts the upper class and their struggles to maintain royal and military status, with the peasant class who toil simply to survive one more harsh winter. In the end, it questions the choice between life and death when Anna's emotional world collapses, and her place in society is adrift."

I could see Aaron trying to process this. I don't think it was the type of book he'd expected. I was sure by his reaction that he'd never read it.

Nevertheless, I felt I somehow passed the test, if that's what it was. Aaron smiled as we parted ways.

CHAPTER 4

THE INTERNET AGE

"The difference between a vision and a hallucination is that other people can see the vision."

MARC ANDREESSEN

Over the next few days, I dwelt on my conversation with Aaron. The possibilities for a new paradigm in personal finance software intrigued me, and Aaron was captivating. But the elephant in the room still bothered me. Were the conditions favorable to disrupting Quicken's dominance? Sure, there was room for improvement, but wouldn't Intuit crush an upstart?

Scott Cook, who founded Intuit, was a former Procter & Gamble marketing manager. Cook knew from observing his wife at their kitchen table that she detested paying household bills, balancing the checkbook, and recognized a universal problem ripe for a software-based solution. He met Tom Proulx, a computer science major at Stanford, in 1983 while recruiting engineers on campus. They settled on the name "Intuit" for their company (meaning to understand by instinct) and "Quicken" for their product—which Cook had found in a Palo Alto bookstore by looking up "fast" in a thesaurus.

Thanks to a friendly, simple product design based on a checkbook and born of Cook's user interviews and customer-first ethos, Quicken outran more than forty competitors to become the number-one selling consumer financial software product in 1988. And in the '90s, they'd even taken on the mighty Microsoft and emerged stronger.

Microsoft had introduced a competing product, Money, in 1993. Seeing sales pale compared to Quicken, Microsoft, true to their strategy of seeing what products emerged in new markets and then moving to "embrace, extend, and extinguish" them, tried to buy Intuit. In October 1994, Microsoft agreed to acquire Intuit in a merger valued at about $1.5 billion—the software industry's largest acquisition ever by the world's largest software company. But the US Justice Department filed and won an antitrust lawsuit that precluded the merger. As an independent company, Intuit became one of the rare companies to have taken on Microsoft in packaged software and lived to tell the tale. Intuit partnered with banks on electronic banking to complement its direct-to-consumer products and went on to dominate the personal finance race into the first part of the twenty-first century. By 2006, when I sat down with Aaron, more people had bought Quicken software than any other personal finance software combined.

So Aaron's chances didn't look great, but they weren't impossible. Quicken was still a desktop-only product, and now upstart Silicon Valley companies proved that widespread internet access to information and services was the new frontier. New internet-based products and business models were emerging, and venture capital was flowing in. Netscape, led by 24-year-old cofounder Marc Andreesen, was the catalyst. Its Navigator browser gave the world access to information and services over the internet. Despite having no apparent business model, the company saw its stock double on its IPO in 1995. Microsoft's Internet Explorer gradually extinguished Netscape, which became a footnote in history. Still, its breakthrough led to the first internet boom, driven by web 1.0 companies like Amazon and Salesforce that delivered valuable applications and services over the internet directly to consumers and businesses.

It also led to a rush to launch other types of overvalued and unproven digital companies to market, resulting in the dot-com bubble that burst at the turn of the century. It caused a significant stock market crash in the technology sector that sent Silicon Valley reeling.

But Google emerged from the wreckage, propelled by its algorithms and monetization of search. Google IPO'd successfully in 2004, six years after being born, and kicked off the rapid emergence of Facebook and acquisitions of web startups like MySpace and YouTube. It was now game on for web 2.0 entrepreneurs and Valley VCs.

All this set the stage for a new generation of young, digitally-native entrepreneurs to start working away furiously in dorm rooms, garages, and apartment bedrooms across the country. Each of them hoped to create internet applications and services to stake their claim in this new digital gold rush. Among them was Aaron, a young man with a vision for a better way for consumers to manage their finances on the internet. Taking inspiration from Google and those that came after, Aaron would offer Mint for free. "It's the best price," he would say.

It would make for a great story. I couldn't help but see some of my own in it. The same ripples of the internet boom had brought me to chase opportunity in the Valley as well, albeit in the web 1.0 explosion rather than 2.0, and from much farther than Indiana.

In 1994, I worked for a boutique French law firm called Giroux, Buhagiar & Associes, located in Paris's prestigious sixteenth arrondissement. Our firm represented multiple US investment banks and European corporations raising money in the international capital markets, and I, as a native bilingual English and French speaker, assisted the partners on many of these deals. One was the IPO of Business Objects, a French company cofounded by a Stanford graduate. Business Objects decided it would act like a Valley startup: It raised US venture capital, used stock options to recruit experienced high-tech executives, and enlisted technology-savvy US investment banks to shepherd its initial public offering. Our firm worked with the Palo Alto-based Wilson Sonsini, the Valley law firm emerging as the advisor and representative to entrepreneurs growing tech companies, VCs, and investment banks.

The Business Objects IPO was a success, leading to a flood of French startups trying to follow the same path—and more business for us, and more cooperation with Wilson Sonsini. They also represented Netscape in its IPO a year later, further cementing the reputation of

Larry Sonsini. He became known as the godfather of Valley-style law and the personal counsel of Steve Jobs. And my relationship with partners at his firm grew.

Soon Frank Currie, a partner at Wilson Sonsini with whom I'd worked on several deals (and brother of Netscape chief financial officer Peter Currie), offered me a job. I'd mentioned to him that I'd proposed to my American girlfriend Jennifer, and we were considering a move back to the US. Frank thought I'd be an asset to Wilson Sonsini's growing business with European companies seeking access to US capital markets.

Several months later, I packed up my belongings and left Paris for Palo Alto. The energy, optimism, and opportunity of this new world drew me in. I wasn't the only one. There were people like me arriving from all over the globe, many of whom were among the finest minds of their generation with a passion for technology and innovation, all seeing opportunity in the Valley's digital gold rush.

Aaron came to the Valley during the internet's second act, armed with only an idea and drawn by the same gravity and opportunity I felt a few years earlier. Yes, taking on Intuit was a tall task—one that even Microsoft couldn't complete. But the internet revolution had paved the way for a new model of service delivery. And the Valley's short history was already populated by stories of others who had beat even worse odds if those existed.

So why not Aaron?

CHAPTER 5

READY TO RAISE

"The secret to getting ahead is getting started."
MARK TWAIN

After my first meeting with Aaron, he invited me to explore the most pressing challenges he faced. The following week we were back at Cafe Borrone to discuss how I could best help him. We dug into a range of issues. Among the first few was his selection of a law firm and an attorney to represent the company.

Aaron had already met Rob Claassen of Wilson Sonsini via an introduction from Relik. I'd connected Relik with Rob after leaving the firm and passed my portfolio of clients onto Rob. Rob, the man who started the events in motion that found me partnering with Aaron, was coming back into the picture.

Aaron thought Rob was smart and personable, but he didn't want to go with Wilson Sonsini. I wondered why. Aaron was making a judgment call based on the firm's lobby in their headquarters; it seemed too extravagant for his taste. He thought that Wilson Sonsini represented big Valley companies and that his fledgling startup would be overcharged and underappreciated.

He wasn't wrong—Wilson Sonsini's lobby was on the grand side of things, and it regularly saw some of the Valley's most significant deals and players pass through it. It was a Valley revolving deal door. It was natural that the lobby was imposing.

And Aaron was nothing if not frugal. He'd been burning a deep hole in his savings for the past year and was not about to blow the last of it on fancy lawyers. He already understood one of the startup game's basic rules: "First, don't run out of cash!"

I guided Aaron to a more informed decision. I told him about the Wilson Sonsini business model and how they were able to work with startups. They deferred initial incorporation and other fees up to a predetermined amount, typically in the range of $25,000, until the client's first round of funding. In exchange, Wilson Sonsini won the right to invest a token amount in the venture round if and when it occurred. It was a win-win deal. Some of those early investments paid off handsomely for the firm over the years, which helped justify their lavish offices.

I also assured Aaron that it was as much about the lawyer as the firm. He'd have to work closely with his counsel and feel confident he was receiving sound advice from someone he could trust. Someone who understood how the Valley worked and who appreciated the intrinsic potential value of early-stage startups and knew how best to work with them. Rob had all these bases covered. Aaron saw the rationale and agreed to return to Wilson Sonsini and hire Rob Claassen to represent Mint.

I noticed that Aaron was open to good advice if he could learn something from it, even when it corrected his initial analysis. It was another sign of an entrepreneur absorbing crucial new information and adapting to his environment.

We then discussed account aggregation, which would allow Mint to provide users a view of all their financial information. Aaron decided early that he wouldn't reinvent the wheel; he planned to license aggregation software. He'd narrowed it down to CashEdge and another company called Yodlee, two leaders in the industry. I'd never heard of either. One of the challenges would be to choose which provider was right for Mint and negotiate an advantageous deal. I'd have some work to do.

We discussed the algorithms he'd designed to run Mint efficiently. We'd need to think about getting patent rights for them. I thought of Google's Page Rank algorithm, which displayed the most relevant results from its search index for specific queries. That algorithm became the company's crown jewel and is mainly responsible for a market capitalization now passing a trillion dollars. There was precedent for developing the right algorithms for a web service and protecting them as intellectual property.

Aaron also mentioned he was frustrated that he didn't own the domain name for Mint.com. The closest he got was MyMint.com, for which he'd paid a few hundred dollars to own. He was determined to get his hands on Mint.com, as the name was perfect for the vision he had for the service.

Aaron also wanted to pay his first engineers so he could get Mint beyond his prototype. On and on it went. All these tasks were relevant to building a company but a distraction from building a product, and all would require more than our combined resourcefulness. It was going to need venture capital. I could help on that front as well.

It was another excellent meeting. Aaron focused on all the ways I could help him, and I was eager to dive in. The jobs seemed endless, and there was no time to lose. I agreed to work on a prioritization plan to keep us moving forward. It was hard to tell with Aaron, but perhaps somewhere deep down, he was happy to have someone willing to join him on this journey. He'd spent so many months locked up in his apartment in Sunnyvale writing the script for the Mint story that, at some basic human level, it must have been reassuring to no longer be completely alone.

The following week, we met again at Cafe Borrone. We were both keen to work together, but we hadn't yet agreed to terms. Since Aaron couldn't pay me anything in cash, he offered me equity in the form of shares in the company. His offer was fair, and I agreed to it. We were now partners in crime, and it was time to make that equity count for something.

First, we'd work on revisions to Aaron's pitch deck for investors. Aaron was not successful in his first batch of VC pitches a few months earlier. He discovered that VCs are professional skeptics; they can always find some perceived high-risk factor in an entrepreneur's plan to justify turning it down. But when they think they've found the right entrepreneur or cofounding team, all skepticism melts away, and you can almost hear the thunder of a stampede as the VCs rush in to close the deal before it gets away to one of their competitors.

Aaron ran the VC gauntlet but had come out the other side battered, bruised, and rejected. His first meeting was with Roelof Botha of Sequoia Capital. Aaron got the introduction from a former classmate at Duke, who was the son of Pierre Lemond, a retiring partner at Sequoia and Silicon Valley icon. In anticipation of that meeting, Aaron leaped and quit his job at Nascentric, believing that Sequoia would question him as a serious entrepreneur if he wasn't dedicating all his time to this new venture. Aaron had a good meeting with Botha but came away empty-handed. Botha never even asked whether Aaron was working.

As Aaron was nearing completion of the Mint prototype, he tried networking his way to some more venture money introductions from another angle. Aaron joined as many local founder-to-VC social events as possible, including a weekly Wednesday bowling event at an old bowling hall in Redwood City, now long since disappeared. This was a time in the Valley when younger VCs were entering the fray, and they were more comfortable hanging out socially with entrepreneurs that were not much more than ten years their junior. The younger VCs knew that their social proclivities might give them the edge in finding the next boy wonder founder.

Soon, Aaron's pitch found its way amongst the next-generation angel investor and VC crowd, including Peter Thiel, famous as a cofounder of PayPal and one of the earliest investors in Facebook, now with his Founders Fund. Thiel believed Mint would not acquire enough users because consumers would never trust a startup with their banking credentials. Without a proven product and consumers using it, Aaron wasn't cutting it with the investor crowd. Their conventional wisdom did not match Aaron's contrarian view that if you made money management simple, elegant, and powerful and built trust, consumers would opt for convenience and value and overcome their anxieties regarding privacy and security.

Aaron was either the wrong guy pitching to the right investors or the right guy pitching to the wrong investors. I suspected it was the latter.

In light of these challenges, we were determined to build a more robust pitch to overcome all the prior rejections he'd encountered and to keep searching for the right investor who would get it. We worked the deck back and forth, examining every angle and detail of the market, the product, the customer profile, the technology, the competition, and the business model. We tested answers to all the tough questions VCs might throw out. How will you acquire customers quickly and cheaply enough? Why should consumers trust you with all their financial information? Won't Intuit move Quicken online and crush you? How will you make money?

The business model we would lay out for the VCs focused on lead generation. We took every financial services category we could think of, from credit cards to brokerage accounts to mortgages and student loans, and set them down in a product category column. We ran the cost per acquisition (CPA) commission that a financial institution partner would pay us for sending them a customer, anywhere from $15 to $250. We then calculated the frequency of action for a product type, hypothesizing how often an average user would take up an offer. We looked at the user adoption rate for each of these products to determine what percentage of our users would convert on an offer presented to them. All of these calculations gave us an assumed revenue per user per year amount for each product category. With all product categories together, we projected $30 in revenue per user per year.

We worked hard on business model comparables to show there was a precedent for Mint to monetize the service with lead generation. For this, our reference company was LowerMyBills.com, a consumer finance website with a free online service to compare low rates on monthly bills and reduce living costs. Matt Coffin founded the company in 1999 in Los Angeles. LowerMyBills marketed itself as a one-stop destination that offered savings through relationships with over five hundred service providers across multiple categories, including home loans, credit cards, auto and health insurance, and long-distance and wireless services. Consumers could easily research, compare, and lower many of their monthly bills free of charge. The service worked with consumers entering their information into lead forms and then matched users with partner companies to meet their needs. Those providers then contacted the consumer directly to try and get them to sign up for their service.

This online monetization practice became known as "lead generation" because the service provider would pay the website a fee for each consumer lead.

LowerMyBills was acquired in 2005 by Experian for $380 million following an explosive period of growth due to unprecedented sales for mortgage lead generators while the housing market was booming.

There was, however, a critical difference between Mint's approach and that of LowerMyBills. That company focused on consumers who were searching for ways to save money on loans and bills. The engagement model was mostly transactional, one and done. In contrast, Mint would focus on keeping users engaged with regular updates on their financial health. Indeed, many of Mint's users would not be interested in transacting to save money initially. And we were not about to ruin the user experience by filling out forms listing out their personal and financial information. Mint would already have access to all their financial data. Instead, Mint would provide an intelligent savings engine that would scan a user's financial profile data and find personalized opportunities to save money and then present those to users. If the right percentage of our users acted on these over time, the business model would work. Provided we could keep them engaged on the site, the engine might trigger Mint users to act on various offers over time.

The last thing missing from the deck was a human-centered approach focused on the consumer problem we were trying to solve. Money matters are a source of great struggle in many households across the US. They cause frustration and, in some cases, outright fear. We believed Mint could alleviate these anxieties by helping consumers manage their money in a smart and straightforward way. This would give them back some sense of control and security, remove frustration and fear, and lead to eventual empowerment. To represent this human anxiety, we put in a large image of a mom sitting up late at night on the kitchen table struggling with her finances, recalling Scott Cook's wife as she tried to figure out how to pay all the bills due at the end of the month. We included this as the final element of our new deck. Now it was time to get this show on the road and raise some money.

CHAPTER 6

THE ALGORITHM ADVANTAGE

"Concentrate all your thoughts upon the work at hand. The sun's rays do not burn until brought to a focus."
ALEXANDER GRAHAM BELL

As Aaron looked to Sand Hill Road once again, my belief grew that the Mint service promised to be unique. Aaron had done well designing Mint to take advantage of many dynamic new technologies emerging in the web 2.0 environment. Aaron was creating a customer-centric product, much like Cook had in the early days of Intuit—but now, web 2.0 innovations enabled services that were not possible before.

Aaron powered his design aesthetic with raw creativity, so essential to true Valley innovation. Some founders are great at refinement or extending work that has been created before them. Aaron believed that creativity is the opposite of reactiveness. He was never afraid of a blank page. On the contrary, he relished the opportunity to sit for hours with his eyes closed and use his energy to think about what problem he was trying to solve. During these periods of intense introspection, Aaron would visualize the structure of flow charts and decision trees and decide what to include and how, and what to eliminate from his designs. And this is how Aaron designed Mint to provide users with clear insights from the simplification of large, complex data sets to solve the problems they experienced with their money.

It would be Aaron's inventions that truly set Mint apart: his algorithms. Aaron mentioned these when we first met at Cafe Borrone, and their technical prowess impressed me from the outset.

The first algorithm dealt with categorizing transactions that Aaron found lacking in Quicken. Aaron's categorization algorithm meant that Mint would recognize and automatically classify (accurately) any transaction that came in via the bank aggregation feed. Whether the spending was on rent, groceries, gas, or something else, Mint would get it right. Though simple when it works, the processing of payment data contains many back-end, indecipherable codes and references that are difficult for humans and machines to discern if they are external to the payments system of record. Aaron called these codes "bank garbage," and they were enough to ruin a product. This is why Quicken still only got about half of a user's transactions categorized correctly.

The entrepreneur in Aaron said there had to be a better way. The engineer in him said that only software could provide a solution. His star line at our initial meeting rang true: "Good software should do the work for you, not the other way round."

Of the several months Aaron spent locked away in his Sunnyvale apartment, about half of that time was used to develop a new system that could automatically categorize over 90 percent of all credit and debit card transactions. The algorithm would take a transaction string and scan backward, searching for a merchant name, city, and state. Then, with whatever tokens were remaining, it would put them into a search engine that Aaron wrote and let it do fuzzy matching. The results would go into a fast-set intersection algorithm and give a probability of a match to a merchant. For this, Aaron indexed over twenty million US merchants by using the Yellow Pages service, which provides a means for finding businesses close to a particular location. The Yellow Pages data are labeled according to the Standard Industry Classification (SIC) codes assigned by the US government to classify industry areas and identify the primary business.

For example, if a customer purchases Home Depot, then within the credit card transaction, embedded in the string of other indecipherable data, are the words "Home Depot." In that case, Mint's internal dictionary took this into account with all other available data. It categorized the transaction as "Home and Appliances" based on how the Yellow Pages categorized the merchant. Mint would be able to identify thousands of merchants and manage hundreds of spending categories in this way.

Despite the strength of the system, sometimes a miscalculation was possible. In such cases, the user would be able to edit the information quickly in the app, with every effort made to keep this manual intervention to the minimum.

Aaron was a pioneer in using machine learning technology long before that term became part of the Valley vernacular more than a decade later. He designed the categorization algorithm to pick up on Mint's user behaviors by accumulating data on what merchants and products were categorized manually and adding them to transaction categories. This meant that if, for example, Mint grew to millions of users, and approximately 20 percent were actively categorizing or recategorizing their transactions, Mint's internal program would be watching and learning as it happened. Then, if thousands of users categorized a transaction that contained the word "Burger King" as "Food," any purchase from any user that included the phrase "Burger King" would be auto mapped and categorized to "Food." This improved the system and further eliminated the need for manual user intervention. Aaron's design meant that, as Mint accumulated more data and users, the categorization program would learn faster, and the product would improve exponentially. That was a built-in competitive advantage.

Wesabe, which was Mint's most recognizable competitor at that time and was also beginning to pitch their product to investors, tried to solve managing consumer spending data by inviting users to tag all transactions themselves. Aaron knew from his experience using Quicken that this was a painful, complicated process and that few people would want to do this continually. It's like counting calories for weight loss—it becomes tiresome quickly and is unsustainable. Aaron believed that automation efficiency and elegant user experience (UX) would always be the winning formula, and he was sticking to his guns.

Aaron knew categorization was only a feature and not enough by itself to take on and beat Intuit and Microsoft. But if a Mint user could understand his or her spending, then so too could Mint. Moreover, Mint would be able to comprehend spending in aggregate across all its users. Aaron knew that if he could build software to tap into this data to optimize a user's finances, it would be more than just another feature—it would differentiate Mint and provide its business model in one fell swoop. To achieve this would require the development of a second algorithm.

The savings algorithm would use offer matching processes. Mint would be able to sift and sort through most of the financial products and services available in the market and find the right one for a particular user based on their unique financial profile and spending stream. For example, if a user were to have $10,000 lying around in a bank account earning little to no interest, Mint's smart savings system would recommend a high-interest rate savings account from E*Trade or HSBC that could mean $660 or more in that user's pocket each year. In ranking the best savings account, Mint considered any associated minimum balance requirements and monthly fees, in addition to the interest rate, to net out the savings.

For credit cards, Mint went further. For example, Mint calculated a better return for the user among cards offering 3 percent cash back on gas, 5 percent cash back on restaurants, and 1.25 air miles for every dollar spent. Mint could also find the best balance transfer card with no interest for twelve to twenty-four months for those users who were struggling to pay off their balances. It all depended on the individual user's financial patterns; Mint would know this and do all the work to calculate the best-personalized savings offer. It even considered those minute details like maximum rewards, balance transfer fees, and 0 percent introductory rates that expire six or twelve months from the time of the offer.

The Mint smart savings system would only show offers calculated to save a user a minimum amount of money, and the system prioritized the one calculated to save the most. Aaron estimated that Mint's algorithms would typically find $500 to $5,000 in annual savings for each user, with the average at $1,800 (or $150 per month). Not bad for a free service!

To "feed" the savings engine, Mint would maintain the latest interest rates and other terms for hundreds of bank accounts, credit cards, and other financial products and services. The algorithms would then crunch through all these prices to find savings opportunities. When a user clicked on a savings offer, the process was entirely anonymous, and a user's information would never leave the site. No information passed except that the click came from Mint.com. Mint would make a tidy referral fee or commission from financial advertising partners on some of these offers. This would allow the Mint service to be free for users while the company monetized the service.

Aaron was determined to build trust with Mint users in this smart savings system. At the risk of sacrificing sponsorship money, the system design surfaced the best savings offer for a consumer whether or not Mint had a paid relationship with a provider. Mint's ranking algorithm would be agnostic to sponsorship—it would find users the best interest rate or lowest price regardless of its origin. For each offer on Mint that came from a partner who would pay a commission, Mint indicated that it was "sponsored," so the user understood we would be getting paid for the referral. The Mint system's beauty was that we would only make money if we found ways for our users to save money, and at the same time, for our financial partners to acquire a customer. If Mint could not find a meaningful savings opportunity for a given user, no offer would be shown to that user. This customer-first approach to web monetization was revolutionary.

As part of the smart savings system, Mint would build in consumer advocacy and encourage users to move away from banks that paid no interest to those that paid 2 to 3 percent and to move away from credit cards offering no rewards to those paying 3 to 5 percent cashback on specific categories. Mint would quantify its savings offers for the user to determine if acting upon an offer was worthwhile.

In the end, the categorization and savings algorithms were complementary since a deep understanding of a user's spending from precise categorization would provide data from which to generate personalized savings offers. It was Mint's use of the data for the benefit of its users that led to compelling and unique value creation. From this analysis, I now believed that, despite the odds, we had a fighting chance of finding at least one venture capitalist who wanted to see this service offered to the world. And soon, because Aaron already had engineers to pay.

CHAPTER 7

THE FIRST ENGINEERS

"Pleasure in the job puts perfection in the work."
ARISTOTLE

As Aaron and I spent more time together, I mentioned coming from a run one morning, and Aaron wondered if he could join me on one of my weekend runs. Perhaps Aaron was looking to add a little variety to his intense gym routine, or maybe he was looking for another way to connect. "Sure," I said, "let's do it."

Aaron began to stop by my place in Menlo Park on the weekend, and we'd run from my house. This allowed him to meet my family. The kids wondered who this new guy was as they looked up from playing with their legos and toy cars on the floor. I'd quickly throw on some running gear, and off we'd go jogging.

At first, Aaron was surprised at how far I took him on the run. We'd start from my place in Menlo Park, weave across the San Francisquito creek through downtown Palo Alto to Stanford's Palm Drive. We'd then veer around the front right side of the university on the ascending Campus Drive loop that would take us gradually up to the Stanford Dish trail behind the campus. There, with the Santa Cruz mountains rising behind us in shades of gray and Stanford's Hoover Tower standing tall like a lighthouse over the mission-style campus below, was where a personal relationship between Aaron and I started to coalesce.

After completing the Dish trail, we'd make our way back to Stanford, looping around to the front of the campus and then back home. By the end of the run, Aaron would be exhausted, but he seemed satisfied to have been pushed to his limits.

On one of our weekend dish trail runs, Aaron mentioned his time spent alone in his Sunnyvale apartment working on the building blocks of Mint. This period of Mint's incubation and Aaron's isolation must have been lonely and, at times, discouraging. It seemed as though it was only his unyielding vision for the Mint service that kept him going, but in his revelations, there was a hint of the occasional moment of self-doubt along the way.

At another level, I sensed that the introvert in Aaron found some comfort in the safety of this period, with its purest form of deep thinking, focus, and inner reflection. Aaron's brain processing power and ability to delve into deep problem solving were at their best away from people and places and their distractions. He knew he had to go through this trek to design the Mint service in a unique and compelling way. I knew that very few humans on the planet were this intense and capable of such monk-like discipline.

But that period was over. It was time for Aaron to come out of his shell. As CEO and fundraiser in chief, Aaron was about to be pulled in dozens of different directions. He would inevitably devote less time to visionary and abstract thinking, service design, and coding. Now, he needed helpers. It was time to go beyond Aaron's prototype and write some code for the alpha version of the Mint service. We had to hire some engineers, beginning with a front-end developer and a full-stack engineer.

A front-end developer produces HTML (Hyper-text markup language), CSS (cascading style sheets), and JavaScript for web applications. The objective is for users to see the information in a format that's easy to read, relevant, and pleasing to the eye. Our frontend developers would also need to ensure that Mint.com would come up correctly in different browsers, on different operating systems, and across different devices.

The back-end is under the hood of the website, such as the database and content management system, and most users are not aware of it. A full-stack developer works across the front-end and back-end parts of a website. They know enough about the code across the entire stack to dive in anywhere as and when needed.

On another of our runs, Aaron told me that his roommate, Matt Snider, had begun work on Mint's front-end development. Aaron met Matt through a founders' hiking group centered around Stanford University. The group organizer was Jawed Karim, who had joined ex-PayPal colleagues Steven Chen and Chad Hurley to found YouTube a year earlier in 2005. Since Aaron and Matt were both keen hikers, you might say that their paths were bound to cross.

On a late spring day in 2006, the group set out for a hike in the Santa Cruz mountains. Aaron caught wind that Matt was a front-end developer of considerable skill. He was determined to corner Matt on the trail and recruit him. Matt's claim to fame was that he'd built SUpost, a Craigslist classifieds clone used by Stanford students to buy and sell stuff. It's still in use today. Matt was working on another startup named Trippert, which was a communal blog for travel writing. Like so many startups, the service was struggling to gain traction. In the meantime, Matt was of no fixed abode and spent his time Couchsurfing with friends. The conditions appeared to be favorable for Aaron to approach Matt about helping him with Mint.

Not holding back, Aaron interviewed Matt on the trail. They were outdoor kinsmen and fellow engineers who bonded over the web and code as they hiked along behind the rest of the group.

After they'd formed a rapport in the initial conversation, Aaron impulsively challenged Matt to stop on the trail and climb up a giant coastal redwood tree with him. Aaron was a natural-born tree climber and had a passion for climbing since he was a kid.

Matt was keen to follow, so they clambered high up the tree together. Matt panted heavily to catch his breath at the first point of rest. Then the testosterone kicked in, and they challenged each other to go higher. The rest of the hiking group stopped and watched; Aaron and Matt heard the shouts of concern and the appeals to reason from far below. They looked at each other with a hint of defiance and a glint of rebellion in their eyes and chuckled. Perched high, Aaron invited Matt to look out from the treetops across the horizon to the glimmering, vast blue waters of the Monterey Bay in the distance. Then Aaron asked Matt to join Mint. It was a great setting and perfect timing. Matt was hardly in a position to say no, and he agreed. Like that, the Mint engineering team doubled from the top of a *palo alto*, or "tall tree," high up in the Santa Cruz mountains.

After their hike, Aaron set up a Skype call with Matt to go over some final technical details and agree on employment terms. Aaron was ready to pay Matt about $1,500 per month in salary. This would further drain his savings. Matt could also take the spare room in Aaron's apartment in Sunnyvale, rent-free. To top it off, Matt could use an old Ford Contour car that Aaron had, as long as he paid for gas and some maintenance. But what sold Matt was Aaron's vision for Mint and the opportunity to work on a project that had personal meaning for him. Like Aaron, Matt tracked his finances diligently, though he did so in an Excel spreadsheet rather than in Quicken. He could smell the opportunity to deliver a next-generation personal finance service using the power of the web. He wanted into a venture where he could have an impact.

Matt was to be Mint's lead front-end developer. He was a specialist in client-side development with a focus on building javascript-driven applications. His mission was to make the Mint web app a great experience from both a performance and a design perspective. In those early days of the web, most websites were flat in their design with a basic point and click functionality. However, by 2003, open-source Javascript libraries emerged, such as Prototype, jQuery, Dojo, and Ajax. Fast forward just a few years, and these new javascript libraries now allowed developers to create interactive web pages providing rich new experiences for web users to enjoy.

There was no better time for Mint to utilize these technologies to demonstrate new experiences in personal finance management (PFM). We knew that inspiring trust in the Mint service would be crucial. So building an experience that felt simple, secure, and elegant was a high priority. By the late spring of 2006, Mint had just hired one of the best up-and-coming front-end developers in the Valley to do just that.

Matt moved in with Aaron and began working on the code. His first job was to polish up the Mint prototype so it would be presentable to investors. Matt's room had no bed, so he curled up on the floor in his sleeping bag for the first few weeks. During that time, he noticed how meticulous Aaron was as a flatmate. Aaron would make his bed in the morning, cook his meals, and always clean up after himself. While Matt was Couchsurfing with other friends, he'd never seen anyone so organized and domesticated. Most mornings at his other host locations, the kitchen sink would be full of dirty dishes and the counters full of empty beer bottles and takeout food scraps. With Aaron, Matt was duty-bound to clean up his act.

Then there was the work Matt had to do on Mint. It seemed never to stop. Aaron was driven and relentless and seemed to love to work; there were times when Matt found it suffocating to keep up. He longed for some occasional downtime, but there was no letup.

As I got to know Matt, I recognized that he was a nice, quiet, unassuming guy who worked hard with real commitment. He had no apparent ego. Over the next few years, I'd marvel as he stood silently at his desk, tapping away at his computer, always with his headphones on tuned into his music and writing clean code that made the Mint service shine.

One break Matt did catch was when a friend of Aaron's, Poornima Viyjayashanker, showed up at the apartment and brought him an old air mattress she had lying around. She couldn't bear to think of Matt sleeping on the floor every night at Aaron's place.

Poornima would be Mint's next hire as a full-stack engineer. Poornima brought brightness and positivity to the team and was always ready with a smile. As a girl growing up, she never thought of engineering as a career, even though the men in Poornima's family were all engineers. She enrolled in economics at Duke University but quickly became bored. She decided engineering might fit after all and ended up double-majoring in electrical engineering and computer science.

Poornima also happened to be Aaron's ex-girlfriend. They first met at Duke in the engineering department. They'd split amicably after arriving in the Bay Area together, and she'd stayed in touch. Aaron wanted her to be part of the formative team. Many would advise against this because of residual relationship complications, but Aaron believed in his ability to compartmentalize, and he valued Poornima's coding skills.

After all, it was Poornima who coined the name "Mint" for the company. On an earlier ski trip to Lake Tahoe, Poornima asked Aaron what he would call his new company. Aaron said he wanted something that would represent "money intelligence." That's when Poornima came up with "Mint." It was pure inspiration. Never mind for now that it was probably going to be impossible to get that domain name. Mint.com—it was too darn good.

Poornima, too, identified with Aaron's vision and the company mission, and she was confident in Aaron's ability to do something remarkable.

As the first female employee on the Mint team, Poornima knew she'd be in for a special ride. She'd experienced the Valley's exclusive, male-dominated engineering climate in prior roles and was determined to affect change from the ground up. She also had founder aspirations of her own, so joining Mint in its infancy was an opportunity for education and a blank canvas that she couldn't pass up.

With Aaron, Matt, and Poornima, the nucleus of an engineering team was taking shape. Aaron, ever resourceful, did what he had to do with the little money on hand: He tapped his roommate and former girlfriend as engineering recruits, he used his apartment as Mint's first office, and he brought on a business guy with Valley insider experience (yours truly) for business development with equity and no cash. The company was running on fumes, but we'd need to keep growing and step on a full tank of gas to go faster. For that, we'd need to raise money and find an investor who bought into Aaron's vision; an investor who was willing to take a long-odds bet on the future of web-based personal finance. That investor was out there somewhere. They had to be. We just needed to find them.

CHAPTER 8

THE SEARCH FOR A WHITE KNIGHT

"I don't think a lot of people have been entrepreneurial about venture capital."

JOSH KOPELMAN

Aaron was in the twilight zone with his venture and was running low on cash. We all needed some money injected into Mint quickly. If not, we might see another startup competitor run away from the field before we got out of the starting blocks. And none of us could continue working on a shoestring budget for very long. It was time to test the new Mint positioning and investor pitch deck. Aaron responded to the challenge by doubling down on his Valley networking forays.

Soon enough, Aaron returned to tell me of James Slavet, an ex-Yahoo senior executive and a new partner at Greylock Partners, whom he'd met at a STIRR event. Greylock was one of the Valley's oldest, top-tier venture capital firms. Slavet seemed to get the new Mint pitch immediately. This bode well. All of the work we'd done to overhaul the deck was having an impact.

Slavet warmed to Aaron as a young entrepreneurial talent and someone he would be excited to mentor. However, despite Slavet's best intentions, his efforts proved insufficient in securing funding. Slavet was a new Greylock partner, so any high-risk, unknown early-stage deal he brought to the partnership might not get the benefit of the doubt from the other, more senior partners. Also, supreme VC firms like Greylock typically invested in the Series A financing of a new company to the tune of $5–10 million. The size of their funds, then in the range of $200 million or more, dictated investments of these amounts over just a few years. It was about ten times more money than Mint needed at this stage. And a familiar theme reared its ugly head. The primary objection of the other Greylock partners was that Mint wouldn't be able to acquire a sufficient number of customers cheaply enough to grow and justify the more significant investment. They thought consumers were not going to trust a new startup with their online banking credentials. It was the same reason that Aaron had struck out on in his first round of pitches months earlier.

Slavet circled back to Aaron to let him down as gently as he could. They had formed a genuine bond, but the relationship was not to be. Slavet wished us the very best and would be "rooting for Mint from the sidelines."

Although we didn't get the money from Greylock, it felt like a turning point. We'd made a dent at the highest level and come very close. Perhaps our next champion would have more risk appetite, autonomy, and authority to close the deal.

One good result of Aaron's interactions with Greylock was that David Sze, a partner of the firm, introduced Mark Goines, a former senior vice president and general manager of the Consumer Group at Intuit, which included TurboTax and Quicken. Goines operated in this Intuit role for almost ten years up until 2000. Since leaving Intuit, Goines was active as an angel investor. If Greylock didn't write us a check, at least they connected Aaron to perhaps the single best Valley angel investor in terms of understanding whether Mint might succeed against the mighty Intuit.

Goines agreed to meet Aaron at a coffee shop near his home in Los Altos. He'd listened to various crazy startup ideas that were supposed to take down Quicken over the years, and none had any merit. He expected to hear Aaron out and then bat him away politely. But as they chatted, Goines observed two strategic flaws with Quicken that changed the dynamic. Goines knew that Intuit was about to announce a massive acquisition of Digital Insight, a provider of online banking software. Intuit announced the acquisition in November 2006 as a cash deal valued at about $1.35 billion. Since Digital Insight served the banks as customers, Intuit wouldn't be able to use the Quicken data to benefit users in the way Mint was proposing—to have them switch to better financial products and services. Goines knew this approach could well prove disruptive and, if so, Intuit would not be able to respond so long as it owned Digital Insight. The second thing Goines noted was that Quicken took forty-five minutes on average to get started; Mint would take about two minutes. The difference promised to change the dynamic for customer acquisition. Whereas every traditional VC Aaron had earlier pitched believed customer acquisition would be Mint's biggest challenge, here was Goines seeing a clear advantage in favor of Mint in this regard.

But there was still one problem. Aaron had no management experience and no product. At the meeting, he was showing Goines some cards. Goines told him to come back when he had a prototype. And in a matter of two weeks, that is what Aaron did. Goines found the prototype to be excellent even as it was delivered in record time. Aaron and Matt had been burning the midnight oil and had come through extreme pressure to deliver something tangible and compelling for Goines. He was intrigued. Goines felt that now was the right time to go after Quicken as Intuit would not be able to respond quickly.

In the end, Goines was so impressed by Aaron's approach and intellect—his way of talking about what he was hoping to achieve—that he wanted to work with him. Goines committed to writing a six-figure check. All Aaron had to do was find an institutional investor to lead the round.

Aaron was so impressed with Goines that he confided that he saw him as a potential mentor and independent board member of Mint. Aaron wanted to soak up his combined operational and personal finance domain expertise in any way he could. I couldn't wait to meet Goines; I sensed he'd be a key figure in our journey.

Aaron soon informed me that he'd met with a small venture firm named Clearstone, an LA-based VC with a Silicon Valley office, and they were impressed with the Mint story. Clearstone mentioned a term sheet, and Aaron thought we'd soon get one. A Valley term sheet is generally about two pages and allows VCs and entrepreneurs to agree quickly on terms in principle. It's nonbinding but outlines key financial terms like the investment amount, the price per share paid by investors, and the voting rights investors receive in return. Both sides sign in good faith as their lawyers proceed with drafting and negotiating the entire funding contract.

Over the next few days, Aaron's optimism was proved correct, and we received a term sheet from Clearstone offering to invest $1 million in Mint. There it was, right before our eyes: money ready for the taking to fuel Mint's growth and fulfill Aaron's dream. But we hesitated. I'd never heard of this fund or the partner; they were an LA firm, and I was not familiar with how they operated. I preferred a VC who had a prior track record as a successful founding entrepreneur, someone who could advise and empathize as a fellow entrepreneur first and as an investor second. I also wanted a VC with a cutting-edge investment track record, someone recognized as getting into the best deals. I knew this would be a signal to other investors, who would then clamor to get in on our deal. We were looking for what the Valley refers to as the "smart money"—a VC that added real value beyond the dollars invested and who could impact the company's growth trajectory and subsequent valuation. It wasn't clear that Clearstone fit the bill.

We had to decide whether to take this money off the street or be patient and keep it warm while finding an investment partner that would get us more excited. I counseled Aaron toward the latter, albeit knowing that beggars could not afford to be choosers. It was a risk, as we'd only have a short window of two to three weeks before Clearstone realized we were stalling, and the term sheet would expire. If we didn't find our white knight investor in time, we'd come up dry and might live to regret our decision. We started networking with urgency.

As it happened, Aaron was a regular attendee at STIRR events, which were networking and emerging technology showcase events for the web 2.0 arena companies. STIRR's Founder Mixers were invite-only events that brought founding teams together with a blend of members from the tech community. These included startup-savvy engineers, journalists, service providers, and investors, who were encouraged to interact, socialize, and swap thoughts and ideas. STIRR was an alternative to the infamous *TechCrunch* parties, led by Chief Party Officer Michael Arrington, that had become too big and glamorous to network effectively.

Often, as with many networking meetings, these amount to no more than schmoozing. But, in some cases, lightning strikes.

One of the next events on the roster was the STIRR Founder's Table Dinner that hosted up to seven startup founders in a facilitated roundtable to discuss business challenges and forge relationships. Aaron's forays into the VC circuit, albeit unsuccessful, had generated a little buzz. The folks at STIRR decided he would be an excellent fit to rotate into this particular event. He was invited to Fanny and Alexander's restaurant in Palo Alto, an establishment now long since defunct. Aaron was seated next to Josh Kopelman, the founding partner of First Round Capital, a new seed-stage venture firm in Philadelphia.

Aaron and Kopelman were soon chatting about Mint. Aaron impressed Kopelman, a natural-born entrepreneur himself, with his understanding of the problem set, the elegance of the product concept, and the depth of thought he'd put into it. Kopelman also observed in Aaron a robust quantitative and analytical approach, just as I noticed in our initial meeting. The clarity and power of Aaron's vision struck Kopelman as exceptional.

As Aaron and Kopelman became absorbed in the possibilities of Mint, Aaron decided on the spur of the moment to run out to the parking lot and grab his laptop from the trunk of his car. He had a server running the Mint prototype on it. When Aaron got back to his seat, he fired up the Mint demo for Kopelman, who liked what he saw.

All those lonely hours leading to months that Aaron spent in his Sunnyvale apartment were about to bear fruit. Kopelman asked Aaron to send him a business plan. At the same time, he stepped away to call his new San Francisco-based partner, Rob Hayes. Kopelman asked Hayes to come down and check out this guy because "he's interesting." Hayes had no car at his office in the city, so he raced to catch the next Caltrain headed south down the Peninsula corridor with a stop at Palo Alto. It was a major trek for Hayes and showed his eagerness to please his new boss. He'd arranged to meet Aaron at the downtown University Cafe (now closed) later that evening.

Once there, Aaron took Hayes through the Mint demo. Hayes was quietly blown away by the completeness of Aaron's vision. Aaron knew what he wanted to build, and the granular level of detail in the design was astonishing. Hayes knew he needed to move quickly and invited Aaron to present to the full First Round partnership the next day. Aaron agreed.

Hayes rushed to catch the last train back to the city to make his final Bart connection back to his home in the East Bay. It was going to be a long night, but something told him it would be worth it.

The next day, Aaron connected to the First Round partnership on a Skype video call. Once again, he walked them through the pitch deck and demo. Kopelman thanked him and said they'd let him know their decision after an internal review.

Kopelman shared his thoughts with his partners that Mint represented a significant transition away from manual products requiring much user input to more of an automated product that needed almost none. Everyone agreed that Mint was attacking a problem most people had—very few people knew what was going on with their money. No one else was combining account aggregation and transaction categorization. This was difficult work and would break new ground if successful. The partners agreed that Intuit had lost its way with Quicken, and the product sucked. And the way Mint was going to make use of the data it aggregated was intriguing for them. They didn't necessarily buy into the data as an asset aspect of the pitch that suggested it had separate value. Still, the use of a consumer's financial data to make the service intrinsically better was revolutionary. Kopelman was also intrigued by the contrarian notion that users would not have to visit the site to get value. They could get an update of their finances in an email generated by Mint. There was no need to log in. This ran counter to conventional approaches to web businesses that were determined to keep users returning to their sticky sites and keep users on them for as long as possible. Yet, here was Aaron creating a service with the functionality of a gas station. The objective was to fill the car's tank so you could journey further and do this by getting in and out in just a few minutes.

But it was not a rush to yes. The First Round partners expressed concern that Aaron was a first-time founder and that he was the only founder; it was conventional thinking among investors that founders' teams were generally more successful than sole founders. However, this concern was minimal relative to how impressed the partners were with Aaron and the Mint project. We didn't know it yet, but the First Round Capital team decided they were in and that Rob Hayes would negotiate the terms of their Mint investment.

The next time Aaron and I met at Cafe Borrone, he told me he'd met this seed-stage VC, Josh Kopelman. He thought Kopelman's interest in Mint was genuine, and he felt like a deal might be on the cards. Aaron explained that Kopelman was himself a former entrepreneur. He'd launched Half.com, a marketplace for second-hand books, and had successfully sold it to eBay. I don't know why—call it intuition—but I had a clear sense that Kopelman was our guy and that First Round Capital would lead Mint's first round. Kopelman fit nearly all of the criteria we were looking for in a VC investor.

Aaron mentioned that he was from Philadelphia, which I found a bit strange. So I did some research and asked around. I'd lived in the Valley for several years and had seen so many deals pass through it that I fell into the trap of thinking all respectable venture investors were based here. I was wrong. They did, however, need to be active here. In that regard, Kopelman was known as the "Redeye VC" because he was always on a redeye flight back to Philadelphia from Silicon Valley. He was a Valley outside insider.

Kopelman's entrepreneurial journey started while in college at Wharton. There, he cofounded Infonautics Corporation in 1992 and took it public on NASDAQ in 1996. As the internet took shape, he envisaged a world where anyone could buy and sell used books, music, and DVDs online, and so launched Half.com in July of 1999. The company was snapped up by eBay only a year later, in July of 2000. After serving his time at eBay, Kopelman hatched one more company called Turntide, which created the world's first anti-spam router. Six months later, Symantec acquired Turntide.

After the Turntide acquisition, Kopelman stepped back to reflect on his operational years. He realized that it was the very early stage value creation process that most excited him about company building. That unique one-to-two-year period at the start of a new venture was the most fun, challenging, and lean. It's also when the culture of a company takes shape. He found that this incubation period made the most significant difference for everything that came after. If he was going to start to venture invest, he thought it only natural to work with entrepreneurs at the seed stage. Here, he could help other founders make the most of the blank slate they have at the very beginning.

Kopelman sought to bring an entrepreneurial approach to building a VC business. The new class of web 2.0 entrepreneurs that had grown up in their teens with the web were much younger than their predecessors. Moreover, the costs associated with starting a company had dropped dramatically in just a few years. This was known as the "capital efficiency shift." With each innovation cycle, it cost less money to get to the first product ship. This was due to lower computing costs from on-demand cloud computing infrastructure, open-source code frameworks, rapid prototyping techniques, API-driven tools and services, and a range of other factors. It was now possible to start an internet company and prove a concept with as little as $250,000-$300,000. The new class of entrepreneurs and the companies they were building didn't fit the mold for the classic Sand Hill Road style VC such as Greylock and Sequoia and didn't need a Series A funding approach of $5–10 million as the first round. The economics of the large venture firms needed to change. However, instead of shrinking to adapt to new market realities, the average size of a VC fund had tripled in the previous ten years. They were committed to making even more substantial investments.

Kopelman realized that the technology industry was becoming ten times more efficient while the venture capital community was raising more capital and deploying it inefficiently. Kopelman had launched three companies, all of which cost successively less to build. Since then, he'd made about forty angel investments in early-stage startups with his own money. These angel investments are different from investing as a VC fund or firm on behalf of third-party institutions such as pension funds, insurance companies, endowments, foundations, family offices, and high net worth individuals. Now, Kopelman saw the gap in the venture market and was confident he could exploit it with a new seed-stage fund. He would raise money from institutional investors who would become limited partners in his fund. Still, the overall fund size and the investments it would make would be much smaller than traditional Valley VCs. This would be seed-stage venture investing at its finest.

Kopelman launched First Round Capital in 2004 with his partner Howard Morgan. It started as a sub-$10 million fund, ten to twenty times smaller than the traditional Series A-focused Valley venture fund. Kopelman and Morgan both lived in Philadelphia and decided they'd run the fund from there. The philosophy of the new fund was to be there at the "first round." This way, they could help their portfolio companies and make a lot of money in the process. First Round Capital became Kopelman's next startup.

Kopelman had a built-in natural buffer to being caught up in current Valleythink. He was deeply connected to the Valley, having worked three years at eBay and having made those numerous angel investments. But Kopelman was an entrepreneur first, and this meant he was naturally unconventional. Besides that, by not being physically locked into the Valley, Kopelman had space and freedom to think differently about his investments. His concept for a seed-stage fund was contrarian, and so too would be his approach to investing.

Kopelman was well aware that Mint had been passed on by many prominent Valley luminaries, as the conventional wisdom was that Aaron's product wouldn't be able to win consumer trust. Nevertheless, he was prepared to look at the deal on its merits and saw possibilities others didn't. For Kopelman and First Round, the most critical thing for an investment was the founder and founding team. First Round typically invested before the product build, before the company had customers and a data set on which to measure the business model. They needed to believe the product and the proposed business model comprised an exceptional approach at the right time and in a big market. But when they invested, the only thing tangible was the people on the team. This gave Kopelman an advantage over other seed investors. As a successful serial entrepreneur, he could better identify people that were like him. He understood the product and market approach would likely change. Still, if the entrepreneur had the right character, motivation, strategic and tactical intellect, and sheer force of will, then that entrepreneur was worth backing. Kopelman and Hayes believed they'd found these characteristics in Aaron.

After the First Round partner meeting on Mint, things began to move quickly with Kopelman and Hayes. They proposed a term sheet to lead Mint's seed financing by committing $300,000. They confirmed they would be able to bring as much as twice that amount from other Valley angels they typically syndicated deals with so that the round would pan out to around $600,000. Since we hadn't signed the term sheet from Clearstone, we moved forward on the First Round deal. They were the "smart money," and though this meant we'd take in less money from them at a lower valuation, we bet we'd achieve more growth and a higher Mint company multiple in our Series A funding with First Round on our side.

Happily, First Round's term sheet was straightforward and no-nonsense. Just as the Clearstone term sheet was about to expire, we agreed to First Round's terms, and Aaron signed the term sheet. Immediately afterward, Aaron called Clearstone to let them know.

CHAPTER 9

SYNDICATING THE SEED ROUND

"To see things in the seed, that is genius."

LAO TZU

Hard on the heels of signing the term sheet with First Round, a combination of referrals from First Round and Greylock injected Aaron into the spotlight. It led to investment commitments from several angel investors that would top up and complete the round. Now it was a question of who we would let in before pulling up the tent stakes. We were looking for angels who had extensive networks and entrepreneurial chops that could add value to Mint and increase the smart money coefficient. These angels would not take a board seat due to investing small amounts of money in many companies, but they had skin in the game and would help us as and when they could.

We thought that somewhere around $1 million would be the right amount to raise. We wanted enough money to get Mint out of the aircraft hangar without giving up extra ownership in the company too early. It was better to wait for the Series A and a higher valuation based on more momentum and less risk in achieving takeoff. This would minimize dilution.

Next up was Jean-Francois "Jeff" Clavier, the founder and managing partner of SoftTechVC, a seed-stage fund (since renamed "Uncork

Capital"). Clavier, a French native, immigrated to the US in 2000 and started SoftTech in 2004, the same year First Round Capital was founded. First Round and SoftTech knew each other well and often co-invested on deals. Like Kopelman, Clavier was a former angel investor whose success had led him to start investing institutional money from limited partners into startups with a micro-VC fund. Kopelman and Clavier were pioneers of the seed stage fund revolution.

In some ways, our round would not have been complete without including the Valley's ultimate angel investor, Ron Conway, and his SVAngel fund. I'd heard of Conway from my time at Wilson Sonsini. He seemed to have faded from the headlines during the dot-com era meltdown but was now back on the scene with the resurgence of internet companies, and he was riding high from his early investment in Google. Conway pioneered an approach to investing in many startups early on, not to miss a big winner. This strategy later became known as "spray and pray" as angel and seed fund investing increased in the Valley. Conway would pump small amounts of money into hundreds of startups to hit some winners along the way to pay for all the rest and more.

Conway was known as the consummate Valley networker and an absolute "super angel." He was always on with a social life that revolved around the Valley's conference, party, and charity fundraiser circuits. Each of these events was an opportunity to build the "Ronco" Rolodex that included some of the Valley's most important players. He generally got tipped off to the startups with the most potential and made it a habit to be in on the best early-stage deals. He was an early investor in Google, PayPal, Facebook, and Twitter, among others. If he wanted in on our deal, then we were only too glad to have him. Aaron and I discussed his style of investing. We knew that he wouldn't get involved in Mint's day-to-day day and would not burden us with reporting requirements or insert himself at inappropriate moments. But when called upon to help us with something, he'd be all in. We took his money and added it to the round.

Next was Aydin Senkut, an ex-Googler who had a small self-funded firm called "Felicis Ventures." Senkut, a native of Istanbul, joined

Google as a fresh graduate of Penn. He was one of sixty employees at the time. When he decided the company had grown too big for him and left, he was one of more than three thousand.

With help from Roy Conway, who knew Senkut from the former's Google investment, he became a full-time angel investor. When he met Aaron and heard the Mint pitch, he wanted to invest some of his Google money.

Our other angels included: Geoff Ralston, founder of Four11, the precursor to Yahoo Mail; Paul Buchheit, another Googler who was responsible for Gmail, the AdSense prototype, and Google's "Don't Be Evil" motto; and Bob Pasker, who built Weblogic, which evolved into a worldwide enterprise platform for Java. Ralston would be a product resource for Aaron; Buchheit would push Aaron on site performance and speed; Pasker was brought in for technical due diligence by Kopelman and would be a technical adviser.

Once the round filled up to the tune of $800,000, we were ready to close it, bank the money, and get back to building Mint. That's when Kopelman broke the news to us that Rob Hayes, not he, would be joining Mint's board of directors. Hayes worked in San Francisco, and it made more sense for him to manage the firm's investment than for Kopelman to try and do so from Philadelphia. Kopelman reassured us that he'd still attend board meetings remotely as an observer. Hayes was a less-known quantity, and to be honest, had less investor mojo, but it was a *fait accompli*. Because of Kopelman's physical distance from the Valley and increasing investment rate, he was beginning to extract himself from the day-to-day affairs of many of his Valley investments. Hayes would cover this base.

So Hayes was our guy. He'd been Omidyar Network's first investing partner in the venture firm started by eBay founder Pierre Omidyar. Hayes was a product guy; earlier in his career, he was the product manager of Palm OS, the operating system for the once-hot Palm Pilot personal digital assistant. We hoped that Hayes would gel with Aaron personally as Mint's first outside board member and that Aaron would benefit from his years of product experience. From Kopelman's perspective, the Mint investment was an early opportunity to get to know his new partner Hayes and to stay in touch with this young, exciting entrepreneur he'd uncovered.

With our roster of investors finalized, all that remained was to complete due diligence. This is the process where the investors' attorneys review all the financial, legal, technology, and business records of the company to ensure it is compliant with all applicable laws, that it owns its technology, and has no pending or potential lawsuits against it lurking under the hood. Diligence didn't take long as Mint had a short history. Soon after, the legal paperwork for the seed investment was complete. The documents were signed, and the investment dollars hit the Mint bank account like blood flowing through the company's veins.

When the round was complete, Hayes invited us to a closing celebration dinner at Tamarine, a new, upscale modern Vietnamese restaurant on University Avenue in downtown Palo Alto.

Goines was able to join us that evening, along with Hayes, Clavier, and Senkut, making up a fair representation of our investors. We spread out seated in comfortable grey leather chairs on either side of a long rectangle table covered in white tablecloth with full silverware and white napkin place settings.

Frenchman Clavier curated an impressive wine selection, and Hayes ordered for the table. We dined family-style on smaller plates of tuna tartare, green papaya salad, and tea leaf beef, followed by larger plates of lemongrass sea bass and hoisin lamb chops with roasted broccoli, among others. It was Mint's first taste of high life. I glanced across at Aaron, who seemed more relaxed in conversation among his investors than he did with this opulent atmosphere. The pomp and circumstance of fancy restaurant dinners ran counter to his frugal nature, but at least he wasn't paying for this one. Hayes closed the evening with a toast to Mint and Aaron, whose vision had shone through. These were optimistic times, and it was only natural to take a moment to celebrate our capital raise and the company's prospects.

PART II

CHAPTER 10

HELLO YODLEE

*"Some single mind must be master, else there
will be no agreement in anything."*

ABRAHAM LINCOLN

Now that we had money in the bank, it was time to integrate account aggregation to develop a Mint alpha product. I knew it was essential to realizing Aaron's vision of simplifying ordinary people's financial lives. Consolidated financial data derived from a consumer's various financial accounts, delivered automatically and cleanly to our users, would fuel the Mint service.

Our research showed that a typical consumer might have several financial accounts, including a checking account, a savings account, one or two credit cards, a retirement account, and perhaps a brokerage account, a student loan, or a home loan account. Even auto, life, and health insurance accounts were relevant to a consumer's finances. Each of these accounts was accessible online, but often from different financial institutions that would have to be accessed one at a time with different login credentials. Moreover, each of these sites had a different user experience that often confused users. As a result, most consumers rarely, if ever, checked all of their online financial accounts because it was complicated, frustrating, and too much work.

With account aggregation, a user would provide Mint with his or her financial account access information one time only so that an automated system could then gather and compile the data automatically on a nightly basis. This would allow users to see their big financial picture and the details under a single login. Mint's analysis of customer spending habits and Ways-to-save marketplace for cheaper product and service alternatives—Mint's means of existence—would not be possible without reliable account aggregation software.

Aaron chose not to build this aggregation infrastructure due to the cost and complexity it would entail. Instead, we targeted another Valley company, Yodlee, as a vendor. Yodlee was developing a new service tailored to third-party developers to allow an application's users to grant permission to access their financial accounts in one place securely. It was what we needed, but many investors whom Aaron had pitched never believed that Yodlee would ever provide Mint with access to this data. Indeed, dealing with the biggest name in account aggregation software would be a challenge for us—and the first one that fell directly in my lap.

Up until this point, Aaron had not clearly defined my role at Mint. I was generally to take on and relieve Aaron from Mint's commercial and operational side so he could focus on building a product and raising money. I was also serving as his Valley sherpa, helping him navigate the customs of doing business Valley-style. Before our seed funding raise, Aaron wanted to print up some Mint business cards and asked what I thought my title should be.

"Oh, I don't know. How about just "Growth,"' I suggested.

All the other fancy titles just seemed too much for that stage. What Mint needed was growth, or none of it would matter anyway. I was also thinking figuratively of the Mint herb and how rapidly it grew when planted properly. Aaron agreed. We printed a batch of Mint cards for me with the title, "Growth" and our next growth move was to lock in account aggregation. It was time for me to go after Yodlee.

In preparation for my negotiations with Yodlee, I discovered that five former Microsoft and Amazon executives founded Yodlee. All of them came to the United States from India to continue their engineering studies. Yodlee.com launched in 1999 to provide consumers with one-stop consolidated access to their internet accounts, including email, banking, news, travel, shopping, bills, and investments, but eventually narrowed to just financial data. They had substantial initial success, including investment from key Valley players and a significant deal with America Online (AOL) in 2000. But Yodlee suffered from the same devastating circumstances that sunk many companies at the time: the dot-com crash, the September 11, 2001, terrorist attacks, and the ensuing economic hard times.

In 2002, the company slashed its valuation to entice the private equity firm Warburg Pincus to invest $20 million. By 2006, Yodlee was back on its feet as a service provider to banks. Its biggest customer was Bank of America (BofA), and it was also powering parts of Fidelity.com and other financial web services.

Instead of the weakness I'd hoped to find and exploit in our looming negotiations, I found the opposite: Yodlee's growing relationship with Bank of America and recapitalization by Warburg Pincus were strengthening its market position. By the second half of 2006, BofA made its "MyPortfolio" personal finance service, powered by Yodlee, available to the bank's customers. BofA was the first bank to use Yodlee's new MoneyCenter module, launched six months earlier. MoneyCenter was the granddaddy of online personal finance software, providing core services such as budgeting, investment tracking, and more. BofA white-labeled MoneyCenter, adopting it wholesale on their site by slapping their brand on it and changing the name of the service to MyPortfolio. The bank then claimed to be the first to integrate a personal finance service into online banking.

Initially, I was concerned. I wasn't sure how Mint could compete. Why would millions of BofA customers who already had access to MyPortfolio ever bother with Mint, an unknown upstart? If BofA succeeded with MyPortfolio, surely other major banks would follow.

I was a BofA customer, so I decided to access the service and dissect it. I was relieved to discover that, to the uninitiated, it was difficult to find on the bank's site. Strangely, BofA was not promoting the service to its customers. It seemed bolted onto its core banking services, seemingly unimportant.

And thankfully, as with most banking sites, the user experience (UX) for the service was awful. It was evident that Yodlee's core focus and expertise was on data services, not on building beautiful consumer web applications. Moreover, there were no insights or savings opportunities like Mint planned to offer; BofA was not attempting to find its customers better BofA products to cross-sell. It seemed like a wasted opportunity.

My instincts told me this poor UX would be the banks' Achilles heel. Just as Intuit had lost its way with consumers by bolting on more unnecessary features, so too had the banks failed to understand the real-time, essential customer connection they could forge over the web. This is where we could attack their flank by offering a simple, automated, and elegant way for any consumer to manage their finances with purpose, value, and community. Only time would tell if our "less is more" approach focusing on design, customer experience, and financial improvement would bear dividends. But the research left me hopeful that we could take on the lumbering bank giants and make a dent in the market.

In my pre-negotiation research, I also looked for leverage in the form of competition that I could use as a bargaining chip. But there was a reason Aaron had identified Yodlee as our primary target: outside of them, it was slim pickings. Intuit had the capability, but they did not open up application programming interfaces (APIs) to outside developers. The only other company with any credibility was CashEdge. Founded in 1999, CashEdge was part of the first wave of internet banking service providers, and a survivor of the dot-com crash. Headquartered in New York, CashEdge got its start as a behind-the-scenes player that supplied banks with services to allow their customers to move money electronically. CashEdge also developed ancillary financial products, including an account aggregation product called AllData.

Aaron did an extensive technical analysis of both Yodlee and CashEdge and favored Yodlee. They had a more robust tech stack consisting of a range of services to build and run applications, including better programming languages, frameworks, and tools for developers to interface with their applications so they could integrate the aggregation software into a service. It would make the Mint engineers' lives more manageable, reduce workload costs, and provide a better user experience to work with a stack like Yodlee's. Moreover, Yodlee had broader bank coverage and some recent customer wins with major banks.

Aaron wanted to go with the best provider technically and the most recognized one in the banking industry. Mint had to build trust with consumers. Using a technology provider that powered major banks, we could claim to be using "bank-level technology" with "bank-level security" in place. The irony of our situation did not escape me. We were trying to work with a company that had failed with a direct-to-consumer approach due to a lack of trust. Now, we were trying to rely on that company's newly found credibility with banks to reassure consumers that the Mint service was safe.

Aaron managed to get an initial meeting with CashEdge, which had a local office in Silicon Valley. However, he did not come away from that meeting impressed with the company and its technology. Meanwhile, Yodlee remained unresponsive to his outreach.

It was time for me to find a way into Yodlee's fortress. I suspected they would view us as a potential distraction. Bank of America had their attention; we were small fry. The word on the street was that they were negotiating an industry-shaking deal to power the bill pay services for Bank of America. Their white-label MoneyCenter personal finance service for BofA was just an *hors d'oeuvre*.

I searched my network to find someone who might know someone at Yodlee. Eventually, I found a secure connection to Melanie Flanagan, the director of marketing at Yodlee. Melanie responded to my outreach, and we arranged to meet for a coffee. As a Yodlee veteran, she was a potential stepping stone to get access to the right people.

I met her at Peet's Coffee in Belmont and showed her Mint's deck. The high-resolution screenshots of Mint looked stunning in stark contrast to the bland offering served up by BofA's MyPortfolio service. Melanie had seen enough. She spontaneously insisted that we come in and show the Yodlee team what we were building. Melanie assured me there would be a lot of interest. She promised to pass along the message to arrange a meeting. Success.

I called Aaron and told him we'd made good first contact with Yodlee with more to come. Though undemonstrative, I sensed he was pleased.

CHAPTER 11

DEAL MODE

"Wise men speak because they have something to say; fools because they have to say something."

PLATO

A few days passed before an email from Joe Polverari, a Yodlee senior executive, arrived in my inbox. Melanie had come through for us. We set a date for a meeting at Yodlee's offices, and Aaron and I began preparing for it.

We agreed that he would lead the technical discussion, and I would handle the business issues. We went over our objectives for the meeting so that we both had a plan going in and would know if it worked coming out. Our goals for this meeting were to have Yodlee believe that we had a solid business plan for Mint, that we had the technical chops to work with their API, and that we could pay them without disappearing over a cliff. We planned to mention CashEdge at just the right moment to test their reaction to some competitive pressure.

Several days later, on a Friday afternoon, we were on our way to Redwood Shores for our first official Yodlee meeting. Aaron drove his 1994 bottle green Jaguar, a car towards the end of its life passed to him by his dad.

As we arrived at Yodlee's headquarters, set in a light industrial office park on Bridge Parkway in Redwood Shores, my mind raced through all the different scenarios that might play out at this meeting. We needed to nail this, or we'd suffer a setback. It was time to focus, soak up the pressure, and make a move.

Aaron parked the car, and we climbed the stairs to the first floor and pressed the door buzzer. The receptionist let us in and welcomed us to Yodlee. She then put us through a range of security checks to give us clearance to stay inside their offices. Yodlee was working with many banking customers, and it wasn't taking any chances on security. We filled out lengthy forms and handed over our identification cards to receive authorization identity badges at the end of the process.

As Aaron was completing his paperwork, I looked around Yodlee's offices to get a sense of the company's culture. There were cubes everywhere, and it was hard to see or hear any people given the office layout. The atmosphere was corporate, stark, and somber. I wouldn't want to show up for work there every day. The receptionist escorted us to a separate conference room back out through the main doors in the front of the building overlooking the car park. She told us that Joe was on a call and would be along soon.

Joe Polverari was the hard-nosed business guy at Yodlee. He joined Yodlee in late 2000 and was now a veteran executive there. He was an imposing figure at the top of the industry's leading company and the champion behind Yodlee's new strategy to attack the market via the banks. By all accounts, as a fledgling startup, we were a mouse in the lion's den. We'd need to convince Polverari that he should give a damn about our little venture.

Polverari finally arrived with Schwark Satyavolu, one of the Yodlee cofounders and the main man behind its account aggregation technology. He would be the technical liaison for the meeting.

We got up and exchanged greetings. They told us that one of their colleagues was going to join in. He'd be along in a few minutes, and we could start the meeting then. As we sat and waited late on a Friday afternoon, Polverari and Satyavolu began chatting about their upcoming weekend plans. They ignored us. It was as if we were not even in the room.

Aaron and I sat there in silence. There was no implicit permission for us to break out into our own side conversation. We were there to make a business play.

Presently, they told us their colleague couldn't make the meeting, after all, so we began without him. Polverari led and asked us to layout our requirements. As we did, Satyavolu seemed particularly interested in Mint's business model and how we planned to leverage a user's financial data to both improve the service and the user's finances via personalized savings recommendations. Polverari didn't seem to care. He was interested in why they should do business with us.

Yodlee had just completed their new API, and it was not yet thoroughly tested. They were not ready to release it into the wild. Their experience working with startups was not good, and Polverari bemoaned this fact with some disdain. Startups were unreliable as customers; they could barely afford anything and often went belly-up before it was time to pay. I acknowledged this risk but emphasized that our recent funding was from quality investors and was just the first round.

What's more, who would be better than us to test the new API? We'd need little support and could give them valuable feedback to improve it. They could iron out all the kinks with us rather than expose them first to the banks. In Aaron's exchanges with Satyavolu, they could see we had technical chops. I sensed this was the opening we needed. We could be their guinea pig, and I said as much.

Polverari wanted to be sure we'd be able to pay them if they did decide to work with us. He went to the whiteboard and sketched out how Yodlee charged for its service and what its underlying operating costs were. It was a good sign of engagement to see him drilling into pricing. Still, I steered him away from this since we were not ready to negotiate a price. We needed more time to crunch the numbers.

We veered back into a technical discussion, and I mentioned our talks with CashEdge. Aaron pointed out a few areas of concern with the CashEdge platform to provide implicit reassurance to Yodlee that we preferred their technology. But the mere mention of CashEdge set Polverari off like a bomb. He launched into a discourse covering how hard it was to build a financial services data platform. Yodlee had been rigorous in its approach, and their leadership was evident just by looking at the banks they had as customers. He had very little time for CashEdge as a serious player in the industry. Indeed, he expected them to go out of business soon. This was the only thing preventing him from lining up a lawsuit against them for infringement of Yodlee's patent rights for account aggregation.

I'd said the right thing; CashEdge was a thorn in Yodlee's side. They were the only company standing in the way of Yodlee having a monopoly on financial data aggregation services. I read it as a good sign that Polverari took so much trouble to dismiss a competitor. It meant that even if he didn't care for our business, there was no way he'd let it slip into the hands of a sworn enemy once his competitive blood pressure spiked.

We discussed the next steps. Yodlee agreed to provide us with access to their platform, documentation, and a test environment to begin our evaluation. Polverari knew there wasn't much sense in going after us for the money just yet. It was better to pounce later. As the meeting ended, we thanked them as we made our way out of the building.

On our way home, we debriefed on our meeting objectives. Yodlee believing in Mint's business model? Check. Seeing us as financially viable? For now, yes. Thinking we had the chops to test their API? Absolutely.

Within a few days, we signed a beta test agreement with Yodlee, and they gave us access to their API. We had to test their system and make sure it would work for us before signing up for a large technology infrastructure and financial commitment.

As I witnessed good progress on our Yodlee testing, it was time to get into deal negotiation mode. First, we needed another horse in the race. Otherwise, Yodlee would skin us alive on pricing. I had to engage CashEdge to hedge our bets and keep Yodlee honest.

I called the CashEdge vice president of sales, who was pleased to put one of his junior guys in touch with me. The young sales guy reached out, and I explained our situation. He sounded excited by the Mint service concept and the prospect of getting a deal done with us. I permitted that excitement to sink in and let him know, in full transparency, that we were also evaluating Yodlee's platform.

Now that I had CashEdge on the hook, it was back to the first horse in the race, Yodlee. From my investigations, I learned that they would charge us a monthly fee for each Mint user. I needed to get that price as low as possible for as long as possible. Otherwise, we might drown the business in aggregation costs. I crunched the numbers on per-user pricing and the total annual amount we'd need to pay Yodlee, depending on various user growth scenarios. Our customer acquisition and aggregation costs needed to be significantly lower than our revenue per user; otherwise, our business model would not work. If the unit economics are wrong, each user added to the system drives the company further into the red. If they are correct, the company can continue to spend on acquiring and serving its users, knowing that it will recoup these costs over time and more. I called around to find anyone who might have worked at or with Yodlee recently to get a benchmark on pricing.

After dozens of calls, I learned two important things. First, Yodlee would hit us with monthly minimum fees regardless of the number of Mint users we had in a given billing period. This was their recurring platform fee and the minimum cost of doing business with them. The second thing I learned was the price they'd negotiated with BofA for account aggregation on MyPortfolio. This service was a loss leader for Yodlee. In effect, they were willing to do it in exchange for the opportunity to set up the grand prize of winning the bank's bill pay business, which would be very profitable. This, then, was their pricing floor. We'd never get them below this. It was inconceivable they'd give us a better price than their biggest customer.

But banks are the worst customers in the world. They're slow, conservative, and bureaucratic. What better palliative than a cutting-edge, hustling startup that's willing to take your still raw software and bang away at it to make it better.

Enter Mint.

We set up another meeting with Polverari at Yodlee's offices. I went alone this time. This meeting confirmed our interest in Yodlee's platform after our technology testing and to negotiate some preliminary terms for a licensing agreement. Once again, Polverari launched into all the things Yodlee would expect from any deal. For the most part,

I listened to determine how hard he intended to hit us and where he might be forgiving. I did not say yes or no to his requirements, but I did let him know that I'd understood what he was asking for and why. I left the meeting with Polverari, allowing him to feel like he'd dictated the terms.

After a couple of days, I received a draft contract from Yodlee. I had some work to do. Their price per user was too high. The contract term of three years was too short. I knew they'd hike the cost after that if we were successful. And on top of that, the monthly minimum platform fees were aggressive.

It was almost as if Yodlee was posturing—here are our terms, take them or leave them. Something told me they wanted the deal, though. It was near the end of the year, and I knew from my days in enterprise software selling that there would be a lot of pressure to bring in revenue to close the fiscal year. I also knew that though they were chasing significant revenue with BofA on bill pay, it might take them months, if not years, to close it. They'd been through a painful restructuring and had landed back on their feet, but now they had to show a return on that investment. The pressure was undeniable during these times. Many private companies operated on a booking basis for their revenue metrics, Yodlee included. They would count our total deal value in the month the deal was signed even though we would be licensing the software over several years. I'd seen crazy deals done with unseemly discounting to squeeze something through. This was to avoid being savaged by the board of directors for missing their quarterly or yearly number—and I saw many a vice president of sales lose their job when missing the numbers.

In light of this, my strategy was to make our deal size and their end-of-year booking as big as possible. In exchange, I'd extract concessions. I increased the duration of the deal, which would add to our total revenue commitment. I also increased the monthly minimum platform commitments and ramp-up progressively each year over the term of the agreement. Expanding the platform fee minimums was a bold, counterintuitive move. There was a risk that we'd end up paying for Mint users we didn't have. I reasoned that if we were not hitting the higher monthly commitments, we'd likely have more significant problems with our business model, at which point all bets would be off. Then, we'd probably renegotiate these fees with Yodlee based on actual Mint user numbers once we knew the realistic trajectory.

Aaron was on board with my approach. Even though he was not an experienced dealmaker yet, I loved how his mind wrapped around the big picture quickly, and he was decisive. I also appreciated his trust in me to get the job done. So I went back to Yodlee with our counterproposal in an email, setting the stage for head-on negotiations. I pushed the deal value just above the total package amount I was shooting for to make it almost too tempting for them to turn it down. Now came the hard part. We were not a bank and could not afford to pay them a high per-user fee. While we were confident in our business model, we didn't know how it would play out. We needed relief on unit pricing. This was our squeeze, and the deal I sent back reflected a significantly lower per-user fee.

On a follow-up phone call to haggle over our respective positions, Polverari appeared disgruntled that he was not getting everything he sought. However, I pointed out that I'd given him more than he asked for on some points. Perhaps understanding this, he did seem to soften his stance. I decided I'd done just enough in this communication. I'd put a big, tempting deal on the table for them to take just ahead of their fiscal year-end, but I'd cut back dramatically on the per-user fee that could come back to bite us hard, and I'd pushed for a longer deal term. I wanted to leave them some time to salivate on the higher total deal package. The final battle setup on per-user pricing was complete, but I left it for another day.

As the last week before the holiday season arrived, I went back to close the deal. Polverari picked up the phone, and we haggled again. As I tried to push the per-user pricing lower, I declared that we might be the company that gets account aggregation right, which would set off a stampede of demand for Yodlee's platform. Polverari was skeptical. He'd heard this one before. He declared that Yodlee was like a utility, and customers, including Mint, need to pay the grid price. I told him that at our proposed pricing (which was equal to what they'd agreed to with Bank of America), I could get the deal done now, and Aaron would sign it. Beyond that, we'd probably be into next year and need board approval. That would take time, and who knows what might intervene in the interim. Polverari considered this and reluctantly agreed that our price was acceptable. We had a deal. I put down the phone and breathed a massive sigh of relief. The agreement was signed, sealed, and delivered before the holidays.

After the deal closed, I paused to reflect that we didn't own this aggregation technology, which would be an essential part of the service we were building. This left a lingering trace of unease in my gut. Our service's infrastructure seemed too important to be beholden to some third party, particularly as they had a reputation for being difficult, even hostile, given the opportunity. I knew Aaron's decision to fold in Yodlee's technology rather than reinvent the wheel was a pragmatic design decision. It would accelerate our launch, and from that perspective, it made perfect sense. Yet, I wondered why our investors hadn't raised this as an issue. For me, that was both reassuring and disquieting at the same time. Perhaps at this early stage of the investment cycle, they were comfortable with multiple risks, and this was merely another one for them. Maybe they saw aggregation technology as a utility that we could always secure in the market somehow. I wasn't so sure. I'd dealt with Yodlee over these past few months, and they'd acted like a wounded bear. They were aggressive, arrogant, and protective of their technology. But there was no time to look back and linger on my doubts. With the Yodlee deal—and my first big win as czar of "Growth"—under our belts, we turned to 2007, the year we would launch the Mint service.

CHAPTER 12

NEW FAMILY.

"I have the simplest tastes. I am always satisfied with the best."
OSCAR WILDE

After securing our seed funding and account aggregation technology, it was time to expand the team. True to Aaron's meticulous nature, he was going to be very selective. He wanted people who were startup-ready and distinguished experts in their field. Mint was on a mission, and Aaron would avoid mercenaries for people who were passionate about personal finance and inspired by his vision for Mint. He sensed that the core team he formed would lock in the company's cultural DNA and set the pattern for future hires.

Aaron was a fan of author Brad Smart, who developed the "Topgrading" process for hiring A-players and wrote a book about it.[1] Topgrading assumes that some job candidates fake resumes and manipulate interviews to obfuscate their lack of qualifications. So Aaron would do a deep dive into a candidate's past educational and career choices to examine their decisions. He believed this would reveal the candidate's underlying character and make it easier and more reliable to decide whether to hire or not. The theory was that candidates willing to discuss the entirety of their careers provide broader insights to interviewers. Patterns of encountering

---

1 Brad and Geoff Smart. *Topgrading (How to Hire, Coach and Keep A Players)*. Penguin. April 1, 2005.

and solving problems can also reveal a wider variety of competencies. Aaron was looking for people who had made these choices and could clearly articulate why. For him, this demonstrated strength of character, intellectual rigor, and fields of inspiration and purpose.

Although Matt and Poornima were both strong hires, they were young and too inexperienced for engineering management. So Aaron was looking for an engineering leader who could further architect the service, integrate Yodlee's technology seamlessly, and build a first-class engineering team. Aaron wanted someone who would set the highest standards for developing code, including selecting APIs and programming languages.

At the next STIRR event in the city, we fell into a discussion with a slight young man with blue eyes and sandy hair whose name tag read "David." He saw us chatting with our investors and seemed intrigued to learn more about our startup. We couldn't tell him much as we were still in stealth mode, the period when a startup builds a product in secret to gain a competitive advantage before it launches. We did, however, hint to David that Mint was something to do with money. David seemed even more curious. Aaron asked him what he did, and we learned he was an engineer. Now Aaron was interested. He told David that if he signed a non-disclosure agreement (NDA), they could meet and discuss Mint. David seemed keen.

Soon, Aaron and David met for lunch, followed by one of Aaron's "topgrading" interviews over Skype. David went over his education and career moves in detail and passed the test to Aaron's satisfaction.

The interview showed that, as an expert in designing and building secure, distributed systems capable of internet-scale, David was right in the zone. A New Jersey transplant with a master's in computer science from Stanford, David's resume also featured several early-stage startups, including GeoCities, where he built one of the first internet ad servers. David also implemented performance and scalability features for NetDynamics, the first Java-based application server (acquired by Sun). He was at PGP Corporation, where he managed the engineering teams behind the company's flagship encryption products. We were impressed with David's credentials.

A few days later, David traveled from the city down the peninsula to Aaron's apartment in Sunnyvale for an interview that would introduce him to the other Mint engineers, Matt and Poornima. The meeting took place at Aaron's kitchen table. David knew these were the people that would be the first members of his team if he joined Mint, and he tried earnestly to show leadership and be respectful at the same time. For their part, Matt and Poornima knew David had stellar engineering experience, but they wondered what kind of boss he would make and how his joining would change their relationship with Aaron. While there was some hesitation on their part, Aaron knew David was the right guy and pushed for their acceptance, which they ultimately provided.

The last person to vet David was me. We met in the evening at Cafe Borrone a few days later. As we chatted, David struck me as bright and ambitious. He seemed willing to take on a raw startup's full risk and responsibility to achieve a quantum career breakthrough. He admitted to being skeptical at first that we were just a me-too copy of Quicken. Happily, as he spent more time with us, Mint's unique differences appeared stronger to him.

The more David got to know Aaron, who was younger than him, the more he wanted to work with Aaron. He'd worked for some non-engineer CEOs, and they didn't always appreciate the complexities and constraints of building web infrastructure and applications. He was impressed by the technical and architectural choices Aaron made for Mint thus far. He'd decided on an object-oriented programming language and had carefully selected some of the best available APIs, including Hibernate. He felt that Aaron had the foresight and patience to ensure Mint wouldn't build up technical debt in its race to launch.

David was also intrigued that Aaron's first paid executive hire would be an engineer. Engineering was something Aaron knew the most about, yet he was willing to give it up first. David appreciated the self-confidence of such a move. After our meeting, I gave my thumbs up to Aaron, and within a few days, we had a firm offer out to David, who accepted. We now had our vice president of engineering and a new member of the executive team. Now that David was on board, we could focus on hiring more engineers. We were on a roll.

With the core engineering team developing, it was time to bring in a marketer to build an audience ready for our launch. That's when Noah Kagan appeared and shook things up.

Noah first met Aaron at an event hosted by Women 2.0, an organization founded in April 2006 to advocate for gender equality in the tech world. Noah didn't think much of Aaron other than to notice he seemed full of himself.

A few months later, their paths crossed again, courtesy of Dave McClure, who First Round connected to Aaron. Dave was a well-known character in the Valley with a popular tech blog called "500 Hats," recognized by its distinctive Dr. Seuss red-and-white striped top hat logo. Dave was a former director of marketing at PayPal. As Noah was looking for consulting work after leaving Facebook, Dave advised Noah to check out Mint.

Dave brought Noah to Aaron's apartment one day in November 2006. Noah's second impression of Aaron was the same as his first—he came across as holier than thou. Aaron could indeed appear austere on the surface; such was his intensity as a driven founder determined to succeed and was nothing if not self-assured. To some who didn't know him better, this came off as arrogance. For my part, I found Aaron to be more of a down-to-earth guy, albeit somewhat severe and socially awkward at times. These character traits seemed to be minor inconveniences and just part of the natural makeup that made him seem extraordinary. I could see that people would either love him or hate him at this level; I could also see that he didn't particularly care either way. Yet, as Noah began to understand what Aaron had accomplished by himself locked away like a caveman in his Sunnyvale apartment for a year, he couldn't help but admire this lone wolf and unapologetic trailblazer.

Noah was doing anything he could to scratch and scrape for money since he no longer received a steady Facebook paycheck. After learning that Aaron offered a $5,000 finder's fee for new hires, Noah quickly ran through his Rolodex and came up with a few quality candidates.

Noah came in one day with a developer candidate to present to Aaron. While Aaron ran through a demo of Mint to explain the service, Noah ended up being blown away by what he saw. After that candidate left, Noah hung around for a few minutes to chat with Aaron. Noah turned to Aaron and said, "Why not hire me as your marketer?" Aaron's response was a flat no. He didn't see Noah, an Intel analyst, and a product manager at Facebook, as a credible marketer.

But Noah's hustling instincts kicked in as he got creative and came up with a proposed no-lose deal for Aaron:

"Give me a week to work on a marketing plan for you for free. If you like it, then hire me as a marketing consultant to execute it. No strings attached."

Aaron agreed. He was ever the scrappy entrepreneur looking to utilize a free resource that might prove useful, and he was, perhaps subconsciously, open to being proven wrong. Aaron had faced rejection multiple times from VCs as an unqualified entrepreneur with a crazy idea that would never work. Still, he eventually overcame the odds of achieving a successful funding round. Perhaps Noah might surprise him.

Noah locked himself away for several days and worked like a madman on the Mint marketing plan proposal. When Noah returned to Mint's offices in early January 2007, plan in hand, he presented Aaron with something audacious. Noah set a goal of acquiring eighty thousand users and one feature in Tier-1 media within six months of Mint's launch.

Noah had thought about Mint's target audience and selected young professionals as the best match. They don't want to waste time and prefer an easy way to stay on top of their finances. He felt they would also be looking for deals and would be comfortable scouring the web for them. This group would be Mint's early adopters. Noah also proposed targeting people in debt who were looking for constructive tips to get themselves out from under and start saving money. His last segment would be new families with mothers who would like to know they could save for their goals.

Noah created a list of blogs and forums that targeted personal finance, moms, young professionals, and tech audiences that Mint would seek to partner with to make up our content network. Noah designed a marketing metrics dashboard and a streamlined registration process as part of the marketing plan. He also laid out the various creative elements to be included on the Mint home page, including sketched diagrams. Noah described how he would make sure the alpha site had the basics of search engine optimization (SEO) implemented, with meta descriptions, titles, and an appropriate URL link structure. To complement this, he would contract with specific bloggers in various verticals of information to have a library of content indexed for SEO and provide useful resources for users. The marketing plan continued for five to six pages covering all aspects of an alpha, beta, and public launch strategy, as well as a thirty-day post-launch plan. Noah had worked hard during the week he took to develop the plan and showed he was motivated to roll up his sleeves and do his best to promote Mint.

One way to convince Aaron you could do something was just to do it. Aaron felt that Noah earned the right to execute what he'd designed with this comprehensive marketing plan. Noah was soon a regular at the Mint offices in Mountain View as our first marketing consultant.

A little later, Aaron decided to enlist Dave McClure as a senior marketing consultant to Mint. Aaron knew that Noah was raw as a marketer and thought Dave might be the chief marketing officer (CMO) we'd eventually need to launch our service. Dave came up with the initial idea for Mint to create a network of personal finance bloggers that would contribute content to Mint's blog and vice versa, an idea that Noah picked up on and ran with to its full potential. We didn't have the money to splash out this early on a big executive hire, so we brought Dave on as a part-time consultant.

The first time I sat down with Noah in a small conference room one evening at Mint's headquarters, we exchanged ideas for building Mint's audience. I soon realized he was way ahead of the game—that he was a web marketing savant. His knowledge of the dark art of search engine optimization was but one example. He was putting this knowledge to build a content marketing strategy for Mint to show up organically in

Google searches. When it did, this would drive web traffic to our site. It was best to get out of his way and let him work his magic. Mint needed to build an audience quickly to lead in the new online market for personal finance, and now we had a plan and a man to help do just that.

Noah was a graduate of UC Berkeley and had degrees in business administration and economics. He was in his early twenties and sported short, curly brown hair, a wispy beard, and a huge grin. Noah had his ears pierced and wore double earrings in both. This look accentuated his already wild demeanor, and, on-brand, he came to work on a high-powered Suzuki motorcycle. Noah didn't seem to have any fixed abode; he preferred to couchsurf. I wasn't sure if he was trying to save money or if he just cherished the vagabond nature of living this way. Perhaps it was the combination that appealed.

Noah was an extrovert with keen curiosity and intelligence and an avid reader and learner. He always had a book propped up in his cube and was ever ready to chat about the latest things he learned. At the time, he was among the first to recognize and prize *The 4-Hour Workweek* by Timothy Ferriss.[2] This book repudiates the traditional, deferred model of working and saving for retirement in favor of delegating and automating to escape the nine-to-five and enjoy life now. Noah was always looking for new ways to hack work and life, and the book captured his imagination.

I was impressed with Noah. I thought he had the disruptor tendencies that Mint needed to build an audience and launch with some buzz. But there was the elephant in the room: Why was he fired from Facebook?

Noah landed his first job at microchip maker Intel in Santa Clara. During one of his early interviews, his Intel manager asked him where he wanted to be in five years. Noah's response was, "Not at Intel!" To his relief, his manager laughed, admitting he felt the same way. True to his promise, after just over a year with the company and when Noah turned twenty-four, he left Intel to join Facebook as the company's

---

2 Timothy Ferriss. *The 4-Hour Work-week*. Crown Publishing Group. June 25, 2007.

thirtieth employee. Facebook was only a year old since its founding in 2004, but its growth was kicking in. It had a few million users, which increased to the tune of fifty thousand new signups per day. On his first day at Facebook, he happened to bump into Mark Zuckerberg, who stopped to inform him his manager was just fired. "Don't ever try to sell my company—welcome to Facebook!" declared Zuckerberg. It was a warning shot.

Noah went on a whirlwind ride at Facebook, soaking up all the energy and excitement, working flat out hard, and learning everything he could. But in his youthful exuberance, he made a series of mistakes that led to his demise.

Noah let his penchant for self-promotion, usually one of his great strengths, get the better of him. He would host startup meetups at Facebook's headquarters to showcase where he worked, and he regularly blogged about Facebook's business on OKDork. This caught Zuckerberg's attention, who took Noah aside and let him know that he'd have to choose between Facebook and his self-promotion activities.

Already on a tenuous footing, Noah's biggest mistake was getting drunk at Coachella and leaking information to *TechCrunch* founder Michael Arrington that Facebook was about to open up its service. It would go beyond college students and form a professional social network for large tech and other companies. The public relations (PR) plan was for the news to be announced the next morning in an orchestrated press release. Instead, using Noah's intel with no apologies, Arrington put out the story that night. Noah was horrified.

Facebook fired Noah. It was a lesson learned at a shocking price. Watching how he'd apply the lessons he'd learned at Facebook to his Mint journey was going to be interesting.

We trusted that Noah would not make that kind of mistake twice.

One advantage of having Noah around was his network of eclectic young web 2.0 pioneers. In February 2007, Aaron decided it was time to launch Mint's blog to the public, and he wanted to deliver the best user interface (UI) and user experience (UX) on the site. That's when Noah introduced us to Jason Putorti, and Mint found its visual identity.

In his early twenties, Jason was of medium height and build with short, wavy dark brown hair, and eyes sunk into a sculpted, handsome face. Jason graduated from the University of Pittsburgh in 2002 with a bachelor's in computer science and mathematics. He started a Master of Fine Arts degree at Parsons School of Design, but his entrepreneurial instincts took over, and he left to help launch a college guidebook company. Later, Jason started a creative agency called Novaurora. He subsequently decided it was time to head out to California and Silicon Valley to fulfill his dreams properly.

Jason became our lead designer and took on responsibility for the product design, the UX, and everything visual at Mint. He also managed the brand image of the company, from the logo to the website. Creating an elegant and engaging interface for users was the crucial next step in Mint's journey. It wasn't an exaggeration to say Mint's success hinged on it. We needed excellence.

Aaron shared a few of Jason's initial landing page designs with me. They were aesthetically pleasing, but I wanted to understand the thinking behind these designs. So the three of us had a meeting early one evening to review the assets. We all knew that trust in the Mint service would be a make or break factor for Mint, and the design and visual appearance of the site would factor heavily in determining this. You only get one chance to make a first impression. When people visit your website, most won't go through a fact-finding expedition to figure out your company history and what your security technology is just to decide if your company can be trusted. Initial trust is a gut feeling, and the easiest way to achieve this trust is via a well-executed visual design that delivers a first-rate experience to your users. Design allows brands to provide visceral experiences that enable emotional customer connections. Ignore design, and you risk creating distrust of your business from day one and driving up the bounce rate from the site.

Simplicity and responsiveness were some of the organizing principles behind Jason's designs. For Jason, design was more than making buttons pretty. It was about helping users get things done in the most effortless way possible—tools that require minimal effort to operate and that generate maximum output are well designed. Mint customers' ability to get to results quickly was crucial, and our design needed to achieve this. Whereas most online web services at the time, like Flickr, used a flat design aesthetic, or minimalist approach, like Google's home page, Mint would use more 3D designs, mainly to separate essential sections. This made it tougher for users to make erroneous clicks and get frustrated.

Jason laid out his design philosophy as he listened respectfully to my intermittent questions. He responded with a brilliant analysis of why every piece of color, copy, and contour was the way it was. He was not good at looking you in the eye when he answered. There was an awkward shyness in his demeanor, but the strength of his design convictions was clear and compelling. I soon learned that design was not just an art form. It was also a science, and that this guy was a master of his craft. After that, I never questioned Jason on design again. He'd forgotten more than I ever knew on the subject. I just waited eagerly to see what he'd come up with next. I knew we were fortunate to have another extraordinary talent on the team and that, if nothing else, we were not going to be out-designed by our competition.

Our team had outgrown Aaron's apartment. As our ranks grew, we moved into our first grown-up office: a building off Hope Street in downtown Mountain View, a hub for startups, that I found on Craigslist. It was a small, two-story building right out of the 70s that was utterly nondescript except for a giant, towering redwood tree out front. Two ex-Yahoo! product guys were running a startup accelerator on the second floor. It was home. We moved in at the end of February 2007.

CHAPTER 13

CONTENT, COMMUNITY, AND COMMISSIONS

"It's kind of fun to do the impossible."
WALT DISNEY

Now that we had our permanent online home, our focus became bringing people to it. The central tenet of Noah's marketing plan was to build content and community. This was the means to capture users in anticipation of Mint's launch. This approach came to be known as content marketing, and Noah and Jason were pioneers of this new web 2.0 movement.

A Mint blog dedicated to personal finance content was Noah's essential tool. He and Jason worked hard for weeks on its roll-out, and when the blog went live, its design elegance was striking. Jason had delivered. It was the first indication of the brilliant trail he was about to blaze across our service, the financial industry, and the web, in design aesthetics and usability.

The blog site's background color was deep bottle green. It drew you in with warmth and made you feel like you were a member of a private club. Jason also designed a new logo consisting of a Mint sprig with a dollar sign engraved in the central leaf. The word "Mint" looked like it had grown out from the sprig as it unfolded to the right. The font was distinguished, and if you looked closely, there was subtle gradient shading across the letters, with a slight reflection coming off the bottom of each letter. The effect was stunning. Jason's elegant blog design created a sense of intrigue, anticipation, and trust around our company. This would give us an early competitive edge against other start-ups chasing this market.

The goal became driving traffic to the blog to capture emails for an eventual launch. It was Noah's time to shine.

Noah thought of himself as a party promoter whose objective was to get the right people lining up to get into an exclusive event. If he could get a line formed, others would see it and want to join. In the online world, that meant creating an email waiting list of people clamoring to discover the latest web service in personal finance.

Noah's marketing plan focused on targeting personal finance and tech bloggers as Mint's primary traffic sources. He figured that influencer marketing and content marketing were going to be the weapons of choice. They were the most manageable campaigns to implement at the lowest cost and highest potential impact. The reality was that Mint would have to acquire its users without a high viral coefficient, a scalable SEO strategy, or paid customer acquisition channels. Mint was not going to be viral in the way that Facebook and Linkedin were. Users generally joined these services at the invitation of a trusted existing user and then invited others to make the service more interesting for themselves. Our service didn't work that way—it was called "personal" finance for a reason. While cost-effective, SEO would take loads of compelling content built up over time and the proper technical keyword tagging of our site for that strategy to gain traction. We did not have that kind of time. Finally, we could not rely on buying ads to build an audience as competing with cash-rich financial institutions in paid online channels was prohibitive and would not scale.

In parallel to their work on the blog, Noah and Jason teamed up on designing online landing pages to attract web users and capture email addresses and user insights. A mix of Adwords (which would become Google Ads), blog sponsorships, and some organic Google traffic from our blog drove customers to these pages. The headline links for this content included such phrases as, "Put money back in your pocket" or "Navigate the credit card jungle." At the foot of each landing page was a prominent call to action to provide an email address "to be notified when we go live." This was the promise of early, exclusive access to the Mint.com beta service when it launched.

Noah and Jason ran many a/b tests on different messaging on these pages to determine what resonated with users and drove the highest conversion of captured emails.[3] These landing pages yielded valuable data providing us with insights into what people wanted most from the Mint service. The pages also allowed us to identify our users' core demographic and financial profiles. Were they looking for more ways to save money or an essential budgeting tool? Did they want to be notified when something significant happened with their money? And so on.

Noah also kicked off a campaign with personal finance and tech bloggers with that same originality. In exchange for early VIP beta access to the Mint service, these bloggers promoted Mint to their readers by posting Mint digital badges on their blogs. This Noah hack created a buzz around our small team, and I had to see what all the excitement was about. I entered the URL for a blog run by Paul Stamatiou, an emerging Valley designer and product geek who hosted a technology-focused blog. There it was, clearly displayed above the fold in the right-hand margin, a digital badge that read "I Want Mint." I navigated to another blogger's site to find another badge that read "My Money's on Mint." Amazing. The Mint service wasn't yet live, and prominent personal finance and technology bloggers were eager to promote it across the web to their loyal audiences. The underlying message was that a very cool personal finance site was coming soon, and they couldn't wait. You, too, could get early access and join the line by clicking on a Mint badge. Because these badges were linked back to the Mint blog, they gave us more free traffic and increased our Google ranking. Momentum would build further once these bloggers got beta access and wrote positive reviews about Mint.com. Noah and Jason

---

3 A/B testing (also known as split testing) is a process of showing two variants of the web page to different segments of website visitors at the same time and comparing which variant drives more conversions.

pioneered new forms of web marketing that our product would have to live up to eventually. The bar was indeed high.

To Aaron's credit, he gave Noah plenty of autonomy and resources to implement the marketing plan. He recognized Noah's energy and creativity, paired with his background in product management. Noah's tests yielded invaluable data in tailoring Mint's product to its customer base and increasing trust in the process. By allowing Noah the resources and freedom to employ then-unconventional approaches like Adwords, Aaron reimagined our pre-launch marketing. He placed Mint ahead of its time with leadership and team members willing to break the mold.

Aaron decided to hire Noah full-time. Noah's disruptive approach was what our scrappy startup needed to take on the industry titans. He became one of Mint's first half dozen employees.

With Noah at the helm, the MyMint blog continued to grow. We started a feature series called "Trainwreck Tuesdays," about people recounting their worst financial disaster. The idea was that learning about other people's blunders made readers feel better about the ones they'd made. It helped build our community. "Have you ever done something dumb with your finances?" we asked readers. "Had they ever held onto a few stocks for too long, bought a car from the wrong person, or suffered through other twists and turns?" We directly engaged our readers by inviting them to submit their stories, and if selected for posting, they would get a free Mint t-shirt from the Mint team. The best comment on the story would get the same prize. Stories would be posted regularly and anonymously on Tuesdays.

We saw our readership grow and become more active, so we followed Trainwreck Tuesdays with another series called "What's in Your Wallet?" Noah would interview someone, like Aaron, one of our investors, or another well-known blogger, and talk about what was in their wallet and why. We'd discover what this said about their personal finances and them as a person. We were looking for creative ways to make personal finance more exciting and relatable to our burgeoning audience. We brought in prominent guest bloggers to write for us, as we couldn't afford to pay for content at the time. They contributed blog articles in exchange for a link from us back to their site and exposure to our audience. At the end of every post, we invited our readers to provide their email for an invite to our beta product.

As we started adding more people to the Mint team, we interviewed new hires on the blog. We called this sequence "The Mint Team Spotlight." This allowed our readers to peek behind the scenes and get to know the real people working on this soon-to-be-launched service. It helped infuse the product with personality and added it to the trust layer we were trying hard to develop.

The Mint blog was a success. It gave us a site we could point our audience to and a voice while the service itself was still under covers in stealth mode. The content marketing network we created allowed us to gather more than enough consumers for our private beta service. This would let us stress test our service ahead of a public launch and give us more valuable product feedback. It also created a significant backlog of users who were ready to join upon launch. After all, if you're going to throw a party, it's better if lots of people show up.

To be ready for launch and for our business model to work, I had to make sure the party was worth staying at. My job was to build commercial relationships with financial partners, so our smart savings engine would be fueled up with offers to present to our users at launch. And because we were still unknown, I'd have to go through the gatekeepers: the affiliate networks. These networks aggregate financial products and services and serve as intermediaries, so the financial partner doesn't have to deal directly with many small, long-tail web publishers.

Affiliate networks emerged with the growth of affiliate marketing and lead generation alongside the commercial internet. In the case of financial services lead generation, or "lead gen," the financial advertiser requires the consumer to complete an application form for a product or service. For example, if a consumer wants a new credit card, they must complete an application form for that card on the card company's site. In this way, the card company receives a lead (the consumer) from the web publisher (Mint). The publisher gets a commission if the card company accepts the consumer as a customer based on completing the application form.

The two leading affiliate networks were Commission Junction (CJ) and Linkshare (now Rakuten Marketing). Before reaching out to Commission Junction, I created a Mint account on their network to test it out. There were a handful of banking products that were generally available to all publishers without getting approval from a CJ agent. Among those first products, I was able to pull an HSBC high yield savings account and a Discover credit card down onto the Mint service. I got these offers on the site in time for our private beta. A few days later, someone in engineering emailed me that a Mint private beta user acted on our first savings offer. It was a surprise. We placed the links simply to test that offers would load and present on the site correctly; perhaps we'd get a few clicks to validate that the offer was functioning. But after a click, one of our users went to HSBC.com to sign up for a new savings account, giving us an affiliate commission of $45. Kaching! A few days later, this happened again with another user for the Discover credit card. Our lead generation system appeared to be working, which meant our business model could work.

This motivated me to go out hard and capture as many financial partners and associated saving offers as possible; we'd need them when we opened the gates at our public launch. From there, I was able to make successful presentations to credit card teams at CJ offices in Santa Barbara and New York and make inroads at Linkshare's annual conference in New York. Once again, Mint's value proposition and execution were shining.

Another essential savings product we wanted to present on Mint was the high-yield savings account. At the time, several outlier banks offered decent interest rates on their savings accounts, in some cases up to as much as 1.25 percent in annual interest, compared to Bank of America's 0.0025 percent.

First Round set up a meeting with ING Direct and me at their headquarters in Wilmington, Delaware. That's where our lightbulb moment happened. ING had the highest yielding savings account with the lowest fees and had the type of product we felt would greatly appeal to Mint's target audience of young, online-savvy professionals. Their CMO encouraged us to present all competitive banking products and services in our Ways-to-save marketplace. He thought we should do this even when we did not have a paid financial partner relationship with the banks behind those products and services. This would reassure Mint's users that we would always present a transparent, comprehensive list of the best financial products and services available in the market.

I knew this was a great idea as soon as I heard it. We could mark the offers for which we would receive a commission as "sponsored." All other offers would be unmarked.

The ING meeting proved remarkable in that they showed such confidence in their products and services that they encouraged full transparency and ranking, which affected Mint's Ways-to-save strategy. This transparency would help Mint build trust with our users and build a deep relationship with those disruptive financial institutions seeking a transparent marketing playing field. Like Mint, they were content to put their product up against any competitor—even the massive incumbents. In that, we were allies.

CHAPTER 14

MINT.COM

"What's in a name? That which we call a rose by any other name would smell as sweet."

WILLIAM SHAKESPEARE

Mint was growing, and although we did not have a firm date for our launch yet, we wanted to get out before 2007 had come and gone. The launch of a startup is the milestone that moves a company officially into the public marketplace with a generally available product that anyone can access by typing the company's URL in the browser. The launch announces to customers, investors, market analysts, the press, and the competition that you're open for business.

Mint's launch would be about getting our story out into the marketplace in a compelling and differentiated way to connect with users and grow our business. As a result, it was now time to reckon with our domain name. We desperately wanted to replace the MyMint.com domain that Aaron had purchased for a few hundred dollars as a hedge while working on the prototype. We needed Mint.com.

Aaron and I both believed that the company's name was crucial to the trust we were trying to forge in the brand. Aaron used to ask, "Offhand, who do you trust more: Mint.com or MoneyAnalyzr.com?" The latter was a name he made up to illustrate his point. It shocked him how little most web 2.0 companies paid attention to their name. "They misspell, have long, cheap domain names, and lose trust because of it," he would say.

Mint.com also made the most sense from a traffic perspective. A convenient but otherwise unrecognizable domain name risked killing word-of-mouth virality. But an excellent, short, memorable name would improve our website rank and boost site traffic. Mint.com was easy to pronounce, easy to spell, and easy to remember. It was clean, fresh, and pleasant sounding. The benefits seemed clear to us—and our hearts were with Mint.com. We thought our end-users would prefer it too.

The only person who couldn't fathom what all the fuss was about was, ironically, our marketing guy. Noah was dead set against us chasing down Mint.com. Noah didn't think Mint's users would care. In his opinion, all that mattered was to have a great product, and the users would follow.

And so we debated. Our marketing guru's opinion held some weight, but the most significant case against obtaining Mint.com was the cost—it was a quality domain name. It would be a high cost for a cash-poor startup that had earmarked its seed funding to build its team and perfect its product.

As we'd just taken on new investors, Aaron was concerned that he should appear as a scrappy, frugal entrepreneur and not one about to spend lavishly chasing after a vanity company name. But Kopelman would have none of this false modesty. As a consummate marketer, he knew the value of a great brand name, and he subscribed to the Valley philosophy of going all out for something to get big fast when it mattered. Kopelman encouraged us to go for it since it would help us build trust in our brand.

Aaron listened; he was learning and adapting to Valleythink at warp speed. He'd heard "no" enough times on Sand Hill Road to realize that building brand trust would be priceless. Indeed, he scoffed at other companies with contorted and contrived names, including early Mint competitors like "Wesabe," "Geezeo," and "Buxfer." And so we resolved to go after Mint.com, but at what cost? We had no cash to put up. Instead, we would offer shares in the company.

We found that Hite Capital Management, a New York hedge fund founded in 2000, owned the "Mint.com" domain. "Oh, great," I thought. "We're going to have to negotiate with guys who don't need any more money. This is going to be tough."

Hite Capital took its name from its founder, Lawrence D. Hite, one of the forefathers of system trading and trend following on Wall Street. Hite cofounded Mint Investment Management Company in 1981. By 1990, Mint was the most significant commodity trading advisor globally in terms of assets under management, and Larry Hite was a Wall Street legend. Jack Schwager dedicated a chapter of his 1992 bestselling book *The New Market Wizards*[4] to Hite's trading and risk management philosophy. According to Schwager, Mint's objective was never to make the most significant percentage return. Instead, Hite aimed for the best growth rate consistent with rigorous risk control. Hite summed up his investment philosophy with two basic rules about winning in trading, as well as in life: "One, if you don't bet, you can't win; and two if you lose all your chips, you can't bet."

With this philosophy, Mint delivered consistent success. In 2000, after years of successful investing, Hite decided to step back and focus on his family office activities. Former members of the original Mint team joined to form Hite Capital Management in 2001.

Learning about Hite Capital would inform how we approached them to negotiate for the Mint.com name. I emailed them to open the discussions. I was pleased when Alex Greyserman responded and agreed to an introductory call. Aaron and I jammed into a small conference room at the Mint offices and huddled around a Polycom star phone as the line connected. Greyserman introduced himself as a partner of the firm responsible for operational and commercial matters. Greyserman's strong Italian New York-New Jersey accent stood out.

I explained the Mint service and its value proposition. Greyserman listened while asking questions intermittently. When I finished, the reaction was muted. Either he was unsure about the opportunity, or

---

4 Jack D. Schwager. *The New Market Wizards: Conversations with America's Top Traders.* Wiley. January 12, 1994.

he was unimpressed. Greyserman explained how they'd acquired the Mint name years earlier and that it represented "market intelligence." They were no longer using it, but that didn't mean they were interested in selling. They'd been contacted by many companies over the years looking to acquire the name, and they'd turned them all away. They had no good reason to part with the Mint domain. I wondered why they'd agreed to our call, given this history.

It was then that Larry Hite chimed in with a question directed to Alex about how and when they still made use of the name. The man himself was on the line, and we didn't know it until he spoke up. His voice was low, gruff, and husky, with a hint of frailty. I detected from the way Greyserman answered Hite's question that they were not in the same room. Although Hite was a passive participant, it was a good sign that he showed up. I doubted he'd make an appearance just for Greyserman to kick us to the curb.

Greyserman thanked us for providing context on our Mint venture. They'd go away and think about it. I was relieved they didn't say no outright.

After a few days passed, I reached back out to Greyserman. He agreed to another call just between the two of us. Hite would stay in the background, above the fray. In preparation, I worked on a spreadsheet with different scenarios under which a small share of the company would be worth a meaningful amount. Some Googling showed that Greyserman held an MBA and Ph.D. in statistics from Rutgers; trying to play a numbers game with this guy was a brave, if not brazen, move.

Beyond that, I sensed my biggest challenge would be to reconcile an east coast, Wall Street negotiating approach with the west coast, Silicon Valley-style of doing business. I knew from my days at Wilson Sonsini that the two worlds were often far apart. The Valley's style was all about speed and getting the deal across the line quickly. Markets, technology, and competitors were moving too fast for deal dithering. Valley deal makers, therefore, focused more on the big picture and the essentials of a deal with a healthy risk tolerance. I'd observed the east coast dealmaking style to take all the time necessary to be thoroughly deliberative, emphasizing downside risk protection and exhaustive examination of edge cases. This could be slow, painful, and costly.

On our call, Greyserman listened as I walked him through the various upside scenarios. Greyserman played his cards close. He feigned disinterest on the call. Being a risk management guy, he struggled with how he would hedge this bet. He didn't want to lose the Mint name if our venture turned belly up. My approaches failed to draw Greyserman out; we ended the call respectfully but with no progress. Yet, once again, I sensed they were implying "no" rather than affirming it. If I could find another approach, there might be a way through.

I gave Aaron an update. "Look," I said, "we're dealing with a couple of guys with a Picasso in their attic. They know it's valuable, but they can't even be bothered to hang it on the wall." What could they want?

Then it hit me. Hite and Greyserman had built a beautiful life on assessing risk and making smart bets, and a small Valley startup on a seed round was about as risky a gamble as it gets. But if we structured the deal with a hedge, they might go for it. We could allow them to retrieve the name in the event of our company's bankruptcy, minimizing their risk. Aaron thought this was worth a try.

I reconnected with Greyserman and hinted that we'd come up with a structure that offered them insurance. It was enough for him to agree to another call. I ran the bankruptcy retrieval idea by him over the phone; he was gruff but reluctantly accepted that this approach was better. He'd think about it.

I called Rob Claassen, Mint's attorney, to check this approach with him. Rob offhandedly endorsed the structure as fine with him; he seemed distracted and didn't do the deep dive we'd expect from him, but that was all we needed to move forward.

I worked on a proposal, and with the language for their hedge in place, I clicked send, hoping it would be enough for them to engage us seriously.

Several days passed in silence, so I prompted Greyserman. I got an email indicating their lawyer thought there were issues with the bankruptcy clause. I was scratching my head. I checked with Claassen, who ran it by one of the firm's experts. He confirmed that, indeed, bankruptcy laws prohibited anyone from making a deal that would allow retrieval of an asset in light of bankruptcy. Other creditors in bankruptcy have a right to a fair distribution of the company's remaining assets to settle all debts. If an asset is sheltered from the bankruptcy proceedings, everyone will attempt this, and the system would break down.

There was no way around it: we'd hit the wall, and the responsibility was mine. I'd proposed an invalid deal structure, and we lost credibility with Hite Capital in the process. I needed to salvage the situation. Fast. Though my Yodlee victory was still fresh, I was far from untouchable; the margin of error for Valley founding teams is minuscule.

Mint's new board member, Rob Hayes, was growing frustrated. He wasn't seeing results on this deal and was looking to assign blame. I was in his line of fire. Hayes was unsure of me to begin with since he regarded me as an unproven web executive, and this gave him an excuse to put more pressure on me. Hayes started to introduce Aaron to a stream of business development rock stars from the First Round network, presumably one of whom might replace me. Hayes was flexing his muscles as the lead investor.

Aaron was aware of the situation and supportive of me. "The problem is you're not part of their little club," he said. I felt that this remark showed leadership maturity beyond his years. He was going to support me or not based on the merits, not based on VC groupthink. Now I needed to repay his faith in me.

I poured over the scenarios and numbers to see if we could be more aggressive in our projections and make the deal more appealing for Hite. When I got Greyserman to agree to another phone call, it didn't go well. He was unimpressed with the various financial scenarios I was peddling. They considered the deal too complicated for them to bother with. Greyserman then hit me with a couple of gems. "We're pure math guys," he said. "We don't get out of bed in the morning for anything less than $2 million." With that, the call ended.

I took a day or two to reflect. It struck me as odd that they were so disinterested, yet Greyserman was spending a good deal of time with me on negotiations. He might want to get to some kind of deal. If only I knew the formula.

With a new approach in mind, I emailed Greyserman for one last call. I let him know that if I couldn't resolve his issues, it would be the last time I'd bother him. That hook brought him back to the table.

On our call, Greyserman backed away with the usual talking points. They didn't need to sell; the deal was complicated; the math wasn't clear. This time, I interrupted and challenged him. "You're thinking about this the wrong way," I said. There was silence on the other end. My adrenaline started to pump. I wanted to jolt him, but I didn't want to go so far as to insult his intelligence. "You told me that you were pure math guys," I continued. Greyserman acknowledged this. "Well, what's your do nothing cost?" I asked. Greyserman was unsure of my meaning. "What's your cost of doing nothing here? How would you calculate that?"

Again, there was silence. I knew I'd stunned Greyserman. The underlying implications must have streamed into his mind. Of course, there was no way to calculate the cost. If our Mint turned out to be a runaway success, they wouldn't suffer too much from the loss of profit. They were rolling in money already. However, their egos as dealmakers would suffer a terrible blow. I had a future image of either one of them sitting at the breakfast table in his pajamas reading the morning's headlines about how our company was acquired for hundreds of millions of dollars. The realization would then set in that they didn't make a dime from the deal or share in an inch of the glory. But of course, they still owned the Mint domain that they weren't using. What a missed opportunity!

I knew it was a good time to end the call and to leave him with a few days to think about this particular math problem.

I thought about how he'd apply Hite's investment philosophy to this situation: "1. If you don't bet, you can't win. 2. If you lose all your chips, you can't bet." I thought Hite Capital could afford to lose the Mint name as a chip while they retained the right to use it for regulatory purposes, but if they didn't bet on us, they'd never win. I turned the tables in this game of poker. I went from being the chaser, on the defensive, to the offensive. I'd moved them away from pure math into a zone where there were no right answers—into behavioral psychology, where they needed to confront deep and complex human emotions. Of course, their simple solution could have been, "Since we can't calculate the value of your cute little personal finance venture, we're out—thanks, but no thanks." However, the fear of missing out can be terrifying and potentially full of regret. It was not so easy to walk away now.

With the tide now turned and Greyserman backpedaling toward the ropes, I got some help just in the nick of time. We'd made progress towards our Series A venture round to add more money and credibility to our startup coffers. Shasta Ventures looked to take the lead with one of their managing partners, Tod Francis, at the helm. I engaged him, and Francis understood our crusade to obtain the Mint.com domain. He agreed to join a call with Greyserman to help nudge him along.

I was relieved that I hadn't offended Greyserman during our last conversation, where I had to be brutal to get through, as he agreed to the call with Francis. After Francis and Greyserman spoke, Francis called me. He thought it had gone well. Remarking on Greyserman's accent, he said it felt like he'd been talking with someone from *The Sopranos*. Francis explained to Greyserman why his firm was lining up to invest in Mint. He saw it as a unique company in the making. Their do nothing cost was going to be higher, much higher, after this conversation. However, Francis was quick to point out that I still had work to do to get them over the line.

When I reconnected with Greyserman, he was receptive, albeit in his gruff manner. We agreed that I could put together another proposal and keep it clear of all the bankruptcy garbage we spilled the last time. It would be a clean deal. We'd get full ownership of Mint.com, and they'd have no recourse. Once it was ours, it was no longer theirs.

I sent the new proposal with an offer of a set number of shares in the company. With the pending Series A investment from Shasta, these shares were now more de-risked and worth more per share than previous offers. This could only help. Their lawyers confirmed there were no legal issues. We agreed on the amount of stock they would receive in the company. It was aggressive but not insane, and Mint's board, consisting officially of Hayes and Aaron, with Kopelman in the background, gave its approval. I waited a few days to go in for the close. It would be a long time before they found another company attaching so much importance to this name and so committed to having it. If they were ever going to sell the Mint domain, now was the time to do it. If we were ever going to acquire it, now was our time.

On our next call, Greyserman was grumbling again about how complicated the deal was. He was exhibiting all the signs of cold feet. His new excuse was that they needed to keep the Mint name for SEC regulatory reasons as they had to respond to inquiries about previously managed funds under a Mint email address. I told him they didn't have to own the domain to maintain those email addresses and that we'd agree they could keep using the Mint name for this. Greyserman appreciated that but was still wary about the overall deal. I sensed this was a play to squeeze a little more juice out of the deal. It was a classic move and implied that if you give me a little extra something, all this trouble will be worth it. I didn't have explicit authority to go higher on the equity offered, but I decided to do it and add some more shares into the deal. It was in the range of another ten basis points (or one-tenth of one percent in the company), which I considered a stretch, but still within the acceptable bounds. I calculated that if we could get a lock on the domain, these additional shares would go unnoticed. I made it clear this was my final offer. Greyserman was now out of excuses. He finally agreed that we had a deal.

I'd taken the call outside on a bright sunny day. As I got off the phone, I walked around for a few minutes with a mixed sense of happiness and relief. I'd gone the distance in a prizefight and came out as the winner, and my bruises were worth it. It was a massive win for Mint and its chances of future success, and me. I'd proven Hayes wrong, made Aaron proud, and earned some security in my role. We'd launch our company in a few months as Mint.com. Now that was a remarkable thing.

I let Aaron know we'd done it. True to form, he did not reveal too much excitement, but I could tell he was pleased. The word started to spread among our small team and back to our investors. They were thrilled, and I received my fair share of congratulations. Happily, I never heard a single complaint about the number of extra shares I'd thrown in. After a few days, Aaron let me know that even Rob Hayes was satisfied with the win and thought I'd achieved something significant. It was a good feeling that came with a sense of relief. I'd struck the ultimate bargain with Yodlee on a long-term, cut-price aggregation deal and had now captured the Mint.com name for a bargain. I'd shut down the doubters.

CHAPTER 15

THE SHASTA SERIES A

"Judge a man by his questions rather than his answers."

VOLTAIRE

Noah's marketing efforts were drumming up demand for Mint, which drove our focus back to where it all began—our product. Seamlessly integrating Yodlee's account aggregation platform in anticipation of a private beta became our imperative, and we'd need more engineers to do it. First, we hired Atish Mehta to work on the backend of the Mint system as the lead data aggregation engineer. He'd also carve out time to work on data analytics and internal tools and help David with scalability and security issues associated with the service.

Like Jason Putorti, Atish was a Noah connection. He was a brilliant young engineer with a computer science degree from the University of Southern California. Atish became part of the city contingent of Mint employees, starting with David, who commuted down from San Francisco to Mint's office in Mountain View. They would roll in anytime after 10 am and stay until about the same time at night before hauling their weary bodies back up to the city. These city slickers contrasted with Aaron, who was content to live a quieter, cheaper, more sober life, renting and commuting from neighboring Sunnyvale. I thought of the city commute as daunting, but they were young, free, and footloose. These young techies weren't going to settle for life in the boring suburbs of Silicon Valley when they could be up all night bar hopping or clubbing with their friends in San Francisco. And as long as their job performance didn't suffer, more power to them.

Atish was deep into techno music and spent occasional nights sitting in as a DJ at some of the hottest techno music events in the city. He also kept an old electronic keyboard and mixing control panel by his computer at work. On some late nights at the office, when all the engineers were working furiously to push out the next release, Atish might help everyone let off steam by firing up his music. He'd let it blast out around the office for a while before everyone got back to work. I enjoyed the eclectic vibe he brought to the company.

On the same day as Atish started, Tuan Le joined as Mint's lead architect to help scale the service.

I was excited to see the team grow; it was fascinating to watch the cast of characters begin to shape our culture. They were starting to eat together in the evenings as they worked late. Aaron, Matt, Poornima, David, Noah, Jason, and Tuan each had their unique personality, and our working environment was still small and open enough to get to know everyone well. Aaron nurtured the team bonding by taking us all out to lunch every Friday at one of the many restaurants in downtown Mountain View.

At this juncture, we had to say goodbye to the first person on the team who didn't work out at Mint. Dave McClure had given us some great marketing insights and been an influential mentor for Noah.

But after observing him strictly as a marketing consultant over the past several months, Aaron didn't think Dave was rigorous enough. From Aaron's binary engineering perspective, Dave's approach was ramshackle, even though Dave knew a lot about the web and marketing. Perhaps Aaron noticed a sharp contrast between what Noah, a novice marketer, could produce and what Dave, a seasoned marketer, delivered. Aaron was always going to judge on the merits, not on reputation. Noah would be able to operate the ship for a while longer, and he was about to bring on some freelance help to keep the blog rolling. So Aaron had the hard conversation with Dave that there wasn't a realistic prospect of him joining to lead marketing for Mint.

I remember Jason, in particular, being amazed that Aaron would take such a hard-line decision. Aaron ignored the fact that Dave was part of the First Round club, which suggested that Mint should be lucky to have him. But, in Aaron's mind, Mint was a meritocracy without compromise. While I was disappointed for Dave, I was impressed with Aaron's determination to make a tough decision when needed. Aaron's commitment to a sharp Mint launch was turning into a force to be reckoned with, and Dave had to go.

For our push into Series A territory, Aaron was getting plenty of help from Hayes, Kopelman, and Goines. By this time, Aaron had convinced an initially reluctant Goines to join Mint's board as an independent director. Goines had established a great mentor relationship with Aaron, meeting with him at least every week at Mint's offices for one to two hours. Somewhere along the way, things fell into place, and Goines agreed to join the board, much to Aaron's relief.

At our next board meeting, we discussed the funding strategy. Kopelman dialed in and spent some time reassuring us that one of our perceived weaknesses was, in fact, a strength. He advised us not to be too concerned that we didn't yet have real users or performance metrics from the primary site. "There's nothing like numbers to fuck up a great story," Kopelman declared. We'd built a core team who'd developed and run a successful alpha, and our private beta was in full swing and demonstrating service stability. We had a blog and a fast-growing email waiting list. Aydin Senkut turned out to be the link in the chain to our next funding round.

Senkut was excited about his investment in Mint, and he was looking forward to doubling down in the Series A. So it was that Senkut made the introduction to Tod Francis and Shasta Ventures in hopes of doing just that.

Interested by what he'd heard about Mint, Tod Francis reached out for a meeting. Aaron responded that if Shasta wanted to meet, they'd need to come to Mint's Mountain View offices. Typically, entrepreneurs called on VCs, not the other way around. Francis was intrigued.

Francis looked every inch the consummate VC. He was tall,

muscular, and lean from hours spent in the saddle of a bike climbing the hills of Portola Valley and neighboring Woodside, behind Sand Hill Road. Despite his thinning grey hair, he had an air of youthfulness about him with grey-blue eyes, a strong jaw, and a natural, patrician smile. But I hadn't heard of Shasta Ventures before, which made them a wild card.

Some research showed Shasta was founded only three years earlier, in 2004 by Francis, Rob Coneybeer, and Ravi Mohan. Francis had ten years of experience investing in technology-enabled consumer and business service companies at Trinity Ventures, a firm I did know. While at Trinity, Francis had invested in Starbucks, PF Changs, the Blue Nile, an online jewelry store, and NextCard, one of the first issuers of credit cards online. However, after the internet bust, no one wanted to touch the consumer space in 2001. Francis had to decide whether to change his consumer practice area or leave his current firm. He chose to pursue his interest in consumer and internet investing.

Francis and his partners started Shasta to invest in companies that would improve end-user experiences in the consumer and software sectors. Shasta began investing its first fund of $210 million in early 2005. Their typical model was to invest in a company with $3 million to $8 million upfront and up to $20 million over time. The aim was to secure 20 percent of the company going in and maintain that stake with smaller follow on investments in subsequent rounds.

I was up in the city for a conference the day Tod Francis and the team first showed up at Mint's offices in Mountain View. After the meeting, Aaron told me Francis would reach out that evening to check in with me. When the call from Francis came in, I noticed he wasn't interested in diligence questions relating to Mint. Instead, he was fascinated with Aaron. In a show of force and bona fides, Francis had arrived with his partners that day at Mint. As Francis recounted, still somewhat in disbelief, partway through the allotted time for the meeting, Aaron paused and asked Francis to explain to him "why he should continue talking to the Shasta team." To his credit, Francis was not offended by Aaron's brusqueness. On the contrary, Francis marveled at the unique boldness of it.

Francis observed that Aaron was as straightforward as they come. Francis was from the midwest of the United States as well, and this may have had him both appreciating and accommodating Aaron's unique character more than most would. Francis knew that Aaron should be discerning about the use of his time as an entrepreneur, and here he was doing so. Francis and his peers in the venture industry were used to entrepreneurs fawning to impress them in their desire to raise money, but Aaron's approach, though unsubtle, was refreshing. Francis also picked up how hard Aaron was thinking about his business and the problem he was trying to solve. This was a unique entrepreneurial trait and success indicator.

I chuckled to myself, wondering which side of Aaron came through with this play. Was it his geek-like, awkward lack of diplomatic and social skills coming to the fore? Perhaps it was his relative naivete about the way things worked in the Valley? Or was it an ingenious play he contrived to shift the psychological balance of the conversation? I prefer to let history show it was the latter, but to be honest, I wasn't sure. I marveled at his transformation from all those early VC rejections to now leading them on a chase to get into the Mint deal.

Francis took up the challenge and told Aaron that he understood the consumer finance market through his experience and ongoing research and that he would demonstrate this to Aaron. He and his team would build a presentation to show the direction of the personal-finance market and what would be needed to win. Aaron agreed to commit some time for Shasta's presentation, just as he had when Noah offered to write up a free marketing launch plan. I had to do a double-take on this. I'd been in the Valley for over ten years, and every funding instance I'd ever known was of an entrepreneur presenting to investors, not the other way round. Somehow, Aaron flipped this model on its head. I had to give Shasta kudos for being humble and confident enough to accept this state of affairs. I suspected that Francis believed that this was the way things should be in the Valley—that every entrepreneur worth his or her salt should be playing the game the way Aaron did.

A few days later, the Shasta team was ready to present their findings on the online personal finance market, and Aaron met at their offices. One of the essential elements of a successful startup is its timing, which can be even more important than the idea, team, business model, or funding dollars that flow into it. The entrepreneur must be ahead of his or her time, but the market must be about ready to turn so that the entrepreneur's product catches the market wind perfectly. Francis knew this, and his presentation showed how Aaron was doing just that. He astutely observed that most of the banks were online, and consumers were increasingly using online banking. Still, no one had connected the dots to understand how aggregation would provide meaning to all this information. Francis estimated that Mint was about two years ahead of its time and that the tide was turning.

Francis was able to draw on his experience as an investor in NextCard, one of the first issuers of online credit cards in the United States. Francis learned a great deal about the online consumer finance markets that he was now applying to assess the Mint opportunity and Aaron's ability to deliver on it.

Francis began asking folks what they thought about aggregating one's finances for online money management. He got two types of answers, depending on the age range of his audience. People who were over forty thought the idea was crazy. No one would ever trust a startup with this type of information. Indeed, it was probably unwise even to entrust so much information to a single bank. But the people who were under thirty had a very different reaction. They instantly understood the value of the service and wondered why this information wasn't online already. Francis knew we had a target market. He shared those findings in the presentation.

Francis also emphasized the importance of building a brand and trust with your users. He pointed to examples of how to do this, as well as how not to. This time Aaron was impressed. He was ready to accept that the Shasta team and Francis, particularly on consumer markets, knew their stuff and could add value.

Francis recognized Aaron as uniquely driven, concise, and compelling. And, of course, Francis loved Aaron's straightforward, no-bullshit approach. Shasta searched for entrepreneurs with a unique vision and passion in a sector where technology can change the way people do business and improve the customer experience. Tod Francis was convinced Aaron and Mint fit the ticket, and he and his partners closed the presentation by telling Aaron that they wanted to lead Mint's Series A financing. And by now, Aaron felt that Shasta and Francis were a fit. He was ready to make a deal.

Shasta moved quickly to lay down a term sheet and get through due diligence. Mint ended up closing a $4.7 million Series A financing led by Shasta in the spring of 2007. We kept the funding under wraps because we were still in stealth mode and wanted to announce it as part of our launch later that year. As a bonus, the round topped up with a new investor introduced by Kopelman. His name was Ram Shriram, and his fund was Sherpalo Ventures. Unlike many investors who wait weeks, talk to their friends, and bring you back for multiple meetings, Ram promptly said to Aaron at their first meeting, "Okay, I'm in" before Aaron finished the pitch.

Here was a prime example of why we'd chosen Kopelman and First Round over Clearstone to lead our seed round. Kopelman kept delivering investor value through First Round's network. Shriram was not just another wealthy gentleman—he was on the board of directors of Google!

The last person to join the Series A was Dave McClure. When Aaron let him go, Dave asked if he could make a small investment in Mint on his way out the door. Dave knew enough about the Valley and web 2.0 to sniff out a truffle, and he was ready to write us a check. Because Dave made a meaningful early contribution to Mint, and his investment amount would not alter the deal's structure, Aaron acquiesced. I'm sure it helped to soften the blow of Dave's departure on both sides.

After the Series A closing, the money hit the Mint bank account and fuelled us up for future growth.

It was a big milestone and a significant relief for me personally, as now I would be able to draw a salary as an officer of the company. Even though the equity I had in the company was climbing in value, it was not paying any bills, and they were piling up.

We were delighted that Shasta was bold enough to make an early bet on Mint and lead the round. We welcomed Tod Francis as our newest board member and knew he would be a close mentor to the company through our next phase of growth and public launch.

CHAPTER 16

LOADING THE LAUNCH TEAM

"Remember upon the fate of each depends the fate of all."
ALEXANDER THE GREAT

With the Series A funding behind us, Noah and Jason continued experimenting with more surveys, user testing, messaging, and psychological profiles. It was the user testing that provided Aaron with his biggest wake-up call. With the offer of a Starbucks gift card, a few members of the public came back to Mint's offices to try out the product and give us feedback. Once Aaron sat in on some of these tests and reviewed the overall results, he felt like he'd been kicked in the chest. It turned out that account aggregation was a huge problem. We'd focused on the technical integration, but we still had work to do to get everyday users comfortable interacting with this essential part of the service.

Users didn't understand why they needed to enter log-in credentials for their bank accounts, and the language used was unfamiliar. As a result, they got caught up in the pitfalls and not the benefits of doing so. Moreover, while it was simple enough to sign up for the Mint service, the onboarding flow for adding bank accounts was less than intuitive. These accounts need to be connected so the data could flow into Mint with the user then moving from registered to active. We'd also failed to consider the many edge cases and things that could go wrong at the onboarding stage. A user might not yet have an online account for their bank, or they might, but they'd forgotten their log-in credentials. The search functionality could be challenging as entering the name of one bank might turn up several types of accounts without the user being able to identify which one they had. The problem set went on and on without sufficient resolution. Overall, we'd failed to create a user experience that was intuitive and trustworthy even though there was nothing wrong with the underlying product functionality. Aaron immediately knew that he'd have to overhaul the entire experience or risk turning away many frustrated users. The software was not ready for launch—not even close.

Aaron and the team focused on the problem set for days and examined all the angles. Then they developed a series of solutions such as placing bank logos on the site, so the user could identify his or her bank quickly for entering credentials and placing security icons, such as a lock there. Hence, users felt safer with the experience. After implementing the fixes, the resulting onboarding flow slowly but surely began to pass additional user testing, and we kept iterating until the results were stable.

The research and user testing also provided the team with branding, messaging, and usability insights to appeal to a targeted audience of young, tech-savvy professionals. Noah coined the theme, "Take back your wallet." Mint would help these people stay one step ahead of the game, save more of their money, and grow it smarter.

Noah was doing an excellent job, but no one (except maybe him) thought he had the experience to lead the company through launch and go on to build a world-class marketing team. So we kicked off our CMO search.

The search began organically. We interviewed several candidates that came in through our network. No one excited us. A candidate might be a brand marketing expert but not strong enough in demand generation, or vice versa. The search was grinding on, and it became clear we were going nowhere fast. We decided to bring in a recruiting firm. It would be expensive, but we hoped it would be worthwhile.

In the meantime, we also pursued a vice president (VP) of product management, which provided another challenge. Mint was a product-centric company, and bringing on a new leader to take our product forward would be another critical hire. For Aaron, as the founder of Mint and the de facto product manager, the product was still his baby. You could be sure that he wasn't going to cede the reins to just anyone. Yet, as with hiring David Michaels and giving up one of his core competencies in engineering, Aaron was ready to surrender the day-to-day product reins. This would allow him to focus on his broader CEO responsibilities and to grow the company.

An independent recruiter brought us Aaron Forth as a candidate for VP product management after getting a referral from First Round Capital. Forth had previously worked with Kopelman at Half.com. When eBay acquired Half.com, Forth spent the next few years there in various product-related roles, where he was when we found each other.

When Aaron Forth first showed up at Mint's offices to meet Aaron Patzer, he was initially put off by the place's pungent odor. At eBay, he was used to state-of-the-art offices; Mint's HQ was a college apartment in comparison. When they met, Forth was not entirely sure what to make of Patzer, who was prone to long pauses as he poured over the Mint pitch deck. Forth noted that this venture was both exciting and risky. He came away unconvinced even though Kopelman had given Patzer the highest recommendation. Forth had subsequent meetings with Noah, whom he found scrappy and brilliant, and then David Michaels, who was able to reassure him of Mint's credentials on the privacy and security front, which was an area of concern.

When it was my turn to interview Forth, I met him in our main conference room downstairs. He was of average height with dark brown hair, cut short, and hazel-grey eyes. He had a pleasant, open face with lightly freckled skin. I noticed his firm handshake as we greeted one another and his direct eye contact. I sat down on the other side of the conference table, and as we spoke, he exhibited an intense focus on understanding the job, who I was, who Aaron was, and the culture of Mint. He sized us up inch by inch and was not about to make any head over heels decision, notwithstanding Kopelman's investment in the company.

Towards the end of the interview, he looked across the table at me and asked, "You're a seasoned guy who's been around for a while—why did you decide to join Mint?" He seemed to be struggling with the risks associated with leaving a prestigious company like eBay and throwing his whole career into a startup. Forth and his wife were planning a family, and he could ill afford to make a bad call at this stage. At the same time, Forth had grown tired of eBay and his role there, which focused on managing people. He wanted to roll up his sleeves and do some real work again, including writing product requirement documents for product features. Working at eBay was like being surrounded by management consultants. It was not easy to get anything done without having to jump through significant planning and review processes that can stifle innovation. Forth's startup experience with Kana Communications and Half.com left him thirsting to get back to a more agile work environment. And he was searching for reassurance from me. I was passionate about Mint, and I was optimistic about our prospects, and I told him so. I was trying to convey, without directing him, that if he was ever going to leap from a big company to a small one, now was the time, and Mint was the kind of company where he should land. He could tell I spoke with deep conviction and appreciated my sincerity. With that, we wrapped up the interview, and I wished him well.

I debriefed with Aaron, and we both felt that Forth was our guy if he was willing to join us. He was a good product strategist and knew how to manage design and development teams. Aaron made Forth an offer to join Mint as our VP of product management.

Kopelman gave us a backchannel heads-up that Forth was impressed with the company and the team, but it would be challenging to get him out of eBay. He was lowering our expectations. Perhaps the timing was not right. We understood but were nevertheless hopeful that the vision for Mint would work its magic on Forth. Hope turned to delight when after a week or two of deliberations, Forth told us he'd decided to come on board. He had the necessary conversations with his wife, and they agreed that Mint was an opportunity not to miss. Forth knew the company was on a mission and solving a big problem and one he experienced personally. There was also the core of a product that he could build on and shape as we drove forward. In the end, Aaron's vision for the service gave Forth the confidence that he needed to make the leap. Once again, against the odds, we somehow got our man and managed to strengthen the Mint team as we continued towards launch.

In the meantime, the marketing search was picking up momentum as we began to look at a trove of potential candidates sent to us by the recruiting agency. Then we saw an unbelievable resume come in from Donna Wells. Donna graduated from the Wharton School at the University of Pennsylvania with a bachelor's degree in economics and from the Stanford University Graduate School of Business with an MBA. She'd spent several years at American Express before going on to be a VP of marketing at Charles Schwab and then VP of marketing at Intuit. From Intuit, she was recruited by Expedia to be the senior vice president (SVP) of marketing. This was her first role outside of financial services, and it took her to Seattle. For whatever reason, the move to Seattle wasn't optimal, and after eighteen months, she left to come back to the Bay Area, where she had a home in Portola Valley. Fate had brought us what looked like a star candidate.

The only question mark was that Donna lacked startup experience. Mint was still pre-launch and had no more than a dozen employees at the time, most of whom were in their twenties. Would this be a cultural fit for Donna, who was much older and seasoned in more corporate marketing practices? Could she lead an innovative, disruptive approach with limited resources? Could she work with someone like Noah and vice versa? We decided to interview her and find out.

I walked into our large conference room to greet Donna, seated at the far end of the table. She rose as I shook her hand. Donna was a smaller woman with a round face, pleasant smile, and blond hair that fell just to her shoulders. She was bespectacled and wore small pearl earrings with a string of matching beads around her neck. Since she seemed steeped in financial technology, I asked her a few questions about which demographic Mint should be targeting and how we might do it. To my surprise, she seemed hesitant in her responses, almost nervous, as if she were taken off guard by my questioning. Did she assume that her resume would do all the talking and that she would breeze through these perfunctory sessions? To avoid an awkward moment, I quickly moved off one question to get her to open up on another softer one, but I got the same reaction. I realized I was in an interview that was not going well for the candidate. She seemed unprepared. I looked for ways to ask a few more questions to fill in time and then wrap it up as quickly as possible. I thanked her for coming in as I got up to leave.

I felt something was missing and told Aaron so. It wasn't just me; he wasn't wowed either. If it had not been for Donna's powerful resume still holding sway over us, we would have passed and continued with the search.

We gave it a few days for reflection. We continued interviewing other candidates, but none were the right mix of strategic and tactical marketer we wanted. We grew concerned that we might be missing something that we would later come to regret. So we agreed we'd both meet Donna together one more time to give it another try.

We arrived at a small cafe for lunch in the Ladera Shopping Center near where Donna lived. This meeting was make or break. If we got the same Donna that showed up to interview in Mountain View, we'd be on our way. Thankfully it wasn't. This time she was relaxed but positively assertive, and we were relieved. Nobody wants an executive search to drag on, and the clock was ticking towards the end of the year. On our way back from lunch, Aaron and I agreed that Donna had done enough this time and that we should hire her. We set the wheels in motion, and within a few weeks, Donna arrived at Mint's offices in Mountain View as our new chief marketing officer.

We were also interviewing PR agencies since an essential goal of any startup launch is favorable media coverage. Ideally, a PR agency gets in on the positioning and messaging process from the beginning to give feedback on what the analysts, press, and market influencers will believe and what won't play with them. We received a recommendation for Atomic PR from Mark Goines, who'd previously worked with Martha Shaughnessy of that firm on a prior startup. The firm had deep experience in technology, consumer, and entertainment markets, along with far-reaching media and influencer relationships.

Soon Martha and a junior colleague arrived at Mint's offices in

Mountain View, armed with the pitch Martha had poured over the night before. Aaron was impressed with Martha, who came across as smart, engaging, and fun, and she clicked with Aaron. Perhaps the introvert in Aaron appreciated the hyper-extrovert in Martha, and it was a case of opposite admiration. For Aaron, public relations and people who worked in the industry were not high on his list of priorities. They were more of a necessary evil. But there was something about Martha that appealed to Aaron. Martha was still going up the ladder in her career, but she'd already picked up many tricks of the trade as she spoke with authority regarding PR strategies for Mint's launch. The meeting wrapped up with Martha sensing that it went well. Aaron's transparency meant that most people knew soon enough whether a meeting was successful or not and whether there was any personal connection.

After hearing the Mint story and engaging with Aaron, Martha was impressed, too. Aaron's clear vision for the service was striking, as was his goal of fixing something important for ordinary people with real problems. He wasn't the Valley founder trying to get rich quick type. He was also the first prospective client that Martha had spoken with, who was younger than she was.

There was a great story and message in Mint, too. Martha was the target user; she was twenty-seven years old and burdened with student loan debt. It was high time she got her financial act together. And she knew that would resonate with millions of people across the country and with the media.

Martha took her excitement back to the firm's chiefs. Aaron's next meeting was with Andy Getsey, the cofounder and CEO of Atomic. Getsey was known as a branding and communications savant. He understood startups, and he knew how to communicate beyond the technology of a company and shape its brand into a story. He could rally an audience around a product to create an authentic community. After meeting Getsey, Aaron knew Atomic was the right agency for Mint. He wanted Martha to be our account manager and lead our PR initiatives with strategic oversight from Getsey. We signed a contract with Atomic, and with Donna now on board as CMO, we had all our pieces in place for launch, even though we had no set platform or date for that event yet. We just knew we had to get out before the end of the year or risk being late to the stage.

Fate and timing were on our side. *TechCrunch* was planning to hold its first startup launch event in the fall of 2007, just several weeks away. If selected, we'd be able to launch the company at that high-profile event. More than seven hundred young companies from around the world were applying to be in the final twenty companies that would present at the event. The word on the street was that we were already on the radar of Mike Arrington, the outspoken founder of *TechCrunch*. *TechCrunch* wanted its first event to be successful, so they were keen to round up what they considered the best pre-launch startups in the Valley. We were in that group—the noise we'd made on the investor circuit, through Noah's marketing, Jason's designs, and our recent hires were already paying dividends. We got some extra attention through Jeff Clavier, who knew Arrington well. Even though the time had passed for us to apply, Clavier ensured that Arrington made an exception for us. A date was set for Aaron to pitch Arrington and his team to approve our entry. At that meeting, Arrington insisted that Aaron show him more than one or two screen captures. He wanted a full-blown demo, but Aaron, well aware of Arrington's reputation for leaking, refused to show him more. It was a bold move because Arrington could have thrown him out of the meeting then and there. Instead, Aaron's move must have impressed Arrington, who had become used to entrepreneurs meeting his demands at the drop of a hat. It left him intrigued. The only way for him to find out was to let us into the event and be on stage during the launch.

Once the news broke that we'd be launching at *TechCrunch* in only a few weeks, I felt the energy surge around the office—for most people. Noah had brought in Viet Dho over the summer to help out as our blog editor and boost our content output. As Viet made his mark, it became noticeable that Noah's presence and motivation at work were shrinking. Something was not right. Perhaps he was resentful that we'd brought in Donna to run marketing. Maybe he looked at

Donna's resume and decided he had nothing to learn from her except corporate conformity. I could empathize at some level. He'd done a fantastic job up to this point and maybe felt he deserved better. He must surely realize that Mint's launch was a milestone, and it was only natural the board would want a leader who'd done this many times before.

Things came to a head when Aaron confronted Noah. To his credit, Noah didn't beat around the bush. He confessed he'd been working on his own startup. While having a side hustle is an unspoken norm in the Valley, particularly among engineers, those who practice this well still manage to contribute fully to their day job until they're ready to take the leap out on their own. Noah was abusing this rule by burning the candle at both ends, and his work rate at Mint declined precipitously. It was deja vu in terms of Noah's exit from Facebook; history was repeating itself. Noah was relying on Viet Dho to cover for him on Mint's content marketing efforts. Viet was doing a good job, but we couldn't accept an employee of Mint retreating from his responsibilities. Since Noah had no intention of changing direction, he had to go. I was perplexed; apparently, he'd learned nothing from the mistake he made at Facebook. Maybe our mistake was trusting that he would. In any case, Noah was committed to his new venture, and he was about to be forced from his second golden startup opportunity for the same sins.

Mark Goines, in his mentor role for Aaron on leadership, encouraged stoicism. Noah was one of those unique characters who were unmanageable, and he wasn't going to change. Aaron talked to Noah and quietly informed him that his time with Mint was over.

I was frustrated with Noah's decision. He was a great talent and personality and immensely helped our team, and I hated to see him leave. I wished he'd been more disciplined and hung in there for just a few more months to earn out his options so he could go with some Mint shares—I wouldn't have begrudged him that.

We'd gained two new executives but lost Dave and Noah along the way. For better or for worse, this was the team that was going to lead us through launch. And though seeing former teammates who made meaningful contributions depart is tough personally, I wasn't surprised at the turnover. As a young company takes shape and grows, some people will inevitably lose the fit and move on. They get replaced by new talent. As with most things in the Valley, change is the only constant.

CHAPTER 17

TECHCRUNCH LIFT-OFF

"Nothing is more powerful than an idea whose time has come."

VICTOR HUGO

I clearly remember the moment when our launch became real and tangible. It was a morning in early August 2007 when I arrived at the office, and Aaron asked me to hop into a meeting room with him. Aaron leaned forward to tell me that Mint would be one of the presenting companies at *TechCrunch* 20.

"That's great!" I said, and I asked Aaron how he was preparing for the event. He'd begun working on his presentation and designing the demo, and I could see he was gearing up to practice it to perfection. Aaron knew he'd be on the spot to deliver, and though he possessed supreme confidence, he was not a polished public speaker who basked in the spotlight. He needed to get in shape quickly. Indeed, the whole team needed to double our focus and execution in the month before launch. The product team would have to decide which features to cut and finalize all requirements and designs. The emphasis would be on stability and simplicity. The engineering team would need to work extra late nights to write the code for the site's launch version. Donna and the marketing team were perhaps under the most pressure as they scrambled to finalize Mint's positioning and brand image. They would need to line up the media to capture maximum buzz from the event.

Our launch was in sight. We had a date, a venue, and a platform. We had to be ready. *TechCrunch* was waiting.

TechCrunch 20 was the inaugural startup launch event hosted by the day's ultimate Silicon Valley tech blog. The man behind the *TechCrunch* phenomenon was Michael Arrington. I knew Mike since he was a Wilson Sonsini alum. Luck would have it that our offices were just around the corner from each other when we both worked at the firm in the late '90s. We were on different teams, but we did know each other. We both left the firm in late 1999.

While we both went to work directly with internet startups, Arrington eventually founded *TechCrunch* in 2005. The purpose of the *TechCrunch* blog was to chronicle web startups in real-time since no one was writing about the explosion in new consumer web companies. Arrington thought it was a gap he could exploit. Getting into character, he mimicked young engineering entrepreneurs and began working sixteen hours a day, seven days a week, to build the *TechCrunch* audience.

Arrington began hosting barbecues at his Atherton home rental. Initially, only a few guests would show up here and there. Then the numbers started to swell to the point of needing to pitch a large tent in his backyard and host up to five hundred people. These events turned into late-night parties and became part of the Valley insider scene. The TechCrunch audience continued to grow, and Arrington became a prominent Valley influencer.

A positive write-up on *TechCrunch* usually meant a sudden spike in website traffic and a credibility boost with the VC community. One example of this phenomenon was with a company called Scribd which Arrington profiled as a YouTube for documents. After the post, CEO and cofounder Trip Adler described how he had ten calls from venture capitalists within forty-eight hours. With strong valuations on offer, Adler took the money and ran.

Arrington earned a reputation as an aggressive reporter who broke the news. He scooped Google buying YouTube in October 2006 and got Noah Kagan to spill the beans on Facebook's plans to open up its platform. Technorati ranked Arrington as the world's fourth-most-powerful blogger. It was only natural that he'd become the catalyst for startup launches rather than just reporting them.

Early in 2007, while attending DEMO, an established annual tech conference for entrepreneurs, Arrington announced that he would create a competing conference on his blog. It was to be known as the "*TechCrunch* 20 Conference."[5] It was a joint venture between *Tech-Crunch* and Jason Calacanis, who cofounded Weblogs' blog network in September 2003, before selling it to AOL in 2005 for around $30 million. The *TechCrunch* format was to have twenty of the hottest new startups announce and demo their products over two days. It would be free for these startups, and they'd be selected exclusively based on merit. Arrington would charge all but the startups presenting a cover price to attend the conference to break even on the event. Arrington would simultaneously boost his blog's brand so that more readers and advertising revenue would stream in.

Back at Mint HQ, Aaron was practicing his pitch for the event. It would be the most critical seven minutes of his life as an entrepreneur up to that point, and he was methodically working on every last detail. He consulted with Andy Getsey and Martha Shaughnessy on tone and messaging, but it was Aaron's design of the script as heavy on a product demo that would make or break his pitch. We were confident in our product and design. Aaron, well-adjusted but an introverted algorithm guy was more of a question mark.

As the big date approached, we began to learn more details. Arrington's choice of the landmark and historic Palace Hotel in San Francisco set the stage for a prestigious showcase. The present hotel structure opened on December 19, 1909, on the same site as its predecessor destroyed in the 1906 earthquake. The hotel was just about to turn a hundred years old.

TechCrunch announced that they were expanding the conference to forty companies, doubling the startups that would be presenting.

---

5 Michael Arrington. "The TechCrunch 20 Conference." *TechCrunch*. February 1, 2007.

This was due to the overwhelming demand and quality of companies wanting to participate. It raised the stakes and increased competition around the event.

In preparation for the big day, Donna ordered bottle green t-shirts for all Mint employees with a front label that read, "I Mint my Money." The Mint leaf logo featured on the back of the t-shirt with "www.mint.com" running underneath. We'd give away some extra t-shirts at the conference to prominent press members and other distinguished attendees.

First Round Capital secured a large reception lounge on the first floor of the Palace Hotel, just up a flight of stairs from the main conference ballroom on the ground floor. This would be the conference home base for First Round's portfolio companies who were part of the event. It was a space where the press, investors, and other influencers could mingle with the attending companies.

The day for the event finally arrived on September 17, 2007, and the San Jose's *Mercury News* ran a headline that read, "The geeks meet at the Palace Hotel for demos at *TechCrunch*."[6] As I arrived that morning and walked through the panoramic front doors into the hotel lobby, I could feel the energy of the crowd building. I walked up to the registration desk as conference attendees milled about with their *TechCrunch* 40 badges draped around their necks. It seemed like most of the new generation of Valley people were there, along with some of the old. New web 2.0 disruptors mixed with the Netscape-era originators, investors with money to burn, celebrities—even MC Hammer, the renowned rapper, was there.

I found my way upstairs to the First Round reserved lounge and was pleased to see the familiar faces of several Mint team members occupying one half of the room. Looking almost like a small army in our Mint t-shirts, the Mint team—employees, investors, and advisors alike—had shown up in numbers and effectively taken over the place and made it our own. There were a couple of other First Round companies in the room, but they seemed insignificant compared to our

---

6 Therese Poletti. "The geeks meet at Palace Hotel for demos at TechCrunch." *The Mercury News*. September 17, 2007.

presence. Conference attendees started drifting up to our place, sensing something was going on and looking for a bit of relief from the swirling, chattering crowd on the ground floor. Many people wanted to know what Mint was all about, but we couldn't tell them as we hadn't presented yet and didn't want to spoil the party. Aaron was off over in a corner with Martha shepherding him through back-to-back sessions with the press and tech blogger community. He was telling them the Mint story under embargo until after he'd presented at the event.

I wandered downstairs to check out what was going on in the grand ballroom. I pushed open the massive wooden doors and slipped into a seat in the back to absorb the atmosphere. The room was full of tech's big players, many of them recognizable. Marissa Mayer, with her unmistakable sleek blond bob, was just a few seats up, and to her left was Matt Coffin, the founder of LowerMyBills. Arrington was up on a well-lit center stage holding court. I pondered for a moment that a couple of years earlier, he was a young, unassuming, completely unknown Wilson Sonsini attorney in the office near me. How things can change quickly and dramatically in the Valley if you're willing to embrace risk and delve into extreme work to get something off the ground.

Arrington managed to pull in a pre-lunch keynote panel of considerable stature. The session featured Mike Moritz of Sequoia Capital, who was the moderator. Moritz, a former *TIME* magazine journalist covering the Valley who had since turned VC, was renowned for his early investments in Yahoo! and then Google. The panelists were David Filo, cofounder of Yahoo; Chad Hurley, cofounder of YouTube; and Marc Andreessen, cofounder of Netscape.

Andreessen, still young but with a shiny bald dome head betraying some advance in years since founding Netscape, opined that for a startup to work, it has to begin with an idea others view as crazy. This is because if it's not off the wall, big companies like Microsoft will have already done it. At the very least, it will be on their roadmap, ready to go as soon as they see any traction in the market. The problem, he continued, is that, out of a thousand crazy ideas, 999 are mad. So that combination of the lunatic and workable business idea is the rare gem that everyone is looking to find.

As the companies lined up in the afternoon to pitch, I pondered which of them would appear to have that lunatic and workable combination and which ones would appear as crazy. Which side of the line would Mint fall into in the eyes of the esteemed judges? It was conventional wisdom in the Valley that the determinative factor for sorting out the wheat from the chaff was the founder or founding team. If that individual or team viewed the market in such a unique way ahead of its time and appeared to have the determination to succeed, that might be the winning ticket. The hedge theory that accompanies this is that if the idea turns out to be crazy, the founders will learn this quickly, pivot, and find another path to successful company building. I liked Aaron's chances.

At this point, Moritz asked the panel which entrepreneur they admired the most. The group all agreed on this: it was Steve Jobs. He created and built Apple into a successful company and then returned from the cold to turn the company around when it was on its knees. Barely a few months earlier, in June 2007, Apple released the first iPhone. No one on the panel yet knew the astounding effect this device would have on the industry and the world.

As the first day of the conference wrapped up, several companies in the batch of forty had gone on stage in front of a panel of judges and pitched their stories. These included Powerset and CastTV in the search and discovery category; Yap, Trutap, and Cubic Telecom in the mobile and communications category; Flock and Tripit in community and collaboration; and Cake Financial in the crowdsourcing category.

The day would not have been complete without a keynote in which Mike Arrington sat down on stage for a fireside chat with none other than Mark Zuckerberg, the young, Harvard drop-out founder of Facebook. Facebook recently emerged as the rising star of the Valley and had just quadrupled in size over the last twelve months. Earlier that year, Facebook launched its developer platform for building applications that would connect to what Zuckerberg began calling the "Social Graph." This concept took the company to another level and saw them leave their arch-competitor, MySpace, behind in their wake.

After Zuckerberg's chat, the day ended. It was time to head back home after a quick, otherwise uneventful drink at the cocktail networking hour. The next morning, Aaron would be on stage to unveil Mint to the world.

I arrived back at the Palace Hotel on Tuesday morning, September 18. Once again, it was buzzing with conference attendees. I checked in with the team upstairs. Everyone's adrenaline was pumping. There was a ton of interest in Mint from conference attendees the day before, and people could see that the press was all over Aaron. Martha was doing a fantastic job corralling them. There was positive tension in the air waiting for release with the launch of Mint later that morning. Three companies were to present before Mint: Xobni, Orgoo, and App2You. Before them sat a panel of judges that included Arrington, Roelof Botha, and Guy Kawasaki. Botha was the former CFO of PayPal, who became a partner at Sequoia Capital, leading that firm's investment in YouTube. Kawasaki was best known as one of the Apple employees responsible for marketing its Macintosh computer line in 1984. He popularized the word "evangelist" in marketing the Macintosh as an "Apple evangelist."

The most exciting company of the second day's morning session was Xobni ("inbox" spelled backward), another First Round company. Xobni brought social activities to Outlook email to make the conversations more personalized and engaging. Their key feature was a sidebar in your inbox that showed profiles of the people with whom you were corresponding. Renowned tech blog *VentureBeat*[7] published a post early that same morning in which it predicted Xobni would win best in show. It made sense; email was the dominant app on the web, and while Outlook was the dominant email platform back then, it was not a popular program. It followed that anything that could significantly improve the user experience would be valuable. It was strong competition, and we were the underdog yet again.

After the next couple of companies, Orgoo and App2you came and went quietly; it was time for Aaron to present Mint at around 9:30 am.

---

7 Matt Marshall. "Email company Xobni launches, may steal TechCrunch prize." *Venturebeat.* September 18, 2007.

I stood to the side of the ballroom, edging close to the front near the stage to get a good view.

A presenter announced Mint.com to the audience. Aaron walked out on stage and strode across to the podium. He was wearing the standard unassuming, yet unique, Aaron package. On top of his Mint polo shirt, Aaron wore a light tweed jacket that one might have imagined more suited to one of his professors at Princeton. He offset this with a pair of faded light blue jeans and brown brogue shoes. He stood erect, young and clean-cut, and the audience fell silent in anticipation as he paused to commence. This was his moment. It was now or never.

As the quintessential product guy, Aaron was more show than tell. He wasted no time firing up Mint.com on his laptop and projected his screen on the giant monitor behind him. Or at least Aaron tried to. At first, he incorrectly typed his password into the program. Still, he stayed calm and corrected this as he uncovered Mint to the outside world for the first time. Mixing stoic calm with a touch of geek gravitas, Aaron smoothly took the audience through some highlights of what Mint was and how it worked. He explained that Mint was a free personal finance web app that was going to revolutionize the way people manage their money and optimize their finances. It would do this by helping them save and make real money. Aaron shared that he had four credit cards and a couple of savings and checking accounts and that it was tough to keep track of all this stuff. He had tried Quicken, Microsoft Money, and even his own Excel spreadsheet, but these were all too much work. These programs wore people down so much that they ended up not keeping track of their finances. On the other hand, Mint connected to more than two thousand banks and fifteen hundred credit cards and pulled in all of your information automatically. Aaron explained that the service was anonymous and didn't ask for your name, address, or social security number. "Mint doesn't know who you are. It knows about your financial information, but not about you," he told the audience. It was a strong start. He had the room's attention, and the audience was eager to learn more.

At this point, Aaron casually began to connect some of his financial accounts to Mint. He started with his CapitalOne business card, followed by his CapitalOne personal card, and then his Fifth Third Bank checking account. All three accounts started to load simultaneously in real-time, which was impressive to see, but at the same time, nerve-wracking. The bandwidth at the conference was spotty, and any one of those banks could have failed to load data for technical reasons at any time. This would have punctured the demo. For now, it seemed surreal that the founder of this young company was about to share his personal financial information, but it added to the drama.

His first CapitalOne card came through, and he continued addressing the audience as the others loaded. He explained that to do the same thing in Quicken takes twenty-nine screens and about one hour. As both card accounts loaded, he pointed out how much he owed on each card and that his most frequent merchant on the business card was Google AdWords. Finally, the Fifth Third account information was loaded, and Aaron was able to take the audience through the Mint overview page and dashboard. He explained that you could see all of your accounts, how much money you had in them, and how much debt. Aaron pointed to a Mint alert that showed he only had $400 in available credit remaining on his CapitalOne personal card. Mint users would be able to get these alerts through email or SMS text messages on their phones while on the go. These alerts would include having a low balance to avoid bouncing a check and paying those nasty bank fees and bill reminder alerts. Mint would also tell you if you've got unusually high spending. For example, you might be spending three times more than usual on restaurants this month.

Aaron then explained the robust technology behind the Mint service, with four patents pending. These were for the system that automatically categorizes and classifies your transactions with 90 percent accuracy. This was no small feat as there were over fourteen million merchants across the United States to classify. Mint could parse all the complex data associated with bank payment transactions into something readable and straightforward. Mint's categorization mastery contrasted with Quicken's misery, which sported about 40 percent accuracy. At that low rate, users don't know where their money goes. Aaron then zoomed in on a pie chart of his spending, which showed the breakdown among gas, groceries, personal care items, and so on. He reminded the audience that only two minutes ago, he was setting up his accounts. Now, he could see a complete breakdown of his spending and where his money was going. For example, he showed how much he'd spent on Amazon in the past three months.

Aaron proceeded to the Ways-to-save section of Mint. This was where users could optimize their finances. Aaron mentioned that in the past three weeks of Mint's private beta, the service had found more than $5 million in savings for several thousand users. He explained that knowing where your money goes is just the beginning of the process. Mint helps users find more money. He showed how Mint just found $2,600 in unique savings for him. Aaron zoomed in on his CapitalOne card, which showed his current interest rate and how much he earned in rewards per dollar spent. Mint showed that if he switched to a similar card from Discover, he'd make over $1,300 in rewards for the same amount of spending.

The audience was stunned. They'd never seen anything like this before. It was all automatic and real-time.

Aaron then switched to his Fifth Third bank account, which showed a balance of $23,000 earning almost no interest. Mint showed that if he changed to ING Bank, he could make as much as 4 percent interest, which was worth an extra $900 per year. Aaron explained that Mint finds the credit card that's right for you. For those who travel a lot, Mint will suggest a miles card. If you spend a lot on groceries and gas, it will indicate a card that rewards you with 5 percent cashback in those categories and 1 percent back on all spending. Aaron then explained the trust system built into Ways-to-save. All of the suggested accounts in the marketplace are rank-ordered concerning how much money the user could make or save. The only offer a Mint user would see is one calculated to save money. For some of these offers, we had an affiliate relationship with the financial institution where we would get paid if the user clicked on the offer. Still, for others, we had no such connection, but we'd show these offers regardless. The intention was to optimize personal finances in a personalized and unbiased way. Most of the audience knew an internet saturated with irrelevant and annoying display ads that interrupted the user experience rather than adding value. This was a refreshing new approach to web monetization. This was "Minty."

Aaron wrapped up his pitch, just a shade under the allotted seven minutes. I breathed a huge sigh of relief that nothing had gone wrong. On the contrary, Aaron had nailed it. The product came across as new, sleek, and powerful. It was easy to understand how it worked, who would use it, and why. The young man who was the visionary behind the product seemed intriguing. Yes, there was something about him that seemed unique. I could feel the audience stir as one after another person turned to the person next to them and whispered what looked like something approving. There was no denying it: they had just witnessed something impressive.

Aaron then stood his ground to field a few questions from Guy Kawasaki, Roelof Botha, and Esther Dyson on the panel of judges. Kawasaki wondered whether Mint should emphasize the saving money aspect of the service or focus on organizing finances. Aaron let the panel engage in a brief discussion as to which was more important. The panel continued to pepper Aaron with questions. Aaron calmly met each with deference, intelligence, strength, and conviction. I realized this was helping to boost Mint's overall first impression. Arrington stood up and thanked him for the presentation, and Aaron walked off the stage to warm applause.

For just a moment, I thought about Aaron Patzer, the founder of his new company, and Roelof Botha, of the mammoth Sequoia Capital, both up on stage. Just over a year earlier, Botha turned down the chance to invest in Mint, and Aaron simultaneously turned down the opportunity to be the first front-end engineer for Youtube. When Aaron first emerged with his Mint prototype and hit Sand Hill Road for the first time (before I joined him), he got an introduction to Botha and Sequoia. Botha, the former CFO of PayPal, had joined Sequoia after the firm had helped PayPal go public and subsequently invested in his PayPal mafia brethren, Hurley and Chen, at YouTube. When Botha first heard Aaron's Mint pitch as an investor, he was still bearing the scars of PayPal's tribulations in the financial technology arena. Botha knew it was a hard industry vertical to break into. Though Botha liked the Mint concept, he didn't rate its chances in the heavily regulated financial services industry. He did, however, recognize Aaron's qualities as a brilliant young engineer and tried hard to recruit him to join YouTube. Had Botha succeeded, Aaron would not have been up on stage that afternoon. However, he would have already been worth more than $10 million, given YouTube's acquisition by Google less than a year ago. With that amount of money in his pocket, who knows if he ever would have bothered to start Mint.

Arrington called out Matt Cohler, formerly of LowerMyBills, in the audience and asked him if what he'd just witnessed was deja vu—it was, after all, another financial service modeled on lead generation. Then Arrington turned to the audience and declared that Mint had done the best pre-launch marketing he had ever seen from a young company. There was so much buzz around the company and what it was going to reveal that he couldn't wait to find out what it was all about. I thought of Noah in that instant and all the brilliant pre-launch marketing work he'd done. It was bittersweet since he was no longer with the company and unable to participate in this fantastic day for Mint.

I headed back upstairs to find out what the rest of the Mint team thought of Aaron's presentation. I wanted to be sure it was not just me seeing things through rose-colored glasses. As good as it was, I daren't imagine that it was capable of winning the show. There were too many other good companies in the mix, and Xobni seemed like a press favorite.

The Mint corner was buzzing. Many conference-goers now knew our location, and they rushed up to do a double-take on the company. I chatted with a few Minters, and everyone agreed Aaron had nailed it. There was no sign of Aaron; he was likely inundated with press interviews after coming off the stage and wouldn't resurface for some time.

After the excitement settled, I realized we were now officially launched. It felt strange after so many months of dedicated preparation to get to this point. Now, anyone could go online and sign up for our service, and the registrations were starting to flow. We couldn't curate and control our audience any longer with private invitations and carefully balanced numbers. Mint was live. It was a fantastic feeling, though tinged with a hint of uncertainty.

The rest of the afternoon at *TechCrunch* 40 passed by in a haze as people swirled in and out of our room. I managed to catch a few of the other contestants presenting but wasn't particularly struck by any of them. As I mingled with the crowds, everyone congratulated me on the company's launch and complimented Aaron's presentation.

As events like these tend to, the show started to fade on the afternoon of the second day. A handful of the Mint team continued to serve Mint Mojitos to conference attendees who were still drifting up to our pod upstairs. After helping pour a few for our guests, I decided it was time to head home. Little did I know that just a couple of hours later, we were about to receive some happy news. Calacanis came on stage with Arrington to announce the winner. It was Mint, not the early favorite Xobni or any of the other thirty-eight rising tech stars, that took the prize.

Aaron went up on stage to shake hands with Calacanis and Arrington and join in a photo op in which Arrington presented him with a massive cardboard check replica for $50,000. Of course, it would be nice to bank the actual check, but Mint was just anointed the hottest new startup in the Valley, and that was worth far more than $50,000.[8]

Overnight and during the next day, the press and congratulations rolled in. The dozens of back-to-back interviews Aaron did at the show with *Forbes, Fortune, Business 2.0, VentureBeat,* and *CNET*, among others, were now bearing fruit. According to Technorati, Mint.com had nearly a thousand posts written about it immediately after *TechCrunch* 40.

As the congratulations came flowing in, so did the new users. More than eighty thousand people visited the site within a twelve-hour window, and over fifteen thousand people signed up for Mint that day. This was far more than we had contemplated. It slowed our site to a

---

8 "Mint Wins TechCrunch40 Top Company Award; Takes $50,000 Prize." *TechCrunch.* September 19, 2007.

crawl, and for what seemed like hours, the site could not be reached by the many who tried. Complaints started to flow into the blogosphere as people wondered what all the fuss was about this new service that they couldn't reach. I asked myself if this were to be our moment of misery, where we'd fail to hold up in the face of everything we'd worked so hard for due to technical failure. I'd been working night and day for over a year since I met Aaron to arrive at this moment, and I didn't want the dream to turn into a nightmare.

Fortunately, David Michaels and Atish Mehta moved into high gear and worked late into the night, rewriting the data provider and increasing MySQL's in-memory database cache. This made it more scalable for the next wave of sign-up spikes. They pushed the new code out overnight, and by the following day, Mint was up and running smoothly.

We'd done it! We'd successfully launched Mint to the world. As Kopelman noted, we'd achieved the entire year's plan for audience growth in forty-eight hours. Now I wondered less about what the future was about to bring, than all the things I needed to do the next day to keep the growth engine humming. The journey had only just begun.

PART III

CHAPTER 18

BUILDING MOMENTUM

"If you want to build a ship, don't drum up people to collect wood and don't assign them tasks and work, but rather teach them to long for the endless immensity of the sea."

ANTOINE DE SAINT-EXUPERY

Back at the office, the feeling in the days and weeks following *Tech-Crunch* 40 was buoyant. We had only circumstantial evidence of our success up until launch, but now it was tangible. That also meant we were in the spotlight.

With this success inevitably came scrutiny and the first challenge beyond handling the traffic of the first night for our Mint service. We shared the fate of much of history's new technology: a public hesitance to trust it. Scattered among the praise on online tech communities were aggressive doubts about Mint's security: predictions that it was vulnerable to hacking and fraud, that banks would block the service and that customers waived the right to their banks' protection against fraud by using Mint. None of this was true, and we'd prepared for this pushback. A disruptive new service must.

We provided a comprehensive section of the Mint site to explain that all data storage on Mint is encrypted. Our servers were also in a secure facility protected by biometric palm scanners and 24/7 security guards. Beyond that, communication between a user's browser and Mint occurred using 128-bit SSL, the highest industry standard, to prevent hacker activity. We used bank-level standards, including encryption, auditing, logging, backups, and safeguarding data. We informed our users that we regularly hacked our site, running thousands of tests on our software to ensure security. We scanned our ports, tested for SQL injection, and protected against cross-site scripting. We also updated and patched our software all the time. We referenced our use of industry-standard, secure account aggregation via Yodlee, the same back-end aggregation system used by Bank of America, Fidelity, and Microsoft Money. We stressed that Verisign independently verified Mint as secure via an audit that confirmed we followed industry security practices. We explained that even if there was a security breach, our site was "read-only" in that no money moved in or out. And we emphasized that Mint was an anonymous service—all we had were emails, not names or social security numbers.

But despite the preemptive steps we'd taken, the negative buzz was enough to prompt an official statement by Aaron extolling Mint's security. We even explored providing insurance to Mint's users via Lloyds of London, more as a strategy to influence the tide of public sentiment than because we thought we needed it. Eventually, the favorable reviews by bloggers and users that kept streaming in were enough to drown out the naysayers and win the court of public opinion. A *Lifehacker* review noted that "after just four weeks...financial management website Mint is already boasting over fifty thousand members and managing over $2 billion of their money."[9] Adam Nash, a former Quicken user, had glowing praise for Mint: "Within the next five to ten years, if Mint stays a free service, most normal people would be using Mint or an application like it."

In the meantime, Mint's earliest and fiercest startup rival, Wesabe, had taken another approach to privacy and security. Instead of enabling their service with your bank's login credentials, Wesabe's users installed a small browser plug-in that allowed them to download their bank statements and upload them to Wesabe. This approach seemed

---

9 Adam Nash. "Is Mint Ready For Your Money?" *Lifehacker*. October 18, 2007.

more secure since users never had to provide their login credentials to a third-party service. However, the thought of having to go online periodically, log into your various bank accounts, and manually do this work was something Aaron was not willing to bet on. He knew that simplicity, ease of use, and time to data that delights must be paramount, and he stuck to his guns on this. Time would tell if he gambled correctly.

To Aaron's credit, he didn't become preoccupied with the noise. He steered us toward concentrating on our bread and butter: moving past beta and developing the comprehensive personal finance service we envisioned Mint to be. Gaining trust was only the beginning; keeping it would be the challenge.

We launched Mint as a minimal viable service. Still, we wanted to improve our categorization, add more banks to our service, analyze investments and loans, bolster our credit card vertical, help users with budgets, optimize taxes, and the list went on. To execute it, we needed more talent.

First, I hired Sid Bhatt as director of business development in October 2007 to be my right-hand man for building Mint's revenue engine. He had business and product skills, combined with financial services industry experience. Sid supposedly lived in an apartment somewhere close to our offices in downtown Mountain View. However, many of us suspected, half-joking, that he lived at the Mint office. Sid would smirk when I asked where he kept his bed kit. At least once or twice a week, an Amazon package would show up at the office personally addressed to him. I'd wonder why it hadn't gone to his apartment. I never found out what was in those Amazon packages, but I'm sure his Mint profile showed some significant spending at merchant "Amazon," category "shopping."

With increased traffic and a larger customer base came the need for the product and engineering teams to expand. Justin Maxwell, who'd played a significant role in the redesign of Apple.com, joined Jason in design and user experience (and Atish as another electronic music aficionado). New hire Daryl Puryear, boasting a master's in computer science from Stanford, was quickly promoted to director of the engineering team so David could focus on site architecture, scalability, security, and growing the engineering team. Val Agostino, who'd just shuttered a social startup based on Facebook's platform, joined Aaron Forth's team. Aaron also added Yahoo! vet Stephen Mann for customer support, George Chlentzos for quality assurance, and Stephan Sochoux as director of technical operations. Donna expanded her marketing team by hiring Stew Langille to accelerate online demand generation.

Our ability to attract and win over this talent was a sign of increasing strength. The battle for talent in the Valley is fierce and not for the faint-hearted. Many other larger, more resourceful Valley companies are competing for those with proven success and potential to grow. Indeed, a company's ability to hire and integrate new team members quickly and successfully is right up there in importance with product-market fit.

The management team was now in place, with Aaron Forth and Donna joining Aaron, myself, and David, and each of us was beginning to build out our teams for growth and scale. Our new team members blended into our pre-launch team to total nearly twenty employees.

Thus far, we'd done well if only judging by the count of awards we were starting to collect at the end of the year. These included: "*P.C. World* 25 Most Innovative Products Award," "*Business Week* 101 Best Free Sites on the Web," "*Lifehacker* Top 10 Innovations for 2007," "*Finovate* Best in Show for Financial Innovation," "The Motley Fool Award for Best Money Management Tool 2007," and many more. Now it was time to make some strategic decisions about how to mold Mint so that our users might never have to visit another financial site online.

CHAPTER 19

SERIES B IS FOR BENCHMARK

"The really big wins are where all the rewards come from."
BOB KAGLE

By early 2008, the time was right to raise additional venture capital to fund the company's continued growth. Like most startups focused on growth, Mint was burning cash every month as the cost of building the business was higher than the revenue we were bringing in. Eventually, our runway would end. The main cost centers were headcount, account aggregation, and customer acquisition, which were all continuing to expand.

From my years of doing venture funding deals at Wilson Sonsini, I knew the fundraising game well. It was customary for an emerging, high-growth startup to be losing money at this juncture. The expectation is that reaching cash-flow positive and, beyond that, profitability would take considerable time. As long as the growth was there, the investors would accept underlying losses. It was par for the Valley course. In the meantime, the investors expect that the cash a startup burned through was invested wisely in growing the business and that the burn rate (the amount of money the company lost each month) should stay at a minimum acceptable standard—considered to be under $500,000 per month at the time. Mint was well under this, but costs were rising.

Another startup benchmark was that a company should always have at least six months of runway cash in the bank when it goes for funding to allow enough time to secure the financing. This serves to preclude investors from taking a hard-line negotiating advantage when the company is on a cash precipice. Planning early for ongoing fundraising was considered wise.

One final consideration was market timing. If the venture market was buoyant, it was always easier to access funding than when the economy turned south and liquidity dried up. And you never knew when that might happen. Mint was hot, the market was hot, and it was an ideal time to raise.

The board of directors and Mint's management team met to discuss the best approaches. To get to a higher valuation, we'd need to have competition for our deal. Whichever firm won our Series B would expect to have their representative partner join our board of directors. This meant we'd be focusing on the strengths, character, and integrity of whoever that lead investing partner might be.

As we put together our funding pitch and leveraged contacts in our investor network, we soon emerged with two horses leading the race: Benchmark Capital, represented by Bob Kagle, and Bessemer Venture Partners, represented by David Cowan. Both firms were Valley heavyweights, and these two gentlemen were the luminaries at each.

Aaron first met with David Cowan of Bessemer Ventures at their offices in Menlo Park. Cowan asked many tough questions and was critical of some aspects of Mint but was nonetheless intrigued. He wanted to dig into preliminary diligence to decide whether to go to the term sheet stage. We were in the game and on first base with a top-tier venture firm.

In the meantime, Aaron was soon to meet with Bob Kagle of Benchmark, who was introduced by Tod Francis. Kagle lived in Woodside, a small town on the edge of the Santa Cruz mountains that is among the wealthiest towns in the US. Kagle counted some of Silicon Valley's most prominent names among his neighbors, including Scott Cook, Larry Sonsini, Steve Jobs, and Larry Ellison.

Kagle invited Aaron to meet for breakfast at Bucks of Woodside, a small restaurant that gained fame as a meeting place for venture capitalists and tech entrepreneurs. What intrigued Aaron was Kagle's focus on him more than on the Mint service. Just as Aaron grilled most of his interview candidates with the topgrading process, Kagle seemed determined to find out who Aaron was as a person and an entrepreneur. Kagle had surely learned from experience that it was entrepreneurial DNA that best determines whether a venture investment is likely to succeed. So Aaron was on the spot under a laser focus.

For his part, Aaron identified with Kagle's midwestern demeanor and hardworking background. A native of Michigan, Kagle earned a BS in electrical engineering from General Motors Institute (renamed Kettering University) while working at the company. He went on to earn an MBA from Stanford and worked his way up through consulting and venture capital before founding Benchmark Capital. Here was a guy who'd made it the old-fashioned way through smarts and flat-out hard work.

Benchmark itself had a contrarian approach that was appealing to a young entrepreneur. It was relatively new and founded in 1995. Kagle and his partners distributed profits equally among them, rather than the "to the winner go the spoils" approach of most firms.

And Kagel was establishing himself as a visionary. He'd made the best-performing venture deal of all time, investing $5 million in eBay for an eventual return of $5 billion. Kagle's personal take from the eBay investment was said to be a cool $170 million—a number worth remembering.

All that was music to Aaron's ears. And we knew the value of choosing the right venture firm to lead our financing. We wanted the smart money—the investor who would be a positive addition to the board and help us grow the most. We also needed someone who would form a positive and productive relationship with Aaron. In contrast with Kagle, Aaron did not gel particularly well with Cowan's personality, which seemed dry and reserved.

Benchmark was well aware of Bessemer being in the race, and they finally came through on valuation. Kagle was not a man to spend any extra money than he needed, but he was not one to hesitate or pinch pennies when he saw a deal was right for the taking. After Aaron presented to the full Benchmark partnership, the firm made the right offer, and we never looked back from there. The Benchmark term sheet came in, and both sides signed it.

While a term sheet can look perfectly acceptable to both sides when signed, the devil is often in the details. Valley venture term sheets are intentionally light, consisting of only one to two pages that set out the essentials of the deal in simple language. This is so they can be quickly negotiated and agreed to lock in a deal pending completion of more robust final legal agreements that can run to hundreds of pages containing dense legalese. If you don't do a deal fast in the Valley, someone else will do it for you in the meantime.

As the full legal agreements were processed, Benchmark included a provision that created a serious issue that was now holding up the deal closing. Aaron told me that Benchmark wanted the right to a set of special voting rights for the Series B stockholders as a class, including the right to veto any acquisition offer made for Mint. At that point, an acquisition was the furthest thing from our minds, and this seemed draconian. This language meant that if a legitimate acquisition offer came in for Mint, Benchmark, as the majority holder of Series B shares, could block the deal despite not owning a majority of all the shares of the company.

Although I felt the deal was far enough along that it was likely to close with reasonable minds ultimately prevailing, this was a severe issue, and Benchmark had big guns. On the other side, it's a hard thing for a founder to accept that when an investor only buys a minority slice of the company, albeit for millions of dollars, they could subsequently block a deal that would otherwise represent life-changing success for that founder. This issue was preoccupying Aaron, and I could see he was anxious to resolve it.

Whatever the rationale on both sides, here we were, at a standoff. I suggested to Aaron a possible compromise. My idea was to let them have this blocking right, but only if the deal adversely affected the Series B investors as a class relative to the other classes of seed and

Series A investors. It was a subtle distinction. Still, it presented a much narrower test and would limit Benchmark's opportunity to block a deal.

The most likely scenario would revolve around a "liquidation preference," which allows venture investors to take back their initial investment, dollar for dollar, from the sale proceeds of the company. It's a hedge for VCs and happens before any proceeds are distributed to common stockholders. Benchmark might get less back on a percentage basis than the seed or Series A investors and move to block the deal in the event of a fire sale of Mint with limited proceeds for distribution.

I could see Aaron's non-legal brain processing this idea, and he seemed to get it. He nodded his approval, and I knew his next move would be to run it by Claassen to see if it had legs. Rob knew that this right was given to Benchmark in any event under Delaware law, which governed since Mint was a Delaware company. So adding specific text to the agreement wouldn't be giving anything away. Within a few days, Rob returned to inform us that Benchmark's attorneys had agreed on this approach. The last hurdle to the deal had gone away, and we were back on track to complete diligence and close within another week or two. I was relieved. Time is money in the Valley, and we needed more of both.

In March 2008, only six months after our launch at *TechCrunch 40*, we announced our Series B venture financing, led by Benchmark Capital, whose partner Bob Kagle would join our board of directors.[10] It was our third round of funding, and this time we brought in $12.1 million in new money, with all of our previous investors participating in the round. Even Hite Capital, who now owned shares in Mint, decided to invest new money based on their pro-rata right to maintain their percentage ownership.

Aaron showed just a hint of exuberance as he let people know that Bob Kagle was "coming off eBay's board to join Mint." I think the reality was that Kagle had been a board member at eBay for almost ten years. eBay was now a mature public company worth tens of billions

---

10 "Leading Personal Financial Web Application to Expand Reach, Functionality, and Service Offerings." *Mintlife*. March 5, 2008.

of dollars, and Kagle's time there had just run its course. Kagle needed to look for the next eBay and not hang around at the old one. Regardless, it was an honor to have him on our board and be part of helping Mint with a new chapter of expansion.

TechCrunch again stepped in to cover our story. As usual, there was a slew of for and aghast verbiage in the *TechCrunch* comments section, but this time we felt no need to chime in and defend what we were doing.

As the Series B money hit Mint's bank account, I didn't dwell on Benchmark's right to block any Mint acquisition under certain circumstances. But one thing should have been clear to all involved: Kagle joining Mint was a signal to expect us to play in the big leagues and hit a game-winning home run out of the park. Nothing less would satisfy the expectations of Benchmark Capital.

CHAPTER 20

BUILDING BEYOND BETA

"The reward for work well done is the opportunity to do more."

JONAS SALK

Next, we scaled. If things start to slow down in the Valley, it's never a good sign. You've got to keep moving faster and growing stronger simultaneously. But that pace of expansion makes for tough decisions about directions and priorities, sets up strain and conflict, and risks diversification, leading to product dilution.

The first move was a clear one: expand our footprint in a vertical that was a proven, key driver of revenue. Our credit card marketplace was the showcase of our Ways-to-save system. We had the best balance transfer cards, cashback rewards cards, airline miles travel cards, cards for building credit, and student-oriented cards—and each conversion by a customer meant a commission of $45–85 for Mint. Because we were making more personalized, quantified recommendations, wrapped in a UX that was easy, clean, and transparent, we delivered more savings to our users and made more money from our service.

But expansion alone doesn't drive success. Our team continued to test and optimize the system. As we analyzed the conversion data we got back from some of our card partners, we noticed a nearly 50 percent drop-off from users who had clicked on a Mint credit card offer and those whose applications were accepted by the card company. What about the other 50 percent that the card companies rejected? We designed our smart savings system to be win-win-win. In these cases of an application denial, the user was not getting the card they applied for, the bank was not acquiring a customer, and we were not getting paid. We were leaving money on the table.

So we did what every successful startup must: recognize an unplanned, organic growth opportunity and iterate quickly.

We hypothesized that we might be showing the best cards to the wrong users. Our algorithm determined the best card for the user based on their current spending, but if the user needed an excellent credit score of 750 or more, but their score was only good, in the range of 700–749, the card company might deny their card application. In this manner, our system had flaws, and the user experience was poor.

So we set up a system to prompt new users to input their credit score. We surmised that many of our users wouldn't know their score, so we grabbed a couple of offers off Commission Junction from companies that offered a free credit score and placed them below the prompt for self-score entry. It was a simple, intuitive flow designed to improve our algorithm's performance.

But few team decisions are unilateral. The product team seemed reluctant with this approach, and the design they provided did not highlight the availability of a free credit score offer. In their relentless focus on UX, the product team sometimes shunned monetization work. They rightly considered that the credit bureaus had an untrustworthy reputation from past controversies that could erode our trust coefficient. So we ran with the product team's design. But test results were poor; some users were offering up their scores, but most weren't, and there were limited clicks on the free score offers. The product team wasn't interested in changing the design, so we, as the revenue team, took matters into our own hands. Sid showed his diverse range of skills by writing up new product requirements and design specs for the credit score prompt. This time, if the user didn't know their score, the prompt to quickly get it for free from one of our partners was prominent as it was placed higher in the flow. I got Aaron to look over the new requirements, and he was impressed both with our initiative and the quality of the work we produced. He gave the green light to the changes, which the engineering team made.

As the data came in during the following weeks, I noticed a significant spike in revenue beyond the average week-over-week increase in our traffic numbers. The redesigned free credit score offers were the primary cause. Our users had flocked to the opportunity to get a free credit score, and we were reaping the benefits from the affiliate payouts on these. Now we were generating additional revenue when users ordered the free scores, as well as improving the credit profile for our users to give them better access to the right offers in our smart savings system—meaning higher conversion payouts on credit card offers for us, too.

It was another lesson that the right user experience, optimized based on experimentation, could significantly improve revenue.

We took the same approach to new verticals. In 2007, nearly two in three American adults reported investing in the stock market. It seemed like a great way to engage them with a personal finance service.

With Investments, any Mint user with investment accounts would see their complete portfolio in one place, with analysis and insights. Some online wealth management sites, such as Fidelity and Vanguard, did offer investment data insights. Still, their design was flat and uninteresting, and they did not aggregate third-party investment data to show users a complete portfolio view. Fidelity tried to incorporate Yodlee's platform, but they could never design something compelling for user engagement. Mint would be among the first to show the total market value of a user's investment portfolio to showcase global portfolio performance and to root out unnecessary fees. Once again, customer-centric design and simplicity would distinguish Mint.

The Investments feature enabled us to offer our users access to better brokerage accounts that would set them on the right track to self-directed investing and save money on trading. Users new to investing would see the best low-cost brokerages on Mint with the best services, with transparency on all fees—and that brought in new possibilities for revenue.

Among the major brokerages, Scottrade was willing to pay more for Mint-sourced customers—the commissions ran into the hundreds of dollars. And their offers resonated with our young, professional, emerging affluent, and online-savvy user base. After Scottrade saw the initial stream and quality of the customers we were sending them, they couldn't get enough of Mint and raised their payouts to us. Soon, word spread of the success of our Investments service, and we began attracting many more brokerages and asset management firms to Mint. Our revenues and the average revenue per user (ARPU) started to climb higher from this new source and stream of lucrative payouts.

Fidelity approached us to build out a dedicated individual retirement account (IRA) section of the site that would be sponsored by Fidelity and under which they'd provide exclusive deals to Mint users. I loved the concept as it was a way to extend the relevance of Investments in the form of tax-advantaged retirement accounts. However, it was inconsistent with our brand to be unbiased in our selection of partners and services. I told them that we would build the IRA service but that it would not be exclusive.

Our Mint IRA center would offer users a choice of institutions they could select to manage their assets based on trading prices. It factored in the minimum deposit amounts required, fees on withdrawing funds, and other incidentals. The IRA center would also provide educational content on the benefits of investing in tax-advantaged accounts and the best practices involved. From there, it was natural to expand into 401(k)s and provide our users the information and opportunity to roll over legacy 401(k) accounts (often with excessive fees and limited investment choices) into a self-directed IRA account that best fits their needs.

The idea was sound; it was a great opportunity that we came upon organically to expand a proven revenue driver into tangential verticals. But it would need scarce product development resources to build, and our supply was not infinite.

Aaron Forth, now known as A4 to help identify him separately from Aaron Patzer, was initially reluctant due to existing workload strain. Patzer would need to decide.

The three of us huddled in the large board conference room downstairs. I presented my case, knowing that data would influence Aaron. Our users had, on average, three investment accounts, and for many, this included at least one retirement account. With IRAs and 401(k)s, our affiliate payouts would be higher, and our users' savings would be substantially greater. We would also start to make Mint more relevant for tax planning, which was core to personal finances. But A4 was rightly concerned about a backlog of user-requested features such as splitting transactions and creating custom categories, and he was wondering how we were going to do it all.

Aaron Patzer then lifted his hand to head level to call for silence so he could think. He'd heard enough on both sides, and it appeared to be time for a decision. Aaron slumped in his chair, leaned his head back, raised both hands to his temples as he thought intensely and silently for what seemed like about three minutes. I wondered if he was prototyping a new IRA center in his brain and creating a visual image that would let him determine if it fit into the overall Mint service design. He came out of his trance and announced that we would do it. Mint would build an IRA service center.

After a hard recruiting drive, we landed some of the biggest and best names in the industry in the IRA center, including Fidelity, Scottrade, TD Ameritrade, and Charles Schwab. And it was a hit with our users. They understood the tax savings and wealth creation message and started opening IRA accounts left and right from Mint.

Scaling must stay grounded in a company's core values and offerings. Our board was calling for a Mint online bill pay service. But I pushed back against it. Bill pay would break our user anonymity, one of our crucial privacy points, and require us to negotiate a new, more expensive deal with Yodlee for the service. It would hurt brand trust and profits. Both were anathema to me—especially when virtually every bank already offered a bill pay service.

In the end, Aaron sided with me on the bill pay debate. One of the death knells for a startup is when it loses focus and tries to do too much, too soon. That startup ends up doing nothing particularly well, which is antithetical to a startup's core advantage: to do one crucial thing at least ten times better than anyone else in the market.

Instead, we returned to our roots in helping our customers understand and improve their finances. We introduced a new "Trends" tab as a comprehensive financial analytics and insights tool without equal. The product and design team of Val Agostino, Jason Putorti, and Matt Snider did some of their best work on Trends. We provided Mint users with access to fresh, interactive, colorful, and compelling insights into their income, spending, assets, and liabilities over time. There were as many as sixteen different graphs from which to explore different angles of one's financial life. With the click of a mouse, these charts spun, danced, and flashed colors across the screen before settling into a deep view state. One of the highlights of Trends was the ability to see your net worth at any given point or over time, a measure that users consistently responded to with praise.

We continued this productivity surge by revamping our Budgets feature in July of 2008, with the redesign championed by Justin Maxwell. Previously, we gave users a snapshot of their budgets on Mint's overview page. We now devoted an entire tab to Budgets. We created default, editable categories based on the user's average monthly spending and then tracked the user's progress against them in a green to red bar chart.

At around the same time, we made another major update on our service by adding support for most types of loans, including mortgages, student, auto, and personal loans. These loans gave our users a complete view of their finances. Our product, engineering, and design teams worked together beautifully; Mint's new features were making it as utilitarian as it was aesthetic.

As we added depth and breadth to the Mint product, we also improved our blog to deliver best-in-class personal finance content and build community. Aaron believed that this would complement the product and provide a complete service to our users. Our blog had been essential in attracting users to our launch; now, it would be a vital educational tool for the hundreds of thousands of users who had joined us.

Donna soon hired Lee Sherman for the role. With a strong background in journalism, Lee was determined to transform our blog into a magazine for your money and life with a strong perspective, but without being overly prescriptive. Other blogs of web companies were much more product-oriented at the time. Our goal was to produce a minimum of two posts per day by a better class of writers and find the right mix between evergreen content, current event pieces, and data stories.

Lee joined Stew Langille in overseeing a redesign of our blog in the fall of 2008, which would now be called MintLife. Taking inspiration from USA Today and Wired, the MintLife Blog became a pioneer of web infographics that visualized data relating to personal finances. The power and clarity of the visuals helped readers understand more about their money in the world around them.

The MintLife blog also began to leverage Mint's data to develop more exciting stories. One example of this was a piece that showed that spending on luxury goods was, in fact, up shortly after the onset of the Great Recession, which was counterintuitive but confirmed by our data. This and other similar data-driven posts led to leading publications like the *Wall Street Journal* contacting Martha to access Mint data to enrich their stories. For this, Mint set up a self-service online data store for journalists to search for and retrieve data relevant to their stories.

To promote our content, Stew and Lee took advantage of social media's emergence to trigger the viral distribution of MintLife content. In the process, they perfected the art of hitting the front page of Digg.com, the best social news site of that era. Thanks to these efforts, the MintLIfe Blog climbed to more than 1 million page views per month, with a healthy conversion of readers to Mint service users.

Despite our improvement of the Mint service in many respects, it was inevitable that we'd make some mistakes during this rapid period of feature development, and "Financial Fitness" was our most glaring. We moved to release this feature in beta in April of 2008, and initially, the press gave us a favorable reception.

At that time, there was an emerging digital trend around gamification derived from the popularity of online games—It mostly offered increasing rewards for hitting a predetermined series of achievement benchmarks. Aaron challenged the team to innovate in this zone.

Our product team studied the rewards systems of games and apps like Warcraft, Nike Fit, and Foursquare to craft our personal finance system. The rules of financial fitness were simple: There were five main principles for our users to focus on: "know your money," "spend less than you earn," "manage credit and use debt wisely," "invest your savings," and "prepare for the unexpected." Each of these principles had tasks associated with it, such as "avoid bank fees." Merit badge awards went to those users who had 100 percent health status for an extended period. The most basic tasks (pay down your debt, check your credit report for errors, ensure you have a three-month emergency fund) were introduced in the first month, with more nuanced tasks (put your excess cash into a CD, for example) introduced later. In that sense, each month was like a "level."

The theoretical basis was there, but the application was not. In a rush to follow the gaming trend, we forgot to do extensive user testing in advance. It turns out Mint's users didn't want to share their financial fitness level with their friends, so we lacked any virality—there's a reason it's called "personal finance," after all. And as *TechCrunch* noted,[11] "personal finance and fun aren't exactly two things that go hand in hand." We should have known better.

Financial Fitness never made it out of beta. It didn't surprise me, given my experience with it. Gameplay should be fun and rewarding, but financial fitness was largely disproportionate and annoying. I could be having an otherwise great fiscal month but choose to pay a $3 ATM fee from an out-of-network bank because I needed cash in

---

11 Jason Kincaid. "Mint Turns Personal Finance Into A Game. It's Better Than It Sounds." *TechCrunch*. April 29, 2009.

real-time, and I'd suddenly incur a points deduction by Mint. It was the same for users who chose to incur a small finance charge on their credit card or overdraft an account because of cash flow issues. Mint added insult to injury.

Money is not a game. The service died a natural death. At least we had the guts to pull it rather than stubbornly persist.

We'd stumbled and missed the forest for the trees. The elegance of Aaron's original "less is more" design for Mint was to recognize most consumers wanted in and out with their finances quickly. Reid Hoffman said, "if you're not embarrassed by the first version of your product, you've launched too late." Perhaps we could have streamlined financial fitness to salvage it. Instead, wisely, we chose to fail fast and kill it. On a positive note, you could say we were practicing the startup art as we should. It's likely that if we were unwilling to take on this kind of risk and be prepared to fail, we were not pushing innovation hard enough.

Thanks to strong leadership that kept us grounded in our core value proposition and mediated conflicts to keep the team focused and lean and thanks to teams that could recognize organic opportunity and iterate to realize or kill it quickly, our rapport with our users exploded in 2008. We were well on our way to becoming the comprehensive personal finance tool Aaron envisioned. Distribution to more customers would be the next driver of growth. But an old foe would rear its head.

CHAPTER 21

A FOOLISH MINT

"The fool doth think he is wise, but the wise man knows himself to be a fool."

WILLIAM SHAKESPEARE

As Mint's reputation grew, many companies reached out to us with bold ideas about working together. One of the more appealing invitations came from the Motley Fool, a company known for providing investors with financial advice. Much of the Fool's online content is free, but it does charge a subscription fee to members of its premium investment letter series.

The Motley Fool team hypothesized that they could acquire more customers by offering free personal finance tools and content. They reasoned that people who cared more about their money were likely to become their future investing newsletter customers. Rather than building the service themselves, they decided instead to partner and planned to offer Mint to these prospective customers. This would occur by placing banners on Fool.com that redirected to the cobranded application at fool.mint.com. There, Fool users could sign up for Mint.com directly, and their experience would always have a cobranded header on the overview page.

This deal meant free distribution of the Mint service to a broader audience, exactly what our board was calling for. We might also use this deal as a prototype for similar, repeatable deals with other primary investing and financial web content sites. Imagine the users of Morningstar, Kiplingers, *CNN Money*, *Yahoo! Finance*, *USA Today Money*, and more promoting a cobranded Mint.com to their audiences. This would create more distribution and elevate our brand as the standard for personal finance management on the web. Beyond that, Mint's users would, in turn, benefit from the content and tools available from these sites.

After flying out to Virginia to meet with the Motley Fool team and hash out the partnership details, the Mint team set about developing the cobranded site and packaging up the marketing assets for the launch of the service.

By April 2008, after weeks of hard work, we issued a press release announcing the partnership.[12] Jonathan Mudd, the Motley Fool's senior vice president of programming and general manager of Fool.com, declared that "Mint has emerged as a real innovator in the online personal finance space, and we are thrilled to join forces with them. Mint will help us give our members an accurate, up-to-date picture of their financial standing, so they're well-positioned to take advantage of the superior investment ideas at the core of our services."

Aaron reciprocated by stating that "the Motley Fool is an unmatched resource for financial advice and fits perfectly with Mint's mission to give users information that helps them do more with their money." The deal meant that we'd be able to offer excellent Motley Fool personal finance and investing content to our users on the Mint blog and that we'd be introducing the Mint.com service to the millions of people visiting the award-winning Fool.com website.

All of this complemented Mint's move to add brokerage and investment tracking to the service a few weeks earlier. It also set the stage for Mint to unveil a new approach for users to understand and do more with their investments that were just around the corner.

The celebration of our deal with the Motley Fool was short-lived. Days later, I received an email from Joe Polverari declaring that Yodlee

---

12 "Combining Great Content With Powerful Tools to Help Consumers put Advice into Action." *MintLife*. April 3, 2008.

considered Mint to be in breach of contract and that we needed to terminate the partnership with the Motley Fool or suffer the consequences. Without laying out specifics, Polverari claimed that the license to Yodlee's technology platform did not expressly permit a Fool-type deal.

Yodlee's claim was stunning. We hadn't considered for a moment that this deal would provoke them. I let Aaron know what was going on. We were siphoning users from the Motley Fool over to Mint.com, where they needed to sign up for our service, not a site controlled by the Motley Fool. In doing so, we attached some Fool cobranding as part of the onboarding process, but there could be no mistaking that these Fool users signed up for Mint.com since we hosted the service at our URL.

We could understand if Yodlee wanted to prohibit us from reselling their aggregation service to another website directly without their consent. One example of this would be to offer our personal finance service on the Fool website in a white-label style deal, where the service would be "powered by Mint." In such a case, the service users would be the primary customers of the Motley Fool, which could market to and monetize them as they saw fit. Mint would, in that case, get a fee for providing the service.

But that's not what we were doing with the Fool. Moreover, any Fool users we attracted to Mint.com would increase our aggregation payments to Yodlee, which meant more money in their pockets. That was not a bad thing for them.

Yet Polverari's email indicated they were having none of it. Yodlee seemed to be running scared. We'd negotiated a low price with them, and they didn't want our deal redistributed in the marketplace. That was the perception they were acting on, true or not.

Yodlee's play seemed like a classic case of combined envy and extortion. Yodlee allowed us to slip away into the night with killer pricing on account aggregation, and we'd shocked them with our growing numbers. Instead of being pleasantly surprised on the upside, they seemed appalled at how much money they were losing out on had they only struck a better deal with us at the outset. So they decided to seek petty revenge.

I reviewed the Yodlee contract with our lawyers, and it did not expressly permit us to partner with another site to promote Mint.com. However, it did provide that we could use all available marketing methods for customer acquisition, and our deal seemed to fall within that construct. It would be messy to unwind the Motley Fool deal after a public announcement. Beyond that, Yodlee could block any other type of standard internet distribution deal we might want to do. It became clear that the technology that was powering our aggregation was also our Achilles heel.

I reached out to Yodlee to discuss the issue. A few days later, on a call with Polverari, while insisting that we were in breach of contract, he was already proposing a new pricing package that would be acceptable to Yodlee and would cure the breach. It would mean hundreds of thousands of dollars per year in additional costs and potentially millions more on higher traffic numbers in the ensuing years. He'd shown his hand; this was a shakedown and cash grab.

While I listened to Polverari's demands, the one marker I put down was that our engineering team was far from happy with their aggregation platform and the lack of support we were getting when and as needed. Polverari responded that since Yodlee catered to the banks as customers, they did have a premium support package they could offer us if we were willing to pay for it. This need for support was an area of common ground. I ended the call by letting Polverari know we'd review the situation internally and return to him.

A few days later, I met Aydin Senkut for one of our regular mentoring check-ins at a small neighborhood cafe in Menlo Park called Cafe Zoe. Senkut was one of our earliest angel investors, and he was keen to get more involved with Mint. Because of his international business development experience with Google, Aaron thought it would be good for the two of us to discuss ways to grow Mint's reach and revenue regularly.

I let Senkut know what was happening with Yodlee, and his face fell. As an investor in Mint, this cannot have been happy news for him. It seemed like a situation that could implode—seeing his reaction underscored the need to find a way out of this mess. I knew we'd need to promptly bring this to the board's attention, as it was a material event that could adversely affect the company.

We did raise it at the next board meeting, and to my surprise, the board noted the seriousness of the situation but did not seem fazed. Perhaps Aaron had tipped some of them off ahead of the meeting in private calls, and it was intentional on their part not to appear anxious about this. They seemed content with letting us deal with it—perhaps because it was uncharted territory for them, or maybe because I'd earned some measure of trust in negotiating the Yodlee deal and domain name, or perhaps some combination of the two. I waited for Mark Goines to chime in with an offer to help by having a word behind the scenes at the highest levels. After all, he had a longstanding relationship with Bill Harris, who was the chairman of Yodlee. But there was no offer of help. I'd have to go and figure this out myself.

I started to plan our strategy. The first thing I needed to do was to buy more time. This meant concealing from Yodlee that we were not going to submit to their extortion. Instead, we would be reviewing the situation and coming up with a plan to work through it. I told Polverari as much; he was patient and complacent. He had us in a headlock and didn't see how we would wriggle out of it. He would bide his time, licking his chops.

In the meantime, I knew we needed a contingency plan if Yodlee went nuclear and pulled the plug on their aggregation service. I'd recently met the VP of sales at CashEdge at a financial technology conference, and he lamented they never got the chance to work with Mint. I called him up, and we started working on a plan that would provide immediate aggregation redundancy to Mint and an eventual replacement of Yodlee. This was not going to be easy for our engineers to work through, but it might be necessary. Even if we could hook up the CashEdge aggregation service, it did not appear as complete and robust as the Yodlee system. We were not relishing all that work to find that the replacement platform would be less performant.

Meanwhile, if we were to continue with Yodlee, we did want a higher standard of service and technical support, so I set a plan to work through that side of the deal immediately. We were going to pay more money for this each year, but we were okay with that as we were getting something in exchange that we needed. This helped send a signal to Polverari that we were serious about working through the process with Yodlee—for all he knew, we were considering his massive new payment plan. In reality, our base deal with Yodlee for per-user aggregation wouldn't change as he wanted; it was the increase in service quality we'd agree to pay for.

The first meeting was held with Yodlee's engineers at their headquarters and was presided over by Peter Hazlehurst, an Englishman who had risen quickly to head up operations and engineering. The meeting went well. We worked through some challenging issues, and they accepted they would need to put in substantial platform fixes and provide more technical support. Some of the problems we were dealing with included non-supported accounts of individual regional banks, some other supported accounts not updating, individual debit transactions never appearing in Mint's records, and so on. One of the major issues was with the scripts that Yodlee writes to collect data from the banks. If a bank redesigned its website or added a new feature, the old script breaks, leaving our customers frustrated because Mint won't collect new data for them. Yodlee needed to design these scripts better so they wouldn't break so easily, or, if they did, Yodlee would detect the change and put in a rapid script change that would work on the new bank site. Sometimes the breakdown came from the user side when they changed their login credentials. When the username, password, or security questions and answers change, data scraping technology stops working. The system can no longer log in with the credentials it has stored and must look to the user to update them to restore a working connection. We needed better communication protocols between Yodlees's system and Mint's to detect these changes to communicate to our users to reset their Mint credentials.

I don't think Yodlee's aggregation platform had been put to the test by any of their banking customers as much as it was by Mint. For the banks, aggregation was a sideshow. Their users were not dependent upon it, nor did their technical people understand all the issues. For

Mint users, on the other hand, aggregation was critical. If you could not see all of your financial accounts accurately in one place, our service would not deliver on its underlying value proposition. I observed the Yodlee engineers relishing the prospect of building something more robust and performant to conform to our requirements. They seemed like good, respectful folks, and their accommodating attitudes belied the naked aggressiveness of Polverari.

The next move by Yodlee was unexpected. Julie Solomon, who was unknown to me at that point, reached out and introduced herself as Yodlee's director of customer advocacy. She wanted to arrange a meeting. We met for lunch in downtown Mountain View, and Julie explained that she was our account manager and was here to help us be successful on the Yodlee platform and to address any relationship issues. She seemed genuine and professional. We'd become an essential customer for Yodlee, and we were about to up the ante again. Julie appeared to have good empathy for our situation, so I leaned in and indicated that we would be much more open to resolving all this mess with a good deal if we felt like we didn't have a boot on the back of our neck. The implication was that if Yodlee were to call off the attack dogs for a while, we could all work through this. I wanted to drive a wedge between Polverari's approach to have us capitulate or crush us and those inside Yodlee, who favored detente. Julie was reassuring and suggested that we meet with Anil Arora, Yodlee's CEO, as a next step.

At the meeting, Arora was gracious and seemed eager to learn more about Mint. I sensed that this was not the time or place to bring up grievances between the two companies. Instead, it was an opportunity to get to know each other better and begin to heal the relationship between us. Arora closed the meeting by inviting us to Yodlee's upcoming annual customer conference at the Hotel Nikko in San Francisco. Relations were improving, and these were all good signs.

Polverari, on the other hand, kept the pressure on, and he showed no signs of backing down from his initial demands for much stiffer per user aggregation tariffs. Could it be that Yodlee would try to void the contract if we did not agree to these? The PR effect of this would be net adverse and send a chilling signal to any other startup looking to do business with them, and perhaps even to their banking customers. Surely they'd be shooting themselves in the foot.

Then I realized something else: it would be madness to kill us. As I dug into our aggregation numbers and corresponding payments to Yodlee, I found we were their fastest-growing customer and on our way to being their best customer, period. We were already spending in the low millions on their platform annually with our torrential growth, and as each day, week, and month passed, the counter would tick up even higher. Very soon, we would be so important that they'd never dare kill the goose that was laying golden eggs.

As I stepped back and found that perspective, I realized that we were actually on high negotiating ground between the ambiguous breach situation, our customer status, and our contingency planning with CashEdge.

I could now see the light at the end of this long, dark tunnel. I kept CashEdge warm, and we continued to work through more technical details with them, but as we did, I realized we were not going to need to plug them into Mint after all. It was a contingency plan that we'd only use as a last resort, which always seemed unlikely.

Now that the deal was ready to be locked in, it was time to reckon with the last element: the extra ransom Polverari wanted on per-user pricing. To buy as much time as I could, I led Polverari to believe that I would eventually be amenable to his new package of pricing. However, we'd only agree to it once we'd negotiated all other aspects of the deal, including professional services and support and revised license terms. The ploy worked, and he let us keep going as is under the existing license for a few more months while we worked through the other deal terms. As was my plan, this allowed us to grow stronger as a Yodlee customer making it ever harder for Yodlee to go nuclear on us, and it allowed us to put our contingency plans in place in case we ever needed them as a last resort. We decided that we would forgo doing any more deals like the Motley Fool as we focused on smartphone app store distribution anyway, and if Polverari wanted to blow up the Fool deal, then so be it.

I sat down with Aaron to give him the update. The approach reassured him. In winter 2008, several months after Polverari had initially threatened us, I knew it was time to come clean and break the news that we weren't interested in his deal for higher aggregation pricing. He sent another email seeking to get this last aspect of the agreement finally resolved, and I typed out a polite email in response, giving him the news. I let him know that we would not be moving forward with the new package of per-user pricing and additional fee guarantees that he was proposing. On the other hand, we were ready to move forward with the premium support package and the amended license terms. The implication was clear. The ball was in his court, and if he wanted to terminate our current Yodlee license as threatened, that option was now open to him.

He responded that he was shocked and bitterly disappointed. It seemed like he'd sold the deal and the bonus revenue internally, and now he was not going to be able to deliver on it. But while he barked, there was no bite. As I finished reading his email recounting that he felt there was a breach of an understanding that we would get this done, I realized that he had dropped the threat language. The strategy I had laid out months ago when our backs were to the wall paid off. We'd come through the choke down, still standing. We were about to sign a new deal with Yodlee in which we'd get premium professional services, customer success, support, and explicit permission to develop apps on third-party platforms.

I called Aaron to give him the news. I could tell he was relieved and recall him remarking how glad he was to have me on his team. It was a rare compliment, and I accepted it humbly. We signed the final deal with Yodlee on Christmas Eve, with only me and Aaron left in the office late at night, ironing out the last details. To this day, I still have an image of Aaron hunched over the fax machine, manually feeding the contract in for transmission to Yodlee.

CHAPTER 22

THE GREAT RECESSION

"It was the best of times, it was the worst of times."
CHARLES DICKENS

As we launched the Mint service at *TechCrunch* 40 in the fall of 2007, we had no idea that we were at the precipice of what would become known as the Great Recession. Approximately one year later, the filing for Chapter 11 bankruptcy protection by Lehman Brothers on September 15, 2008, would signal the largest bankruptcy filing in US history. In the aftermath, world stock markets would suffer cataclysmic declines, and the global banking system would teeter on the brink of collapse. The International Monetary Fund concluded that it was the worst global recession since the Great Depression of the 1930s, hence the "Great Recession."

The downturn began in the United States in December 2007 and ended in June 2009, extending over nineteen months.

The Great Recession wiped out millions of jobs, took away millions of homes, erased retirement accounts, and pushed many Americans out of the middle class. Unemployment skyrocketed, and the S&P 500 fell 57 percent. The net worth of US households declined by $15 trillion, or 22 percent. It was a mess, the likes of which most of us had never witnessed in our lifetimes.

Everyone could see that the country was in crisis and that politicians and bankers were frantically racing to prevent a total collapse of the global financial system. I wondered if it might stabilize and end soon, or if it might swoon and cast us all into a Depression with echoes of 1929, including breadlines and industrial strikes.

I'd been through Black Monday in 1987 when I was living in London. On that day, stock markets around the world crashed as the Dow Jones Industrial Average fell 508 points (22.61 percent) in a single day.

I'd also lived through the dot-com crash lasting from March 11, 2000, to October 9, 2004, and the September 11 attacks, which dragged the economic outlook even further into the mire. It seemed as if the era of cocky young Silicon Valley techies minting easy millions was over for good.

Both the Black Monday period and the dot-com bust were excruciating for me financially. I lost a job in each downturn, and my finances came under deep strain as I struggled with the exhausting stress involved in salvaging something from the wreckage during long, slow periods of recovery. So, when the Great Recession hit, I anxiously braced for another turbulent period of my life. I worked in an early-stage startup, a high-risk environment to be in at the best of times, let alone amid a global financial meltdown. I had a young family and managed to buy a small house with a big loan in Menlo Park after renting for several years. I changed careers a few years earlier from startup lawyer to startup business executive. It felt like I was still in the middle of consolidating this as yet fragile transformation. I had no real shelter from the storm and wondered how and when I would get hit by the tidal wave of bad economic news that was now coming out daily.

I was also anxious to preserve and grow the Mint service in the face of this economic meltdown—my livelihood and Mint's were at risk. I worried that we might get swept away by events beyond our control. We worked so hard to build Mint into a compelling service. It was a remarkable feat, especially to have done so in a year and change, and yet speculation in the financial sector was threatening to unravel it all through no fault of our own. And we had no recourse other than to heed the advice of our VCs—we must be even more cautious with our spending. The irony of that advice for a company founded on encouraging the same idea in the general public was not lost on us.

Ron Conway, one of Mint's first angel investors, and Benchmark Capital, the last fund to invest in Mint, sent memos to their portfolio companies. One of the critical Benchmark messages was that in market downturns, frugality is a virtue and could be the difference between survival and failure.

Aaron was frugal by nature, and he ran the company on this principle. He kept the burn rate to a minimum while investing in growth. We kept customer acquisition costs low throughout, and we never went on hiring binges or spent money on lavish offices or other perks that many other startups were found guilty of in the past. Despite this impressive fiscal discipline, I wondered if we would have to hunker down even more aggressively and cut our costs back into survival mode to ride out this storm.

While it was easy enough to be gloomy, I tried to reframe and think about some of the positive things on our side. We raised $12 million in our Series B financing several months earlier, so we would not have to raise again for a good while in this harsh environment. Moreover, our service was free, which Aaron always said is the best price for consumers.

It soon became clear that the Great Recession was not going to be bad for our business. Instead, it was good for us—very good, indeed. As the traffic numbers in the weeks and months after the Lehman bankruptcy came in, we noticed substantial and consistent spikes in Mint website traffic and the number of users. Our revenue continued to rise with the tide: consumers were finally no longer prepared to take their money for granted. On the contrary, they were now looking for ways to know exactly where their money was going and how they could find extra savings. It was the perfect storm for Mint.

I thought back to the days before we launched the service when I spoke to friends and family about what we were building. Their reaction was that it seemed interesting, even smart, but they didn't want to know how much they spent on Starbucks coffee and other extras every month. This was the state of mind for many consumers before the Great Recession. That state of conscious complacency was now rapidly changing. People now needed to know what they were spending their disposable income on—because it was no longer disposable.

As our traffic numbers kept rising, we also saw increased attention from the press in covering our service. As more press articles about us hit the wire, our traffic increased even further. It was a beautiful cycle.

They say that luck and timing have a lot to do with startup success, and I would agree, though one can never rely on these factors by themselves. They are merely accessories that help accelerate a startup venture already built on a solid foundation of product-market fit. And when it's time for your luck to turn, the best startups execute quickly to seize these windows of opportunity as they arise. In some ways, the global economic collapse was the best thing that could have happened to Mint. Our service became essential for the public, and our competitive advantages shone because of our strong leadership and sound business practices as other startups on flimsier foundations failed.

It also became clear that the Great Recession would not be as excruciating for me, either. Unlike my circumstances in 1987 and during the dot-com crash, for this recession, I found myself in precisely the right place at the right time. If there was one company set up to thrive in this recession, it was Mint, and I worked there.

There was another silver lining to these dark clouds of economic wreckage that would also deliver favorable repercussions for our brand and business. The institutions that came off the worst in terms of brand dilution from breach of trust were the banks. Many consumers felt the banks had been reckless and wanton in the events leading up to the Great Recession. To add insult to injury, many of these banks were now asking to be bailed out by the government with taxpayer money. This was happening even as many consumers were themselves going under financially and headed to bankruptcy. Although Mint.com was not a site where you could bank, it did stand out in all of this mess as a trustworthy consumer advocate for financial services, and in that sense, as a bona fide alternative to the banks.

In this environment, we stood to attract even more consumers to our service, relying more on Mint for their overall financial picture, rather than checking their fragmented financial information on their own banks' websites. All of this augured well for a bright future provided we continued to execute, which we were determined to do.

CHAPTER 23

THE IPHONE COMETH

"You realize that success will come from doing things ... or even just one thing ... that no one else is willing to do."

STEVE JOBS

In 1997, Steve Jobs returned to the company he cofounded in 1976 and was ousted from in 1985. Back at the helm, Jobs kicked off Apple's "Think Different" advertising campaign and worked closely with designer Jonathan Ive to develop a line of products that would have global success and move Silicon Valley and the technology world into a new era of mobility. Among this product line, the iPhone would change the world and set the company on a course for unprecedented success and market dominance.

Apple began work on the first iPhone in 2005 in secret. Rumors of this new device reached a crescendo preceding the iPhone's first release on June 29, 2007, just a few months before Mint's launch at *TechCrunch* 40. Upon release, the world discovered something magical about the iPhone, which came with a full-color, multitouch screen that enabled pinch-to-zoom and inertial scrolling on lists. These were features that came to define the modern smartphone.

Apple had lived up to its ethos to "Think Different." The iPhone sold a million units in just over two months and *TIME* magazine declared it "Invention of the Year" for 2007.

The iPhone 3G, released in the summer of 2008, replaced the first iPhone and brought three important new features: 3G internet, GPS, and the App Store. 3G meant there was enough bandwidth to run applications when not connected to wifi networks, making the iPhone genuinely mobile. GPS enabled pinpointing user location, eventually opening the way for new location-based apps such as Foursquare and Uber. The accompanying App Store opened on July 10, 2008. At the time, Jobs called it the biggest launch of his career. The App Store's first weekend saw more than ten million app downloads. By September 2008, the store had surpassed 100 million downloads. It was now Apple's world—the rest of us were only living in it.

With all the buzz swirling around the iPhone and the App Store, there was much discussion inside Mint on whether we should build a Mint app for iPhone to coincide with the upcoming holiday season when many iPhones get purchased as gifts. The holidays were also the beginning of the high season for personal finance that would last through tax filing season ending in April the following year.

The primary champion of a Mint iPhone app was Justin Maxwell, a former Apple employee. The product team, including Apple fanboy Jason Putorti, were all in for Mint to take the leap into mobile and take advantage of the iOS platform. Most in the company agreed that it would be cool to have Mint in your pocket. A4 did some analysis based on the number of app downloads in the App Store and determined that if we could make the top four in personal finance, our total user numbers would double.

Still, there were a few concerns about interacting with your money on such a small screen smoothly, and monetizing app usage would be difficult. Aaron Patzer, who was still a contented Blackberry user, was also concerned that chasing after an iPhone app might not be the best use of Mint's limited product development resources. So he weighed in with a split decision. If Justin and Jason wanted to work in the background to get something going on iOS, they were entitled to do it—just not on company time. Justin knew this was sufficient implicit permission for him to move forward and form a small stealth team to fire up a Mint prototype app. Justin became the de facto product manager for the Mint app and designed the information architecture and UI. He drafted in his wife Cynthia, who would also work on a moonlighting basis to write all the client code. Cynthia was working at Apple at the time and had worked on iOS engineering for iTunes. She became our secret weapon when iOS developers were few and far between in the Valley. Jason chipped in with the design and color scheme for the app. This small team met every day after work to make progress on the app, and as they did, A4 and the entire product team became more motivated to integrate it into Mint's official roadmap and release schedule.

Aaron, who was always partial to spontaneous team initiative, understood the opportunity and eventually gave his full support to the development efforts. As for our investors, they trusted us to determine the latest technology trends, and they were willing to follow our lead on this adventure.

Mint was built from the ground up as a web 2.0 company; taking advantage of innovation and opportunity was our heritage and DNA. We knew we'd be challenged by diving into the mobile world with a looming deadline, but in reality, we had little choice but to go there. That was where the world was going.

Our product team reached out to Apple for guidance on how to navigate development on iOS and placement on the App Store. We were pleased to discover via Larry Moss, a fifteen-year veteran of the company, that Apple was excited about working with Mint and supporting our iOS efforts. The App Store was full of games, and while there were a handful of banking brands in there, we would be the first non-bank financial services app. Apple sensed that we might build a beautifully designed app that would take full advantage of its cutting-edge iOS features and that this would showcase their platform to many more non-game developers. This was the highest compliment we could receive from the world's leading design company. It was impressive that Apple seemed to understand the seasonality of personal finance, hence their eagerness to get their hands on a Mint app by the end of the year.

Apple could have gone to one of our competitors, including Intuit, but they chose Mint. There was a hint of historical frustration with Intuit going back to the years when they dropped support of Quicken for the Mac when it was languishing as a platform. Apple knew that we would be more malleable as a partner than Intuit had proved.

Apple promised to provide a developer resource to help us with technical issues and some marketing support when we were ready to launch in the App store. Being Apple, they created their own rules and never made any specific promises as to marketing support. But they would always give guidance as to the best practices that, if followed, would provide the highest chance of the App store marketing team getting behind our product. And that was what every startup dreamed of. A4 was about to receive many calls from Larry Moss, often late on a Friday afternoon, with a request to add another feature or change to our app to put us in a better position for Apple marketing promotion. This resulted in many late nights for our engineers to rush out new builds to meet Apple's requirements. But it was our chance to sprint further ahead of our competition.

The Mint product development team got down to work. We assigned Atish Mehta as our lead mobile engineer, with Jason Yin assigned to the front end. No one knew the Cocoa language initially, but the team quickly went up the learning curve. Our development team headed over to the Apple campus in Cupertino for many secretive meetings to discuss iOS design principles and the best features to develop. The Apple team had plenty of detailed feedback on the home screen design, budgeting features, and more. After incorporating Apple's feedback, the product team shared the Mint designs with the rest of the Mint team. Our designers Jason Putorti and Justin Maxwell, who mentored Jason on Apple's processes, were extra motivated to work on this project, and I was stunned by the results. The Mint app design was beautiful and inspiring. It was Jason and Justin's best work yet.

It was a thing of wonder to see your financial life in the palm of your hand, painted in bright, bold colors.

There was a rush to complete the app and get approved by Apple before the end of 2008. Millions of users would buy a new iPhone over the holiday period, and many of them would think more about their finances in the coming months than at any other time of the year. We had doubled down on user growth with the Great Recession. It was time to double down again with the arrival of the iPhone and App Store. But Apple's review process could be frustrating for developers like Mint. It would often take one to two weeks to get a solid response and clearance from Apple, and their software development kit (SDK) caused some problems for our developers that we needed to resolve quickly.

Along this path, I realized that after our Motley Fool deal and the adverse reaction of Yodlee, traditional distribution co-marketing deals would be out of bounds for us while we were still on the Yodlee platform. But the App store was a new platform for distribution that I hoped would satisfy our board's craving for more online audience reach. This aligned with the user experience we wanted to create, which would be uniquely Minty without meeting the cobranding requirements of another partner website.

Following our submission of the first Mint app to the App Store and Apple's final approval, we announced the release of our first iPhone app on December 19, 2008, on our blog, with the headline, "Money in your Pocket for the Holidays."[13] We explained that "the Mint iPhone app delivers the same simple yet powerful experience as our web service right to your phone and updated automatically." Our users could get access to their up-to-date financial information at any time, from anywhere. It was the first iPhone app to provide free SMS text message alerts of upcoming bills, low balances, and bank fees on more than 7,500 US financial institutions.

On the first day of our launch, Mint became the number one free finance app in the App Store, replacing the Chase Mobile app at the top of the table. We were ecstatic. The financial and technology press sang our praises, including *Finovate*, whose editor, Jim Bruene, announced on December 22, 2008, that "as expected from a company that is carefully using design to help distinguish it from the pack, Mint's new app

---

13 "Money in Your Pocket For the Holidays." *Mintlife*. December 19, 2008.

is great looking."[14] Once again, we found a way to catch a huge wave and ride it as our user numbers soared.

But we were new to this mobile world, and we made a few mistakes along the way. In our first iOS release, we allowed users to download our app from the App Store but then required them to come back to Mint.com to add their accounts on the back end for the app to function with banking data. This disconnect caused too much friction, and we lost many conversions from app download to active users of the service in the process.

Once we saw the data, we quickly moved to allow customers to link their accounts directly. Even after the fix, we still expected that most of our users would use the app while they were on the go for finance snippets and real-time updates, then return to the website to properly review their budgets, investments, and the like, in more detail. Little did we know that there would emerge a growing class of users who downloaded our app and never came to the Mint website. They either didn't think we had a website, or they didn't care. Another class of users engaged with both the web app and the mobile app, and even with these users, we started to notice a mobile app preference.

This increased mobile usage was evidence that we were now entering the age of "mobile-first," and the technology world had changed. Within a few short years, Apple would become the world's most valuable and recognized brand as smartphone sales gradually overtook PC sales, and more online time was spent on mobile devices than on desktop PCs. We were fortunate that the iPhone and App Store came along when they did to grow the world's digital audience and time spent online and provide us with a distribution platform. We ended up with three times the traffic we had planned for in the first year.

We were wise to recognize the mobile opportunity and jump in before our competitors had time to react. We faced the classic "Innovator's Dilemma." We knew that our website had won multiple awards and accolades and attracted hundreds of thousands of users in just over

---

14 Jim Bruene. "Chase Bank, Mint Top the Charts with New iPhone Apps." *Finovate* Blog. December 22, 2008.

a year who loved it. Why not double down and continue to focus on improving the web service and add a slew of new value-add improvements to it? Why were we choosing to disrupt what we already had worked so hard to build? The answer had two core dimensions. Mint was a product-first, customer-centric company, not a profit-first company. This distinction meant we would always choose to innovate and develop what was best for our users. We were not about to deny our audience access to their finances on the go on the world's best device. On the contrary, we were determined to design the best user experience possible with existing technologies. Secondly, we did not want to end up like our legacy competitors, Microsoft and Intuit, who failed to realize that the web would render their lucrative desktop products obsolete soon enough.

Through all of this, I noticed something intriguing about the iPhone form factor: the principle of "less is more" applied. We were always committed to Mint being lean in our approach to software development and user experience. If the service didn't need an extra feature, we wouldn't build it to keep filling up the candy jar. This minimalism helped set us apart from the bloated, feature-heavy desktop software of the personal-finance incumbents, Intuit and Microsoft. With the iPhone app, we took this to a new level as mobile users, with much less screen real estate, would be even less tolerant of things that got in the way. The need for instant gratification from a tap or scroll was at peak demand. Our approach worked beautifully, and in many ways, the Mint user experience on the iPhone was better and more compact. The world was changing, and Mint's innovation culture allowed us to keep pace and change with it, faster and more flexibly than our competition.

CHAPTER 24

INTUIT FIRES A BLANK

*"Whenever you do a thing, act as
if all the world is watching."*

THOMAS JEFFERSON

As Mint showcased the power of its product and growth in the personal finance market, Mint was also reckoning with a growing threat: competition. The giant was awakening. And by mid- to late-2008, it became clear that David would have to go to battle against Goliath. It was only three months after our launch at *TechCrunch* 40 when Intuit announced it would launch an online Quicken service in January 2008 for $3 a month. The world's largest financial software maker for consumers and small businesses was coming after us with all they had.

At the time, some fourteen million people were using desktop versions of Quicken, and about 1.7 million new copies of that software were sold each year. In contrast, Mint had not yet reached one million users, but our numbers multiplied while Intuit's were declining year over year. Against Quicken's annual refresh, Mint updated its online software as a service on a regular cadence measured in weeks, not years. But Intuit seemed to be getting with the times finally. Intuit's new online product would not require customers to install any software, and Intuit designed the software to attract millions of younger, web-savvy consumers. Intuit was targeting those consumers who were beginning to discover Mint.com.

But when Aaron first saw Quicken Online, he thought it looked like it was from 1996, not 2008. I sensed that Intuit still didn't get it from a business standpoint. It was not that consumers couldn't afford to pay $3 per month for software that helped them manage their finances. It was that the wave of free internet services that had emerged after Netscape in 1995 had conditioned consumers to believe that they should be getting everything online for free. Intuit was going against this grain because they didn't know any better and were resistant to change.

The better strategic move would have been to beat back the startup competition by offering Quicken Online for free. Once the battle was won, Intuit could figure out new ways to capitalize financially on the captured audience. The question of whether to take that approach was Intuit's Innovator's Dilemma. They opted for the opposite of Mint. Instead of building a product that consumers would love, Intuit was reluctant to cannibalize the profits it was making from Quicken and attached a $3 monthly fee to its online service. The notion of a free service and the unique requirements of modern internet business models wasn't in Intuit's DNA, which instead seemed to be relying on its brand and reputation to win the battle. *Lifehacker* noted that Quicken Online was unlike new players Mint and Wesabe, putting an assuring, familiar face on the web page that asks you for your online banking passwords.[15] They were correct in their assertion that if a consumer had ever used TurboTax Online, they'd already entrusted Intuit with their financial data online. This existing customer relationship would make the leap to Quicken Online a short one.

Thus, the battle lines were drawn. Mint had a great product but had to earn the trust of its user base continuously. On the other hand, Intuit had consumer trust but now had to win the hearts of its users with a beautiful product that could at least match Mint's design. I liked our odds.

---

15 Gina Trapani. "Manage Your Money with Quicken Online." *Lifehacker.* January 8, 2008.

Intuit had another advantage in that its account aggregation technology was all "in-house." It didn't subcontract aggregation to Yodlee, and it didn't have to rely on that company for data stability like Mint. This advantage had two core elements. The first was that Intuit could control the user experience by adding and maintaining financial accounts. Mint learned that relying on Yodleee's platform for this made a technically challenging situation even more precarious. The second was that Intuit had no per-user aggregation cost, as Mint had with Yodlee. Intuit could afford to disrupt our free offering from this business model position of strength since Intuit was under no pressure to make money in the short term to cover aggregation costs.

But as we progressed through 2008, it was clear that Intuit's strategy was not working, and Quicken online was not growing quickly enough to knock us off our stride. Consumers continued to flock to new sites like Mint, Wesabe, Geezeo, and Buxfer, with Mint taking in most of those users.

Our running battle with Quicken Online reached a boiling point one morning in early 2009 when I came into the office and picked up on a buzz of excited team chatter. Intuit had sent us a formal legal letter questioning our growth numbers and demanding that we provide evidence to substantiate them. The letter was a legal lecture about misrepresenting facts and the dire consequences associated with doing so. Intuit appeared to be threatening to sue us or expose us somehow for falsifying our numbers publicly. They were clearly warning us to desist from the practice of referring publicly to our growth numbers or face the consequences of their ire.

As I looked over Intuit's language, it seemed to be an extraordinary letter for a respected public company to send. Such a letter could not have been written by mere underlings at Intuit and could not have been sent without the approval of Intuit senior executives. Perhaps they didn't understand the risks associated with their actions as they were making a severe misjudgment—we had not misrepresented our numbers. They were real. What had led to this extraordinary miscalculation? Intuit must have been concerned that if the world saw Mint winning, perception would make up the better part of reality, and Mint might end up winning. Since they didn't believe we were winning fairly, they wanted to smash our charade. Just as a lawyer should never ask a question in court that they don't know the answer to, a respected public company should not get into a public fight with a competitor that it doesn't know it can win. Intuit, it seemed, had not learned this lesson.

Intuit's other psychological miscalculation was that when you complain about your competitor's actions, you are telegraphing that those actions are effective and are hurting you. We sensed this, and it only served to encourage us.

A few of us, including Aaron, David Michaels, and Aaron Forth, gathered for a quick lunch at a Chinese restaurant across the street from Mint's offices to discuss the Intuit letter. Amidst the mirthful incredulity of what Intuit had done, the team thought it would be good to respond publicly to Intuit on our blog with a rebuttal message. Instinctively, I didn't think it was in our best interests to get into a public spat with Intuit. I preferred that we keep our heads down, stay humble, continue to execute, and let the numbers speak for themselves. If Intuit sued us or publicly questioned our numbers, we could respond, but not until then.

I was trying to be the adult in the room, but the team was having none of it. They were too hyped up by the occasion and by how ridiculous the claims in the letter were. Out of youthful indignation, they felt the need to respond without thinking through all the ramifications. I tried to adapt and offered that to react on our blog seemed trite. It might come off as self-serving and boastful to respond on our blog how much we were growing. I put it to the team that it would be better to let a third party judge and expose the reality—one that had a vast audience. So why not allow *TechCrunch* to facilitate this?

Suddenly, I realized the team was listening to me as they agreed this was a great idea. Little did I know that it would turn into something more incendiary. Aaron worked with Claassen and the Wilson Sonsini litigation team to construct a carefully worded response to Intuit's letter, refuting their claims and defending our calculations and integrity relating to Mint's user metrics. Once this was ready, we sent it as a response to Intuit's letter. Then Aaron and A4 coordinated with Donna to leak the Intuit letter to *TechCrunch* in the knowledge that we had a great relationship with them and that *TechCrunch* was generally on the side of the underdog startup versus its larger public company competitor.

I thought *TechCrunch* would find it worthy of mention somewhere in passing and that Intuit would receive a slap on the wrist that might hurt for a day or two before everyone moved on. Instead, *TechCrunch* chose to do a full-court press with the story. Their headline, on February 19, 2009, ran, "Quicken Online Can't Believe Mint Is Doing So Well; Sends Threatening Letter."[16] *TechCrunch* had obtained a copy of both Intuit's letter and Mint's reply and included them as links to the article. From Intuit's letter, *TechCrunch* included this passage:

"While we do not wish to suggest that Mint.com is engaging in false advertising, there is a substantial difference in claimed user numbers over a short period…[that] is of some concern. As a result, we're requesting that you provide us with the substantiation and evidence that you rely upon to support the above-referenced claims…before February 6, 2009."

TechCrunch noted the irony in the Intuit claim that it didn't wish to suggest Mint was lying, even though this was the premise of the letter. The article concluded that Mint was snowballing and soon would pass one million users (no doubt spurred by the bad economy and tax season) and that its competitors literally can't believe it. "And for any startup, that's not such a bad thing."

TechCrunch then rubbed salt into the wound by appending Intuit's response to the story from its spokesman Scott Gulbransen:

"We'd like to apologize to Mint.com if our letter came across as anything but a simple request to understand how they count their users. Businesses do this all the time, and we appreciate their reply. We are so pleased with the rapid growth of Quicken Online; we were just curious about how we're doing. And now that we have a common yardstick by which to measure, we know we're doing great based on an

---

16 Jason Kincaid. "Quicken Online Can't Believe Mint Is Doing So Well; Sends Threatening Letter." *TechCrunch*. February 20, 2009.

apples-to-apples comparison…Quicken Online now has more than 650,000 users and has been adding, on average, approximately 45,000 new users a week since Jan. 2009. So now you know…customers are choosing Quicken Online more than ever before."[17]

In June 2009, Microsoft announced that it was discontinuing MS Money. Microsoft had long been chasing Intuit's Quicken and, after the Justice Department had shut down their move to buy Intuit, Microsoft persisted with the product but also continued to trail Quicken's sales. Now it was facing a new wave of internet-based competitors." With banks, brokerage firms, and websites providing a range of options for managing personal finances, the consumer need for Microsoft Money has changed," Microsoft announced.[18] They were folding up shop to focus on other areas deemed more core to their business.

We flirted with ways we might be able to work with Microsoft to bring on their Money users, but they spurned our outreach and decided to go with Intuit. They probably didn't want the controversial press that might be associated with handing off their customer base to a young upstart company or the risks associated with doing so if something went wrong. Instead, the conservative and safe option was to go for like-for-like and send their users off to a trusted public company. But in the end, it didn't matter much. MS Money users were most likely not our type since they favored a more accounting-driven money management style. And besides, we kept growing fast without them.

The battle between Intuit and Microsoft over the PFM market was now over. Intuit, the innovative upstart at the time, was one of the few companies to have taken on the Microsoft beast and lived to tell the tale. Yet, now it was their turn for disruption, as upstart challenges from web-focused startups like Mint and Wesabe were coming at them hard and fast. Intuit was about to discover how smaller, more agile startups can succeed against giant entrenched corporations.

---

17 Marisa Taylor. "Intuit Defends its Threatening Letter to Mint.com." *The Wall Street Journal.* February 24, 2009.

18 Ina Fried. "Microsoft to discontinue MS Money." *CNET.* June 10, 2009.

Intuit then did what seemed inevitable and moved to make Quicken Online free in October 2008. At the time, Rafe Needleman of *CNET* commented that it was a smart move on Intuit's part. However, he also noted that while Quicken Online was a reliable service, the online competitors kept getting better. His conclusion: "It's unclear to me that Intuit's history will translate into market share in this competitive market."

We felt good about our position as we were well on our way to passing the milestone of a million Mint users based on current growth models. If we got there soon, Mint would record the fastest user growth ever for a personal finance software service, whether Intuit chose to believe us or not.

PART IV

CHAPTER 25

UNTANGLY

*"Oh what a tangled web we weave,
when first we practice to deceive."*

SIR WALTER SCOTT

In early 2009, I sat down with Aaron for our weekly one-on-one meeting. I was thinking about our narrow escape from the clutches of Yodlee over the New Year. My gut told me that something needed to change to lessen our reliance on them. The board of directors did not seem to be pressing for this. Still, my recent tribulations with Yodlee left me uneasy that our flank was exposed.

Aaron and I discussed a few things until I found the right moment to tell him we needed to build a proprietary Mint aggregation service. We could not be held hostage again. It was all very well hitting the market fast and early as we had by not reinventing the aggregation wheel, but surely we were at a point where we had to control our destiny as our users multiplied, our headcount grew, and the investment dollars continued to pour into Mint. We couldn't let someone like Polverari put everything we built in jeopardy.

To his credit, Aaron realized I was laying out some hard truths about the business. And in my role as head of revenue and business development, it was my job to deliver them. I'd negotiated the first deal with Yodlee and then prevented them from blowing it up while I renegotiated an extended contract. If anyone could sway Aaron in this situation, it was me.

I saw that it was uncomfortable for Aaron as the reality set in. There were so many other Mint leadership challenges and opportunities in front of him, and now this. It would be a monumental, preemptive undertaking. There were immense challenges to becoming self-sufficient, the first of which was external: the banks. Few financial institutions were offering any way for their customers to extract their financial data. The banks believed that locking in their users' data could work to their benefit because once a customer signed up for checking and savings accounts, the bank could exclusively cross-sell them credit cards, loans, and other services.

Internal execution was no easy task, either. Aaron knew that our current engineering team had too many projects already. We'd need to create an entirely new engineering team dedicated to account aggregation, meaning more cost and management challenges for Aaron.

But despite the difficulties, Aaron recognized the reality I'd delivered to him: Yodlee could hinder Mint's next phase of growth. Yodlee was now a ten-year-old company with ten-year-old technology, and they were calcifying. Even with the premium support package I'd negotiated, the quality of data they delivered to Mint was spotty and did not hold up to our users' expectations. Yodlee also had a reputation for being litigious, and they could erupt at any time. We needed to build our aggregation engine in secret, and we'd need an engineering leader to do it.

So Aaron began an executive search, but the task for our future exec was almost impossible. Yodlee developed its platform with more than a hundred engineers over ten years and with budgets in the tens of millions. Mint's challenge would be to build our aggregation engine with about ten engineers and less than a $2 million budget and deliver something robust within eighteen months.

Jean Sini turned out to be our man. Aaron found Jean through a mutual contact, was impressed by his engineering credentials, and hired him. Jean was a former founder who engineered and led a social web startup sustained by web browsers. And for Jean, there was something about Aaron's charisma and his intellectual energy that he found irresistible.

Legality was the final hurdle in getting the project off the ground. I learned from Aaron that the original plan to have Jean join Mint changed on the advice of our attorneys, Wilson Sonsini. After reviewing Yodlee's aggregation patents and interviewing Aaron on the design he envisaged for Mint's aggregation service, Claassen and the team advised us that we would have a strong defense on the merits of any patent infringement claim by Yodlee. But this didn't mean they wouldn't come after us with everything they had once they learned what we were up to. I recalled Polverari claiming, at our first meeting, that if CashEdge's business didn't fail soon (and he believed it would), Yodlee would sue them for infringement of its patents and bring them down that way. I was relieved to hear that Aaron's design stayed well away from leveraging any proprietary Yodlee technologies.

However, we had one flank that would remain exposed unless we took all possible precautions: Since we were using Yodlee's technology for Mint, they could come after us for a breach of trade secrets if we used any of theirs in our design or process.

Companies often try to discover one another's trade secrets through methods of reverse engineering. Yodlee contractually prohibited us from any such practice as part of the license and services agreement we entered into with them.

Our lawyers advised us that the best protection was to form a separate subsidiary company. That company would hire Jean and his future engineers as a clean-room team who would work in a separate building, with different servers, and otherwise limit their contact with Mint. By the time Jean officially agreed to join us, he knew this would be the structure, and Jean, as the leader, decided to call the new subsidiary company "Untangly."

Several days after Jean started, he reached out to me to set up a lunch meeting. Jean came by Mint's offices, and we went for lunch around the corner on Castro Street. Jean was of medium height and slight, with a wiry build. He had close-cropped black hair, and his dark brown eyes were rimmed by narrow rectangular glasses that maintained just a trace of geek in his appearance. Jean was eager with a smile and seemed naturally optimistic and high in energy. It was precisely the upbeat attitude needed to take on this new challenge we set for him.

I was curious to know why Jean joined our venture and took on this challenge. He put it down to the quality of the team. In a career spanning over ten years in the Valley, Jean said he had never encountered a team as technically strong as Aaron, David, Darryl, and A4, and he wanted to be a part of it. Jean told me a bit more about his Valley story and how he arrived (from France, as I did) in 1996 and joined Oracle Corporation. In 2005, he cofounded Activeweave, a startup operating in the social web arenas, where Jean did extensive work on browser plugins. In April 2008, he sold Activeweave to Buzzlogic. That's when he discovered Mint.

I knew Aaron was impressed with the Firefox browser plugin Jean built while at Activeweave, and Jean began to explain why. A browser plugin was to feature in the design of Mint's new aggregation system. Mint was planning to enroll our users' help to author and edit scripts for interpreting an online banking website so that Mint could retrieve the transaction data. The Untangly browser plugin would be operated by Mint's most dedicated users when they logged into their banks. The plugin would prompt them to identify each page's elements on the bank's website so that the scraper could figure out how to parse the site and extract other users' data on their behalf. The browser plugin would be active during a user's session and track the clicks, text entries, and other activities on the site to author a master script from all these elements. An extensive set of heuristics would be built into the tool to verify for accuracy against HTML and Javascript website interactions. It was a similar approach to how a software QA department writes tests to verify a new website release's integrity. We would start out using a handful of our employees, like QA engineers, to create these scripts before enrolling some of our users to track their online banking activities through our aggregation browser plugin. Using crowdsourcing, we would cover any bank our users wanted to add to Mint and scale the system to meet our users' needs. It was an innovative and bold approach that, if successful, would take aggregation technologies into unchartered territory. When Mint used the Yodlee API for aggregation, it could only read or consume user data from banking sites. With our new approach, Mint would also be able to write data to, for example, affect ACH money transfers, including from a user's savings account to his or her checking account. This write capability could add new dimensions to our service in the future.

As we got a coffee and paid the check for lunch, I asked Jean why he chose Untangly. He excused his English, which I thought was excellent, and explained that it was about untangling the web. By creating a web scraping system, Untangly would be deriving structured data from unstructured data and effectively untangling the mess. We walked back to the office. I thanked Jean for lunch and welcomed him again to the Mint team. I was delighted to have him on board. Jean left quickly to race back to Untangly's offices as he had an interview with an exciting engineering candidate coming up that he was hoping to hire.

With Jean in the pilot's seat, the race was now on to build our new aggregation platform and have it in production before Yodlee got wind of anything and became hostile again. It was a risky but exciting new chapter in Mint's journey to self-reliance and market domination. I was counting on Jean and his team to succeed at all costs.

CHAPTER 26

A MILLION MINT USERS

"Love is the greatest refreshment in life."
PICASSO

As Mint approached the one-million-user milestone, my nineteen-year-old niece Rebecca entered our lives. Before starting a family, my oldest brother Gerard was one of Europe's leading pavement painters. Every summer, he'd travel to Europe from New Zealand to make his fortune collecting money from awestruck tourists. These tourists watched Gerard sprawled out on the pavement for the entire day, painting a giant, Renaissance-style or Dutch masterpiece replica. Rebecca followed in her father's footsteps as she developed her artistic talents, particularly as a portrait artist. After Rebecca graduated from high school, Gerard arranged for her to study in London at the studio of one of England's finest portrait artists the following summer. In the meantime, Rebecca was traveling through Latin America before her London apprenticeship began. I'd offered for Rebecca to stay with us if ever she needed to take shelter in a safe harbor from her voyage in Latin America. To my surprise, in early February 2009, my brother emailed me to say Rebecca would like to come and stay with us. A few days later, she was on our doorstep. Having separated from her French boyfriend, with whom she was traveling, she looked like she needed a place to lay low for a while and pull her life back together.

Even though we didn't have much room in our small Silicon Valley home to accommodate Rebecca, she was family, and we were delighted to see her. My young sons were intrigued by the novelty of spending time with a cousin they barely knew; she'd even be sleeping below one of the boys in a bunk bed.

Rebecca offered to do some light housework for us and keep an eye on the children, but she loved to cook most of all. Soon, she served us beautiful meals, and we were thankful to have her in our home. After a few weeks passed and we had shown her around the Bay area, I sensed that while she was enjoying her stay, she was nevertheless a teenager who must be getting restless for some excitement beyond our domestic family life. I chatted with a few of the young guys at Mint, including Atish and Jason, to see if they might invite her to one of their events in San Francisco. While they were all polite and said they'd think about it, we didn't get any offers.

Then I saw an opportunity to enliven Rebecca's Valley experience by including her in the secret company celebration that my team was planning in light of Mint crossing the million-user milestone. I had the idea to go for a wine tasting day trip to Napa Valley and take the whole company there on a bus. Carrie Cronkey had just joined my team at the start of the year to develop more distribution partnerships. She got together with Ksenia Kouchnirenko, also on my revenue team, to plan and organize the event. Rebecca had developed skills as a photographer to compliment her artistic abilities, and I thought it would be nice for her to come along and take some snaps to capture the spirit of the day. She could be the event photographer. I knew it would be a chance for her to meet some other young people on the Mint team. Her face lit up when I suggested the idea, and I could see she was excited.

On the day of the Napa trip, I drove to Mountain View with Rebecca, where we were to embark on the team bus for the first leg of the journey up to San Francisco. There we would pick up the other city-based Minters before heading across the Golden Gate Bridge on our way to Napa. The event was a surprise; the team knew something was going on, but they didn't know what it was. This anticipation created a good deal of excitement and chatter on the bus on the way up.

They learned we were going to Napa Valley, the world-famous wine region located about an hour northeast of San Francisco.

Before we hopped on the bus in Mountain View, Aaron caught sight of Rebecca for the first time. His face beamed. He had no idea Rebecca was joining us, but he seemed delighted. I told him she was my niece and that she would be taking photographs of the trip. It seemed reasonable that he was curious, I thought—she's a pretty girl.

As we made our way up to the city with the other Minters who chose to embark in Mountain View, including Matt, Carrie, Sid, Justin, and George, we took the Interstate 280 freeway, otherwise known as the Junipero Serra Freeway. This segment of the highway between Cupertino and Daly City has been called the "world's most beautiful freeway" since its dedication in the 1960s. Drivers see scenic views of the Santa Cruz Mountains to the west and, at a few points, San Francisco Bay to the east. Through this segment, the freeway runs just inside the eastern rim of the rift valley of the San Andreas fault line, one of the world's remarkable earthquake zones. I was blissfully unaware that this trip would lead to some significant tremors in my own life.

It was a spectacular way to begin our journey, yet, in one of the most beautiful stretches of roadside nature in the world, Aaron seemed only to have eyes for Rebecca. I sat with Rebecca in the middle section of the bus. She preferred the aisle seat, so I took the window seat. As we made our place, Aaron squeezed in on the aisle seat opposite us and soon leaned over to strike up a conversation with Rebecca. Aaron learned that Rebecca was an artist and volunteered that he was into drawing when he was younger. Their conversation broke off after a few minutes, and as it did, Aaron got out a pad and pencil and started sketching a drawing. When he finished, he presented the picture to Rebecca. It looked like some kind of flower, and it showed some signs of basic artistic technique. Rebecca nodded her approval.

We then arrived in Crissy Field in the city to pick up the rest of the team, clamoring with excitement to get on the bus and learn what the day had in store for them. Donna boarded, along with David, A4, Atish, Jean, Stew, Lee, and others. Including Jean's new hires, the Mint team had grown to nearly thirty members in two years.

Those on board represented the small team that built Mint from the ground up to be the fastest-growing personal finance software service ever. Intuit, who refused to believe that we'd grown this fast, was for now in our rearview mirror. Every Minter took a risk at one time or another to join our fledgling startup, and each was now reaping the rewards of early success. We'd come a long way from Aaron's kitchen.

We headed to Napa across the Golden Gate Bridge, looking out across the bay to Alcatraz Island. Our main stop in Napa was at a beautiful, Italian-style villa winery estate in Yountville, population 3,297. The team disembarked from the bus, and we kicked off the celebrations with a champagne cocktail out on the terraces, where Minters mixed and mingled in relaxed, collegial chatter and laughter. We were momentarily outside the confines of our office, the constraints of our teams, and the daily stress of our startup life. It was time to relax and enjoy it. It was a beautiful mid-March day that was gradually warming up. Across the road were the open, rolling green fields of vineyards intermittently studded with oak trees and shadowed by the Yountville Hills on the northwest side of the town. Later, we sat down for an alfresco lunch protected from the intensifying heat by large cream-colored sun umbrellas placed alongside our tables. After lunch, Rebecca and I broke away from the team to take a stroll along the road to the other end of town to see the famous French Laundry restaurant owned by renowned American chef Thomas Keller. Having been named the best restaurant in the world in 2003 and 2004, and having been awarded three Michelin stars since 2006, it was a must-see while we were in town.

Next, it was time for some wine tasting in the estate's art gallery. Carrie and Ksenia lead those who were more wine-oriented, including myself, Jean, Stew, and Lee, on this segment of the day. As we tasted various wines, a woman gave us a tour of the gallery and explained the works of art hanging boldly on the surrounding walls. There was a sales pitch happening, and I'm sure she thought we were young millionaires from Silicon Valley that could write her a check on the spot should one of the works take our fancy. In reality, most of us were still struggling to pay the rent in Silicon Valley, hoping that one day those times would be behind us.

Not one for wines and galleries, Aaron led a group of guys, including Justin and Matt, also keen outdoors types, to head off for a climb in the hills. Word got out that halfway up the hill, Aaron decided a race would be a good idea, so the hike turned into a run at top speed to the summit.

As the day drew to a close and the first Minters were getting back on the bus, Aaron and his gang of followers came bounding down the hill out of the bushes just in time for departure. They couldn't have looked happier—like kids in a candy store. Charging up and down the hill to get a sweat on lifted their spirits, and they were full of mirth and chatter on the trip back.

The bus arrived back in Crissy Field to drop off the city folks before heading down the 280 freeway back to Mountain View. As the last Minters headed home, Aaron came over to say goodbye. He asked Rebecca if she had a good time, and she said that she did. Aaron added that if she were interested in getting out and seeing more of the Bay Area, he'd be happy to show her around. He also threw in an offer to go hot air ballooning in Sonoma since he and some friends were planning it. I realized he was flirting. Rebecca took it in her stride and was gracious. I chuckled to myself, thinking, "Nice try, but I don't think you're her type." She was a beautiful young bohemian artist, and he was a geek. No offense to Aaron, a well-built, handsome young guy who was likely on his way to becoming a multi-millionaire one day, but I didn't think there was a fit. Yet, beauty is in the eye of the beholder, and the stereotypes we have in our heads are rarely well-founded.

The day was over, and it was time to head home with Rebecca. Tomorrow would be another day at the office on our way to growing the next million Mint members even faster than the first million.

CHAPTER 27

WORK, LIFE, AND LOVE

"Who would give a law to lovers?
Love is unto itself a higher law.

BOETHIUS

Several days later, I drove Rebecca to pick up some art supplies in Palo Alto. As we chatted about some new experiences she might try in the Bay area, she said it could be fun to go on the hot air ballooning adventure that Aaron mentioned. She slipped this in unassumingly as if it were nothing at all but a passing thought. It was so nonchalant that it raised my suspicion, and then the penny dropped. Perhaps she was bored and was merely looking for fun to break up her routine, but it seemed like there was more to it. Aaron caught her fancy.

My head began to spin as I mulled over all the complications a dating scenario might entail, but then again, I was surely overthinking things.

Aaron had recently told me about a new girlfriend. He had moved out of his apartment in Sunnyvale and into a smaller apartment by himself on Alma Street, close to downtown Palo Alto. Aaron was a young bachelor who was starting to unwind and emerge from his introverted shell. This blossoming may have been a function of Mint's success and his growing personal brand, occasionally displayed on the cover of some business magazine as the founder of a hot new Valley startup disrupting the world of consumer finances. Aaron seemed to be growing as Mint grew. He could still lock himself away to work day and night on Mint, but he was no longer fighting the good fight alone. He had a team and investors who could share some of the load, allowing him the occasional break.

I'd seen Aaron in various relationships since I met him a couple of years earlier, and he was still figuring out how to find the right balance. Aaron could write code and get the program to do what he wanted in the world of computers, but in love and life, things were not always quite as straightforward. Aaron had a prior relationship with a woman who decided to move back to New York to pursue studies. Aaron wanted her to stay, but she decided to go. This remote relationship began to go sideways, and I saw Aaron chasing without catching. With his characteristic determination, Aaron was the more committed of the two, but the relationship inevitably came to an end. Aaron seemed down for weeks. He sought to engage me about it, but I preferred to keep my professional and private lives separate.

Aaron seemed to have rebounded and brought that intensity to his new relationship in Palo Alto, so I saw no harm in mentioning that Rebecca seemed bored. I told him it would be great if he and his crowd were up to anything fun in the next few weeks and could invite her along. He was a taken man, after all.

Nothing came from this exchange until one lovely, sunny Sunday afternoon when I took the kids to Johnson Park in Palo Alto, and Rebecca tagged along. While relaxing in the park, I got a call from Aaron. He wanted to know if Rebecca would be interested in going for a sail down at Shoreline, a human-made lake on the southern tip of the Bay in Mountain View. I passed the phone to Rebecca so she could speak for herself. I overheard her agreeing to the invitation before she gave the phone back to me.

Half an hour later, Aaron swung by the park. He was alone. I was surprised by this as he'd said there would be a group of friends all going sailing together, but they were nowhere in sight. Aaron and Rebecca went off. I went back home, and as the afternoon passed into early evening, I began to wonder where they were. Then Aaron called and said that they'd be over to our house soon. When they arrived, he explained that after sailing, they'd gone back to his apartment and baked cookies. It was plausible; Aaron had a quiet, creative side and liked to spend time in the kitchen. It so happened that Rebecca loved to cook as well, and they must have shared some form of bond in baking.

But Aaron was no Casanova on this occasion. As they went out on a small, rented sailboat on the Shoreline lake, Aaron somehow managed to capsize the boat, and both he and Rebecca were plunged overboard into cold, murky, dirty water. They had to stay there, treading water for several minutes as the lifeguards came out to help them get the boat back up on an even keel and hauled them out of the water. It was not exactly my idea of how to impress a young lady on a first date, if that's what it was. Back at our house, Aaron seemed to take it in his stride and even chuckled as he recounted the story. He teased Rebecca ever so slightly by mentioning how she went into a flap about treading water out in the middle of a cold lake while he kept his stoic calm and waited for the rescue crew. They'd then gone back to his apartment to dry off and get a change of clothes while the wet ones dried out. That's when the idea to bake cookies together must have set in.

As dinner time was approaching, Aaron said goodbye and went back to his place. I didn't quite know what to make of it. They'd been on some attempted date, yet seemingly Aaron had ruined it by capsizing them both into the filthy water. I didn't have time to think about where his other girlfriend might be in the picture or where this would lead. Tomorrow was Monday, and my mind started to get in the zone for another week of intense work.

Aaron and I never mentioned Rebecca at work over the next couple of days. It was as if nothing happened. Then, one evening later that week, Aaron called again to speak to Rebecca. This time he planned to take her downtown Palo Alto for dinner and a movie at the Stanford Theatre. I'd asked him to help bring Rebecca out among his friends, but this sounded like another date.

This time Rebecca rode one of our bikes over to Aaron's place to walk downtown from there. I went to bed early that night, trying to keep my mind off their evening. It was none of my business, after all.

The next morning I got up and found that Rebecca had not made it home. She'd stayed the night at Aaron's place.

As I headed off for work that day, it began to sink in that things could get complicated quickly. I had a nineteen-year-old niece staying in our house, and she was now sleeping with a guy who was almost ten years older than her. And he was my boss. How was I supposed to act in this situation? None of it was clear to me, and I knew of no precedent.

In just a few months, Rebecca would be off to London, a world away from our driven existence in the Valley. What would the ramifications of all this be? If it all fell apart, leaving Aaron with emotional wreckage, would I be the constant daily reminder of a painful wound in his heart? I felt an invasion of privacy. Fine, I'd asked Aaron to take Rebecca out, but in a group of friends so she wouldn't be bored, and in the knowledge that he was in a relationship. I felt that Aaron was now forcing a merger between my two worlds. He wanted what he wanted and damn the consequences. This situation was like a massive sinkhole just opening up and getting ready to swallow me.

Over the next few days, I was testy at work and at home. I gave Rebecca a wide berth, and, to her credit, she was mature enough to notice that something was wrong. On the weekend, she sat down with me to discuss the situation. I tried as best I could to explain that this scenario was challenging for me. If she wanted to date some guy at nineteen years of age while living with us, I'd have no problem with that, as long as it didn't disrupt our household. I wasn't a prude, after all. But of all the guys out there, why choose Aaron? Couldn't she understand that I had to maintain a working relationship with him in an intense environment and that this could blow that up?

She listened carefully and seemed to understand. She reflected on the situation and then assured me that she'd take care of it. I was relieved that she'd listened to my concerns and that she was ready to clean up her mess. Yet, Aaron is a persistent guy. As an entrepreneur who'd spent months by himself coding up Mint's prototype and pushing past dozens of no-funding decisions from VCs, he'd demonstrated that. As a young guy looking for relationship experiences, his single-minded determination might transcend even his entrepreneurial convictions. I remained wary.

Over the next few days, Aaron repeatedly tried to reach out to Rebecca, but she found excuses to brush him off. It got to the point where he was so confused that he mentioned it to me. This was the very thing I was not looking for—to be a go-between for him and Rebecca. "I don't pretend to understand women," I shrugged.

Another week went by, and Rebecca stayed in the background as Aaron kept plowing through his days at work. I could see he was preoccupied. The weekend arrived, and I was relieved to get out of the office and retreat home for a couple of days to clear my head and put things in perspective. Late after the kids had gone to bed and we were relaxing, there was a knock at the front door. We all froze. It must be Aaron. Rebecca lept into action and answered the door as we stayed in the background. She saw Aaron off with some excuse, and he went away.

Aaron just showing up like that meant that he was blissfully unaware of the tensions brewing, or he knew and didn't care. Either way, the situation I was trying to avoid was now spinning out of control. When Aaron was safely gone, I read Rebecca the riot act. I said it was all very well for her to travel around the world as a free agent at nineteen, but when you come into someone's home for shelter, there are minimal responsibilities that come with the territory. If she was not mature enough to grasp that, perhaps she should consider whether she was ready to be so independent and at large. She suffered through my lecture, looking somewhat shaken by it, and quietly went off to bed. The following week I'd have to go back to work and pretend none of this happened. It would be a strange act of pretense, and it made me uncomfortable.

I didn't know what would happen next, but I was hoping things would simmer down for a while. How wrong I was. One morning I woke to find Rebecca missing as I readied for work. She snuck out during the middle of the night on one of our bikes from the garage. There was only one place Rebecca could have gone. Aaron had kept up the pressure on Rebecca, and she cracked. She would stay up late at night on the computer out in the kitchen while communicating via

Facebook. The irony did not escape me that the harder I tried to keep the lovers apart, as in a Shakespeare play, it seemed to create more dramatic tension and a deep bond that only drew them more passionately together.

Once again, I had to go to work and pretend as if nothing happened. But it was getting harder to seal up the cracks this was causing in my relationship with Aaron. On the following Monday morning, the Mint leadership got together for our weekly staff meeting to review the results of the prior week and to set priorities for the upcoming one. It seemed surreal that it should be business as usual for other team members like Donna, David, and A4 when Aaron and I seemed to be locked in an unspoken battle of wills. I couldn't wait to get out of there and retreat to my cube and lock myself away in deep work. But then I had to come back home at the end of the day to Rebecca. It was like having a teenage daughter who was rebelling against her overbearing and overprotective father. Except she wasn't my daughter. It seemed absurd. God only knows what happened to the young lady that Aaron told me he was dating and seeing almost every night. My guess is she tired quickly from seeing him too regularly or was swept away in Rebecca's wake.

It was an uncomfortable situation at work and home, and I couldn't wait for it to come to an end. I couldn't have it out with Aaron and demand to know what he thought he was doing. I had to work every day with him, perhaps for years to come. And I couldn't have it out with Rebecca and demand to know what she was doing driving a bus through my work life when she was only passing through town. She was my niece and forever part of my family. There was only one thing to do at this point: put my head down and wait for May to come as quickly as possible. That's when Rebecca would leave for London to continue her art studies. In the meantime, I would give both of them a wide berth and hope to keep the lid on simmering tensions, so there were no unnecessary blow-ups that all of us might regret. Rebecca's departure was only a few weeks away, and I was counting the days.

The weeks crawled by as I gritted my teeth, and we all ignored the elephant in the room. When it was finally time for Rebecca to go, we said our goodbyes without much else as we drove her to the airport. It had started as an enjoyable experience having her stay with us. Somehow, it got turned upside down. After she'd gone, I ruminated on the situation. I thought that at this stage of my life, I was mature, rational, and well-equipped to handle most situations. I was wrong. You can still step in quicksand at any point, and the harder you try to work out of it, the deeper you get sucked in. Only time will allow you to compose yourself and work your way out. In the end, I realized that two lovers falling in love is the most natural and harmless thing that can happen. If I had to do it all over again, I'd let love take its natural course and not try to control it. It was a fool's errand.

CHAPTER 28

CHINKS IN THE ARMOR

"Do what you can, with what you have, where you are."
THEODORE ROOSEVELT

Aaron and I never did speak about the Rebecca situation—and our working relationship gradually returned to normalcy. We both welcomed it. And we'd need to be back on the same page, fast.

Mint's growth from launch was impressive and exceeded expectations. By the time of the Great Recession, our growth accelerated and continued without a break during the peak of the personal-finance season from December 2008 through the end of April 2009, helped by the release of our first iPhone app. We fell into thinking this was the new normal only to find that traffic to our site started to slow down as spring eased into the summer of 2009. Our board of directors had told us that we couldn't ride our PR wave forever. They predicted it would last about eighteen months. We were in month twenty-two since launch.

PR had turbocharged the Mint growth engine. We consistently got high-quality traffic from reputable sites through media coverage of Aaron and Mint. The team from Atomic PR, led by Martha Shaughnessy, who became Aaron's media sherpa, helped Mint increase its coverage by more than 250 percent. This PR blitz would, on occasion, propel us to as many as twenty thousand sign-ups in a single day, such as when Mint appeared on the MyYahoo! home page. It helped turn Mint into the fastest growing personal finance service in history and drove the numbers that dumbfounded Intuit.

Some of the world's leading news outlets and publications had featured stories on Mint, including ABC News, *Businessweek*, the *New York Times*, *TIME*, and The *Wall Street Journal*. Other coverage included broadcast TV, where Aaron would pop in to appear for a few minutes on morning shows such as NBC's *The Today Show*. As early as December 2007, I realized Aaron was becoming a celebrity beyond the *TechCrunch* and Valley audience. He was young, handsome, intelligent, well-mannered, and measured, and he was the underdog disrupting the world of financial services. Aaron would soon be featured in *Forbes* and appear on the cover of *Fast Company*, which drew a novel analogy: "If personal finance for most folks is like personal hygiene–an unpleasant chore motivated by necessity–Quicken is Old Spice. Meanwhile, the Axe Bodyspray of personal finance–cool, fresh, and even sexy–is an upstart named Mint."[19]

Once Aaron realized PR was good for Mint's brand and growth, he spent more time making himself accessible to the media, including going on multiple press tours organized by Martha and delivering over five hundred interviews. When Aaron introduced Martha to people, he would sometimes remark that "unlike most PR people, she's very smart." Martha's presence allowed him to relax a little and reveal a hint of occasional dry wit. Martha became like a surrogate older sister to Aaron. They were opposites: he was introverted and always calm; she was an unabashed extrovert who was hyperactive. Martha helped Aaron adapt to different media situations and use more human mainstream language, such as referencing "bank-level security" instead of "SSL encryption" when discussing Mint's security practices.

On one media tour, while walking together down a New York avenue, Aaron blurted out a question to Martha: "How much do you weigh?" Martha was still processing the matter as he squeezed her arm

---

19 Anya Kamenetz. "Easy Money: Mint.com CEO Aaron Patzer is Merging Personal Finance with Web 2.0." *Fast Company*. December 1, 2007.

and commented, "I think you're denser than most women your size." That was Aaron: a shade socially unaware and a touch geek statistician just trying to process how Martha fit into the female genome matrix he was storing in his head. Martha was too fond of Aaron to take offense. Instead, she chose to turn it into a learning moment for him and explain that it's not always a great idea to talk to women about their weight as some can be sensitive about it and might take offense.

Martha knew two things about Aaron in terms of his learning receptivity. First, processing new ideas were akin to adding original programming to his computer—Aaron matured as he gained experience and added each new code layer. Secondly, Aaron would only accept the input if he saw value in the learning. If he did, then he'd take it in without ego. In this case, Aaron noted Martha's advice and found it useful. Indeed, Martha would encounter many more of these speak out loud before you think moments from Aaron, such as when he confided in her one day, "You're thirty years old. Did you know that more than half of your eggs are now dead?" Martha learned something new that day.

As Martha shaped Aaron into a consumer finance media personality, the media sought Aaron's advice regarding buying a first home and young couples having their first child. When it came time for Valentine's Day, the press wanted to know from Aaron how much couples should spend to celebrate the date. Aaron learned how to take on a different tone for different audiences, sometimes more calm or professional, depending on the circumstances. Aaron's media profile became so hot the producer of *The Bachelor* tried to coax Martha to put Aaron on the show. Martha thought it would be a distraction and rejected the idea. She told Aaron afterward, who understood why she declined the offer even as he felt it was an amusing idea that he half-fancied.

Every Minter felt proud each time there was meaningful media coverage, and there was a fresh buzz around the office at every spike in our traffic. It's fun and energizing to work for a recognized, hot company. Our PR journey peaked in 2009 at Davos, the world's most prestigious economic gathering. Aaron attended the conference in January, where the World Economic Forum named Mint a winner of its 2009 "Technology Pioneers" competition—one of only thirty-four recipients worldwide. Suddenly, we were catapulting beyond Valley backyard recognition to attention on the world stage.

With this avalanche of media coverage, we never anticipated the traffic slowdown that came in our second summer in 2009. Less than two full years had elapsed since our launch, and everything was up and to the right. We were growing exponentially, but we didn't realize that personal finance is a highly seasonal business. We'd eventually understand that a summer slowdown is typical; it's when consumers stop paying attention to their finances and start thinking about getting away on hard-earned vacations to spend their money rather than budget. For the first time, I saw Aaron unsettled. I'd never seen his confidence in Mint waver before. Yet, traffic and revenue were still flowing in, just at a less torrid rate than previously. To be a great sailor, you need to weather the storm as well as the calm, and this period tested Aaron's ability to do so.

At the same time, serious competition began to emerge on our flanks. Credit Karma began disrupting the credit bureaus by offering a free credit score and associated content to customers. They would also present financial products to their users, albeit not the smart offers we made. Billshrink allowed customers to compare mobile plans to find savings. It was founded by none other than Schwark Satyavolu, the former cofounder of Yodlee, whom Aaron and I worked with just months after our first meeting at Yodlee in late 2006. And NerdWallet arrived to educate its users by providing reviews and comparing various financial products, including credit cards, banking, investing, loans, and insurance.

Credit Karma, Billshrink, and NerdWallet went after the same financial services lead generation market that Mint was leading. None of these companies offered a complete, one-stop-shop financial service the way Mint did. Nor did I see any technology offering from them that came close to Mint's smart savings engine. Instead, each of these companies was trying to unbundle one dimension of the Mint service and exploit it with a more direct and in-depth focus. It was a classic Valley play to seek to divide and conquer another successful business.

While Mint appeared stronger across the board as a consumer online financial service, paradoxically, our one weakness might have been covering too much personal finance territory.

In the face of these tests, Aaron was intensifying his relationship with Rebecca. He was not about to let distance keep them apart for too long. They used Skype to communicate regularly, and Aaron found ways to be on the east coast, either for a press tour or a financial conference. He would take a red-eye flight to slip across the Atlantic and land in London for a weekend, sometimes springing a surprise on Rebecca. Aaron, it turns out, was an old-fashioned romantic. Of course, he worked relentlessly as ever while in transit, but it did mean that he was spending less time with the troops and starting to have a hint of life beyond Mint. Some of the earliest Minters noticed this subtle change in his schedule and availability. Others who joined later thought it was the regular duties of an expanding startup CEO keeping him from being in the office daily.

During that summer slowdown, Aaron's younger brother persuaded him to take a break and join him for a short but long overdue vacation in Costa Rica. Since the day I met him, I'd never known Aaron to take any time off other than to tack on an extra day here and there on a visit back to see his family in Indiana. Aaron's work ethic and his ascetic frugality almost precluded the concept of vacation up to that point. This was to be Aaron's first real break in about three years of Mint building. Aaron hadn't had a real break since he was fourteen years old. He graduated from high school early and continued to overachieve through his college years, taking on a triple-major at Duke while simultaneously running a side business building websites. He did his master's in record time and went in and out of a doctorate program at Princeton. Before he opened the Valley office of Nascentric as its lead architect, summer breaks were spent interning at IBM. Then he started Mint. The man needed and deserved a break. So Aaron booked the trip to Costa Rica with his brother and flew Rebecca out to meet him there in the second week of the stay.

I sensed this might be a turning point for Aaron, and I was interested to see if the same workaholic engineer and driven founder would return intact. Who knew what, if any, impact this trip would have on Aaron, but spending time in a tropical paradise beside a beautiful new young love might make them wonder why they were running in opposite directions. The ambitious entrepreneur in Aaron might be merely taking a quick break before returning to the Valley to raise more money, hire more employees, stoke more press fires, and take on all who would challenge Mint. Aaron was the author of a fantastic product roadmap that would take us far into the future of money. The reality was that it would take many more years to build an excellent, profitable company and mainstream brand. And the recent slowing of growth, along with the challenge of building proprietary account aggregation, was imposing. Aaron was less comfortable managing a growing body of employees, all with different needs, than he was burying himself alone deep in algorithms or sketching up new product ideas. Would the daily grind be worth it? What if less was more?

CHAPTER 29

A FORK IN THE ROAD

"Do not go where the path may lead, go instead where there is no path and leave a trail."

RALPH WALDO EMERSON

Upon his return from Costa Rica, Aaron jumped back in the saddle, visibly no different other than the glow of a light tan and a flush of love. Rebecca was back in London. Whatever moments of relaxation Aaron stole while on vacation were gone, and many challenges and opportunities were looming on the Mint horizon that needed his attention. Microsoft was courting us to develop a Windows Phone app, and Google was lurking with Android. Though we'd choose only the platform that emerged as most popular, we knew the specialized resources required to support a mobile platform. Untangly also needed investment for growth. We needed to raise more capital.

The Mint board of directors reconvened with the company's fundraising requirements top of mind. Bob Kagle of Benchmark stepped in and tugged on the firm's network. Kagle had previously received interest in a possible investment in Mint from Dag Ventures. Kagle told Dag that if they wanted in, they'd have to invest at a significant multiple to the company's valuation in its last round.

Dag Ventures slotted in as a mid-stage venture capital partnership and typically led later-stage growth financing rounds in promising portfolio companies of select, early-stage VCs. When Benchmark came calling, they listened. Dag immediately marked their interest in Mint and began diligence with a term sheet based on the Benchmark quoted price. This set Mint's valuation at $125 million pre-money, and with that, our Series C financing had commenced.

That's when Intuit's CEO, Brad Smith, presumably lacking any knowledge of our next funding move, reached out to Aaron. Intuit's fiscal year ended on July 31, and Smith must have had some space to make strategic moves after that. He wanted to talk to Aaron about personal finance education initiatives. The context seemed natural since Mint had recently participated with the state of Ohio to sponsor and include a personal finance section in the math curriculum for state school kids. Martha had garnered some press for this that must have caught Smith's eye. Aaron was both flattered and intrigued. The giant incumbent was taking notice of us in a much different tone than a letter accusing us of fabricating our growth numbers.

With that said, this was not our first experience with outreach from the Valley's giant companies. As Mint rose to prominence, we'd already received many invitations to attend corporate development meetings at companies, including Google and Apple. These corporate development groups seek to acquire companies to feed their growth engines. After attending several of these meetings, we soon discovered that it was standard procedure to check out any company that was hot in the Valley. They'd always act interested in the technology and be highly complimentary before inquiring politely about funding history and any upcoming rounds and associated valuations. This approach was an attempt to gauge whether we might be open to acquisition and, if so, at a favorable price, just in case they might be interested. At this point, the entrepreneur was free to signal that his or her company might be for sale at the right price, at the right time, to the right company.

The situation with Brad Smith was different. He was the CEO of Intuit, and he was reaching out for direct discussions. Aaron consulted with Mark Goines and decided he would meet Smith. A date was set for the meeting at a Hobee's restaurant in Mountain View, in neutral territory. Aaron also called Rob Hayes to let him know what was happening.

Hayes had an immediate reaction: "He wants to buy Mint," he told Aaron. Aaron protested that the meeting wasn't about that, but it was the first time Hayes detected a sheepish reaction from Aaron about anything. Hayes asked Aaron regardless, "Well, do you want to sell the company?" "Of course not," was Aaron's response. "It is way too early."

Hayes then called Kopelman and let him know his prediction that "Smith will give him a number and Aaron's going to come out wanting to sell the company. Just watch." This was a remarkable forecast by Hayes as he and Kopelman had often said that of all First Round's portfolio company founders, Aaron was in it for the long haul. Still, Kopelman was not about to second guess Hayes's intuition. They'd both have to wait and see how things turned out.

Aaron arrived early to the meeting with Smith and sat waiting at a booth. Smith soon arrived, spotted Aaron, and they shook hands as Smith sat down opposite Aaron. After just a few pleasantries, Smith apologized for the legal letter they'd sent to inquire about our user growth numbers. Smith seemed to take cover from his assertion that, in this case, the lawyers got carried away. He did not acknowledge that it happened on his watch and was ultimately his responsibility. Smith soon threw out the pretext for the meeting as he leaned across and asked Aaron point-blank, "How would you feel about us buying your company for $100 million?" The first part of Hayes' prediction was coming true.

Aaron was taken aback and didn't quite know how to react. Then an old negotiation technique I taught him nearly two years earlier flashed across his mind. He indicated that he'd need to consult with his board of directors and his executive team before he could contemplate anything like that. Smith seemed satisfied with the response. He struck with the element of surprise that allowed him to get a clean response from Aaron, who had not said that it was out of the question.

After Aaron's heart rate came back off a racing high, he was able to ask Smith what some of the advantages to a merger might be. Smith rattled off some talking point synergies, including that with a Mint integration to TurboTax, Mint would become a household name for personal finances. As Smith continued to engage, Aaron realized that he was dealing with a man of staggering charisma. Indeed, Smith reminded him of President Bill Clinton, who Aaron had met at a White House event for young pioneer entrepreneurs a few months earlier. Soon the meeting ended, and the two men departed on their separate ways with a mutual promise to stay in touch and keep the dialogue open during the coming days and weeks.

Brad Smith soon reached back out to continue his charm offensive with Aaron; he wanted to meet again. Smith had succeeded in creating an initial bond with Aaron. This time Smith came on stronger. He told Aaron that both he and Scott Cook were hugely impressed with Mint's achievements. While lavishing praise on the Mint service, Smith was also careful to point out how brutally hard it is to build a strong brand in the consumer market. Intuit and its founder Cook knew this all too well from experience. Smith thought it would be excellent for Aaron to meet Scott Cook next time around.

The next day, Aaron and I went out for lunch on Castro Street to discuss what had transpired. This was new territory for Aaron, and he was still trying to process the chain of events. Nevertheless, Aaron wanted to share the news with me in recognition that I'd been working with him longer than anyone. Neither of us contemplated this happening so quickly. I told Aaron that I was happy to keep building Mint but that if we sold, I'd prefer to work somewhere like Google rather than Intuit. Google appealed to me more as a modern, highly technical company, and I also thought Google could help fulfill Mint's mission better than Intuit. In other words, I wasn't enamored with the idea.

I could see being open to an acquisition at the right price. Since we were still a young company, the number in my head was something north of $300 million. It was flattering that Intuit had approached us, but they didn't seem to be within range, so I wasn't going to lose a lot of sleep over it. I told Aaron so, and he took note without revealing anything about where he stood on the subject.

As the Intuit meetings took shape, we got word that Peter Thiel was interested in joining our pending Series C round. David Michaels met Thiel at a function in San Francisco, where he expressed regret that he had passed on Mint's first round a couple of years earlier. Thiel gained his notoriety as the cofounder of PayPal in 1999 and served as its chief executive officer until its sale to eBay in 2002 for $1.5 billion. Silicon Valley circles know Thiel as the head of the "PayPal mafia," representing a classic Valley network cluster of former employees who became founders of their own companies and VC firms. Through this network, Thiel became Facebook's first outside investor, dropping in $500,000 for a 10.2 percent stake in the company. Within a few years, following Facebook's IPO in 2012, Thiel sold most of his shares for over $1 billion.

One of Thiel's post-PayPal ventures was the Founders Fund, a venture capital firm that he launched in 2005. This was the fund that was proposing to invest in Mint's next funding round. Thiel's newfound interest in Mint was a signal that, at least in his view, we could go big and achieve world-class status, even if Aaron might be having his first moment of doubt.

And so we had a choice to make. The board of directors was excited about our prospective Series C funding. Still, since Smith had floated a real number in earnest contemplation of acquiring Mint, Aaron was obliged to bring it up. The board quickly realized that Aaron was open to being led down the path of acquisition. The second part of Hayes' prediction was coming true. Each of them would need to adjust swiftly and start thinking about their respective positions on a potential early exit. As that debate was percolating, Aaron accepted the invitation to meet with Scott Cook.

At our next Monday morning staff meeting, Aaron shared the high-level details of his encounters with the executive team. I could see temptation as Aaron leaned into his Intuit discussions. Everyone else was enthusiastic, even giddy, with excitement. I was alone in my opposition to the deal. I felt Mint was worth much more than $100 million, which I'll admit is a lot of money for any product less than two years in the wild. Why was everyone in such a rush to sell at the first sign of a prospective offer?

The next development shifted the dynamics in reverse. Aaron went back to meet with Intuit's CFO, Neil Williams, to discuss the mechanics of a possible acquisition. Williams had joined Intuit from Visa in January 2008 and was relatively new in his role, though he had over thirty years of experience at other high-profile public companies. In that meeting, as Williams looked over some of Mint's metrics, he declared that the most Intuit could pay for Mint was in the range of $80 million. It was a classic good cop, bad cop play between him and Smith. But it was the wrong hardball move at the wrong time. No one wanted to fold their cards at $80 million, and Aaron knew he wouldn't get any board support for that price. I breathed a sigh of relief, as it appeared there was a gulf between the two companies, and the deal was unlikely to happen after all.

As we went to ground on the low ball offer from Intuit, Smith must have realized they'd made the wrong play and began to try and win Aaron over again. By this time, negotiations with Dag Venture's and Thiel's Founders Fund had progressed to the point where we could close the deal if we wanted it. I sat down with Aaron to discuss the pros and cons of proceeding with the Series C financing. He was clearly in some doubt as it would result in dilution from giving up more of his share of the company, which would be unnecessary if Intuit's acquisition were to proceed. From these ruminations, I could see he was still harboring hopes of a deal with Intuit.

I believed we had to take the Series C financing, and I told him so. If the Intuit acquisition never materialized, we needed more money to continue growing independently. Moreover, I viewed the cost of dilution, while painful, as the cheapest insurance we could buy. If we let the funding slip away without demonstrating that we had sufficient money in the bank to continue growing the company, Intuit would drop the price on us in a heartbeat. And that would be extreme dilution to Aaron. Whereas, if we took the venture money, we would have an alternative to an acquisition in which we could say no if the price wasn't right. We would also be setting a minimum floor on the acquisition price with the Series C valuation of $125 million pre-money, which was well above Smith's first number. There would be no way Intuit could expect to pay less than that amount, and they'd need to pay a premium for outright control of the company. Aaron saw the logic and accepted it. Whatever the outcome, the next chapter of Mint's story would be about our Series C financing.

CHAPTER 30

TO SELL OR NOT TO SELL

"It's easier to resist at the beginning than at the end."

LEONARDO DA VINCI

In April 2009, we announced in a press release that Mint had completed a new $14 million Series C financing round led by Dag Ventures.[20] Included in the round was new money coming in from Peter Thiel's Founders Fund, and all of our existing investors participated pro-rata. This latest round brought Mint's total funds raised to date to $31 million.

TechCrunch ran with the news.[21] Since launching at *TechCrunch* 40 in September 2007, they reported that Mint had grown to 1.4 million registered users, tracking $175 billion in transactions and $47 billion in assets. Mint had also identified $300 million in potential savings offers for its members. *TechCrunch* also observed that Mint was becoming something more than a personal finance tool. Mint was becoming a treasure trove of financial and economic data because of its ability to

---

20 "Leading Personal Finance and Budgeting Software Prepares for Expanded Product Upgrades and New Partnerships." *MintLife*. April 12, 2009.

21 Jason Kincaid. "Full Details On Mint's $14 Million Series C Round." *TechCrunch*. August 13, 2009.

know where people are shopping and how much they're spending. This meant Mint could potentially use this aggregate data to track the performance of entire industries or even individual stores.

Included in the *TechCrunch* commentary was the observation that Mint's brand was going global. The calls were becoming louder for the company to expand the service to Canada, the UK, and many other countries, including Germany and Brazil. In the wake of the Great Recession, it was remarkable that Mint could attract unsolicited new venture money. With the Series C money in the bank, we could hire more people to help us take the Mint service to the next level and beyond—if Aaron chose to.

Yet Mint's Series C Funding did not deter Smith and Cook from their pursuit of Mint. They set up to woo Aaron once more, only this time more forcefully. As their pursuit resumed, Intuit announced another acquisition. It was for online payroll services provider PayCycle, which specialized in serving small businesses. The acquisition would bolster Intuit's goal of moving away from packaged desktop software to cloud-based online software delivery. The purchase price was $170 million; there was the marker. Intuit was ready to splash the cash to buy companies that would help further its strategy of becoming an online financial services software provider.

At the next Mint executive staff meeting on Monday morning, David, Donna, and A4 seemed giddy with the PayCycle news as they anticipated Mint might be next in line. Aaron kept his usual calm, reserved demeanor, but he must have noticed the team's excitement. I was frustrated by such talk. I pointed out that we had a company to run and a new set of investors to reward. From my experience across many corporate acquisitions at Wilson Sonsini, I observed that good companies get bought and don't get sold. We needed to keep focusing on our customers and growing the business either way. In my mind, the $170 million paid for PayCycle was not the $300 million I mentioned to Aaron when we first discussed a possible acquisition at lunch. And Intuit was not Google!

Aaron let me have my say, but he did not echo my sentiment, and I could see he was more inclined to keep dancing with Intuit until the music stopped. Aaron's style was not to contradict or argue. He would allow you to speak. However, on this matter, it seemed like Aaron had made up his mind, and it would take something extraordinary to shift him to a different gear and direction. At the end of this meeting, it was clear where each member of the Mint management team stood on the acquisition. I was isolated. I had to accept that I could influence but not direct the outcome, and now it was up to our board of directors to determine if an acquisition was suitable for Mint at this juncture.

I reflected on how some of the other Minters would feel about an acquisition were they to find out about it. They were not allowed to know since Intuit was a public company, and if this information leaked out, there would be legal ramifications. I had to believe, like A4, Donna, and David, some of them would regard it as a win, a career booster, and a personal financial windfall. Matt, who started on the floor in Aaron's apartment, could buy a house and think about starting a family he could support. Sid could take his proceeds from the acquisition and start a new company. Poornima, too, might take her chances and become one of the Valley's few "femgineer" founders. Jason was unlikely to fulfill his creative destiny at Intuit. No doubt, his options would be plentiful. Atish might take the money and flee with his coding skills to Facebook. And there were many others, all who would face life-changing choices.

Mint's next board meeting focused on whether or not to sell the company to Intuit. Word came back that a split emerged between the early and later-stage investors. Mark Goines was open to the deal. With his Intuit background, he thought that company was the right place for Mint to land, and he understood the strategic reasons why Intuit would pay over the odds. Rob Hayes was also open to the deal. The returns to both Goines and First Round on a $100 million-plus deal, when their initial money was invested at a $3 million pre-money valuation not much more than two years earlier, would be huge. While Mint might sell for a lot more in the future, there was still risk associated with that play. The current price was more than suitable for their seed-stage venture investing model. And of course, each would claim that they were "founder-friendly" and would always back the founder and the team, even if they might have some personal misgivings. They would also argue that they would support the company if it wanted to go on independently and build something big. It was Aaron's choice to sell or not to sell, and they were going to support him either way.

A deal at $100 million-plus would represent a quick, impressive win for Tod Francis and Shasta. However, Shasta was a more traditional Series A investor that typically played a longer game, with bigger bets on the table searching for far more significant returns. Francis, a veteran investor in the consumer technology sector, was a true Mint champion and believed that the company had unique potential. While Francis was always sympathetic to what the management team wanted to do, he was not on the sell-side and opposed the deal in principle. Francis felt that by approving and participating in Mint's Series C financing, he'd done everything he could to say to Aaron and the team, "Go ahead and build a great company. We'll support you." Francis considered that if Aaron and the Mint team were patient, there was a minimum $1 billion outcome there.

Ultimately, Francis was not going to stand in the way of what Aaron and the team wanted. He knew that you couldn't make people work if their hearts are no longer in it. Francis also factored in the Great Recession's psychological effect, which provided a crushing backdrop to this whole episode. These were dark days for Valley investors and entrepreneurs alike, and Francis couldn't recall a significant acquisition exit since the recession hit. Since no-one at that time could see the light at the end of the recession tunnel, it was only normal to consider that this might be an opportune time to take shelter from the storm.

Bob Kagle did not come off the board of directors at eBay to play in a minor league game. He was in the last chapter of his career at Benchmark and was looking for more crowning achievements. He'd also orchestrated Mint's recent Series C Financing in full support of the company going it alone and achieving big things in the future. In the grand scheme of Valley things, if done at $100 million-plus, this deal would be a proverbial rounding error. Benchmark was not particularly interested in cash-quick sales unless a company was showing signs of trouble. Benchmark could afford to swing for the fences and strikeout. Indeed, their venture model demanded it.

This model would often put the venture community at such odds with a founder's interests. Most founders poured blood, sweat, and tears into their companies, and it was a terrifying thing to think of swinging and striking out. These founders do not have several other investments in their portfolio that they could rely on to bail them out in the event of failure of one of them. By contrast, even in a successful venture capital career, you lose all of your bets over half of the time—10 percent of your investments provide 90 percent of your returns. Failure is the norm in venture capital, and if you're not striking out, you're not swinging for the fences. As Kagle put it, "in venture investing, the home runs need to go out of the park and down the street aways." Imagine a major league baseball player leading the league in errors, being struck out the most, and hitting into the most double plays yet still being voted the MVP. That was post-seed-stage venture capital.

But Kagle was a statesman, and he had enough experience to realize how important it was to be mindful of founder entrepreneurs and their needs. He also understood that it was essential to maintain a founder-friendly reputation in the Valley ecosystem, particularly as the VC game was much more competitive. Yet, he wasn't ready to sanction a deal on these terms.

What Francis and Kagle were facing was a shift underneath them in the Valley mindset around exits. The new type of early angel and seed investor on Mint's board of directors, represented by Goines and Hayes, did not show up in startup boardrooms just a few years earlier. They were a new breed, looking for more consistent returns—and open to pulling profits early to get them. They were ready and willing to accept deals like these on Intuit's terms.

Once Aaron understood that he was facing resistance from Francis and especially Kagle, he turned white under the pressure as he realized he was in a stand-off with his board. Over the following days and weeks, Hayes would notice an incredible strain on Aaron, who appeared not to be sleeping. A4 noticed that he started drinking coffee for the first time.

While the debate continued, Aaron got to work in the background to ensure the deal would stay alive and keep all Mint's options on the table. In his next meeting with Brad Smith, he knew he had to convey the message that if Intuit wanted to win this poker game, they'd need to raise the stakes. After he met with Smith, Aaron took me into a small conference room upstairs at our offices and relayed almost precisely what he'd said in the meeting. I listened carefully in amazement. It was a passionate discourse on the future of personal finance, the strength of Mint's product roadmap, and the strategic reasons for doing the deal. I marveled at how he must have prepared this speech and rehearsed it multiple times before delivering it. This preparation was just as he'd done almost two years earlier for his seven minutes on stage at *TechCrunch* 40. It was testimony to his relentless focus, determination, and persistence when he set his sights on something, rightly or wrongly. He had an iron will, one of the critical factors that VCs look for in an entrepreneur. Only this time, it was working against a segment of his investors.

I imagined Smith's reaction. On a product level, it must have reaffirmed Aaron's visionary status, which Smith saw as a critical asset in Intuit's strategic move to the cloud and the mobile world. On a character level, here was a young man less than thirty years old going head to head with a Fortune 500 CEO and carving it up. Smith knew Aaron could improve his team at Intuit immediately and was potentially someone who might lead the company one day. And on a personal level, Smith must have admired Aaron's sincere, youthful courage and conviction to set a course and stick with it. Perhaps Smith saw something of his younger self in the mix. The two of them were beginning to form a personal bond and a sense of mutual trust. Smith was ready to bring Mint into the Intuit family and take Aaron under his wing.

At the next Mint board meeting, once again, the debate broke out about selling the company. By this time, it was clear that Aaron was now firmly on the sell-side. Aaron spent more time with Mark Goines than any other investors and was surely relying on his advice more than anyone during this time. To some extent, he convinced himself that the later-stage VCs were only concerned about their fund's success and delivering returns to their limited partners. This is why they were holding out. Aaron was always a rationalist. He struggled to see the difference between numbers such as $30 million and $60 million as his haul when he'd already calculated that $15 million would set him free for life. Going for $60 million or more was just scorekeeping. Whereas there was a fundamental difference between $0 and $30 million. Aaron knew other founders whose VCs had turned down early lucrative acquisition offers only to subsequently have their companies fall on hard times and sell for scrap. He knew that if he could bank a success here with Mint, no one could take it away.

But wherever the truth lay, both sides had a point. From the VC side, it was disingenuous for the entrepreneur to take their money when he needed it to grow the company, then turn around to sell out early and deny the legitimacy of their business model when it no longer suited.

In Aaron's mind, there was also Rebecca. He was now deep into a long-distance relationship with her. He perhaps felt that an acquisition would relieve him of the time-crushing obligations required to build an independent company. With enough money to never have to work again and more time to court Rebecca, what was not to like about the early exit option? And in the back of Aaron's mind, he was already beginning to dream of more magnificent and daring entrepreneurial adventures. He started discussing more openly his idea to one day start working on a radical transformation in transportation infrastructure that would change our cities and perhaps our world. For Aaron, roads and cars had now become inefficient, and he was itching to work on a "maglev," or magnetic levitation transport system to replace cars in most urban and suburban settings. Aaron fancied himself an inventor first and an entrepreneur second, just like one of his heroes, Thomas Edison. Edison was a great inventor, but he was also a first-class entrepreneur who found a way to market his inventions to the masses. He developed the lightbulb and invented the entire electric grid and power distribution system that went along with it. General Electric, one of the world's largest and most profitable companies, still stands today as his legacy. Aaron's Edison concept was to develop a magnetically levitated system using two-person vehicles attached to a track, driven by a linear synchronous motor. In effect, little pods would move people through the air on an extensive set of tracks built throughout neighborhoods, which could replace a good deal of local car trips.

Aaron had previously discussed this transportation system with Kagle to sound him out on the concept. When I asked him what Kagle thought of it, Aaron, with a wry smile, said that Kagle placed him and the idea in a basket of crazies that various entrepreneurs had pitched him over the years. By acknowledging Kagle's skeptical reaction, Aaron was self-deprecating on the surface, but underneath, you could tell he backed himself to do this. Breakout success for an individual can result in hubris, and it was unclear if Aaron had a clear ingenious plan for this new transportation system or was merely delusional.

Meanwhile, Kagle now knew that Aaron wanted to sell. With this in mind, he took the reins at the board and declared that "if we're going to do this, we're going to do it right!" Kagle had worked his way through a whole series of acquisitions of his firm's portfolio companies, and he knew what doing it right meant. For Kagle, it was time to find the right investment bank to lead Mint through the acquisition process.

CHAPTER 31

CHOOSING OUR BANKER

"Change your life today. Don't gamble on the future, act now, without delay."

SIMONE DE BEAUVOIR

After Kagle made some phone calls, two prominent investment banks lined up to represent Mint in the deal. Kagle would have included Goldman Sachs in the mix, but they were already representing Intuit. The two firms chosen for a run-off were: Credit Suisse First Boston and Allen & Co. Lining up for CSFB was their top dealmaker, George Boutros; lining up for Allen & Co. was Ian G. Smith.

I was surprised that we were getting such big guns to fight over our relatively small deal. It was a sign of the severe economic times brought about by the Great Recession. At least our little company was creating some heat in the market and keeping these hunters' claws sharp until good times returned with fatter prey and much more significant deal sizes on offer.

One of the primary roles of investment banks in mergers and acquisitions, or "M&A," is to establish a fair market value for the companies involved in the transaction. The selling company seeks the highest price possible, and an investment bank will use all of its financial and market research skills to justify a higher price for its client. For the buy-side, the investment bank helps prepare and predict Wall Street's reaction to an acquisition. The bank will do everything it can to create a positive combination story that minimizes the downside and maximizes the upside. The investment banks also structure and negotiate the deal for their respective clients.

The sell-side bank will go out quickly and quietly to a small number of potential buyers and attempt to get a better offer. If the banker manages to get multiple offers, it will lock the buyers in a bidding war until someone emerges victorious. If this does not transpire, the sell-side banker continues to negotiate improved terms for its client with the primary buyer.

Finally, when commissioning an investment bank, the board of directors of the selling company is entitled to rely on the banker's valuation, advice, and negotiations during the transaction to preclude any shareholder litigation that they sold out too cheaply. Similarly, the board of directors of the acquiring company is fulfilling its fiduciary duty to its shareholders by engaging an investment bank that will ultimately opine on the merits of the acquisition for the price paid.

Boutros from CSFB was a star investment banker with over twenty-one years of investment banking experience, during which he'd advised on more than 350 completed transactions. His resume included Google's acquisition of YouTube for $1.7 billion, Sun Microsystems' sale to Oracle for $7.1 billion, and VERITAS' $20 billion purchase of Seagate Technology.

Boutros was renowned for representing sellers in deals and had a knack for driving up prices for his clients. As the selling company's advisers, bankers push for the best price, but they only get paid if a deal closes. Because of this, most bankers end up trying to convince founders and chief executives to accept lower prices than they want. Though Boutros had a reputation for sharp elbows among the M&A community, his willingness to take and stick with an aggressive stance on price was valued by sellers. Boutros could get a 10 percent higher price than anyone else while simultaneously increasing the likelihood of getting the deal closed. This is why his firm commanded millions of dollars in fees when negotiating agreements. Boutros himself would typically walk away with fees exceeding seven figures. The view around the Valley was that Boutros was a fierce negotiator who you'd rather have on your side.

Allen & Co., as a privately held boutique investment bank headquartered in New York City with offices in San Francisco, had a more conservative reputation than CSFB. They deliberately avoided publicity but were considered savvy, if measured, dealmakers and advisors in the entertainment, media, and technology sectors. They had been one of the ten underwriters on Google's IPO and had joined our Series B round as an investor. Allen & Co. was perhaps most renowned for their annual Sun Valley Conference, where dozens of individuals with the highest net worths converge for a private conference nestled in Idaho mountains. The event is one of the most exclusive business conferences globally, with frequent attendees such as Bill Gates, Warren Buffett, George Soros, Rupert Murdoch, Oprah, Larry Page, and other high-profile leaders. Aaron thought of the firm and their event as some part of the Illuminati. Mysterious, blue-blooded bankers were never going to be his cup of tea.

My money was on us selecting Boutros and CSFB to go up against Goldman Sachs, and Boutros seemed to have the Valley edge over Allen & Co.

The two banking teams got to work on their pitch decks, determined to outdo one another to impress Mint's board and win the deal. Allen & Co. had an inside edge as an early investor in Mint, but Boutros had an ace up his sleeve. He had a long-standing relationship with several Benchmark partners, having represented their portfolio companies in various exits. Often, it's better the devil you know.

Each of the banking pitch decks included their recommendations on positioning Mint to the buyer and the proposed sales process. This was a crucial section since it provided insight into how each bank intended to present Mint's assets to close the deal at the highest possible price.

But there was not much to distinguish between their presentations. Both banks highlighted that Mint reached one million users in eighteen months, while it had taken Quicken six years. They claimed that Mint was poised to attack much more extensive market opportunities in the consumer tax preparation market and small and medium business accounting products. Incorporating both into the product roadmap would serve to notify Intuit in diligence that they would have multiple "product sanctuaries under attack."

The banks were smart to do so since, at that very moment, my team was working on a strategic partnership with Intuit's archrival in consumer tax preparation, H&R Block. Intuit's TurboTax was the eight-hundred-pound gorilla in the consumer tax market, but H&R Block was aggressively transitioning its network of brick-and-mortar tax studios into an online service. They were keen to launch a comarketing campaign with Mint for the upcoming tax season. I pushed the deal far enough along where we needed to include it as a material business item in the diligence package shared with Intuit. I knew Mint's emerging partnership with H&R Block represented a ticking time bomb for Intuit. If Mint were to go after Intuit's tax franchise the way it went after Quicken, billions of dollars in annual revenue would be at stake.

Both banks would try to create the perception that there was a window of opportunity to purchase Mint at a modest price relative to Intuit's market capitalization and cash position. But there was a risk to Intuit that an outside, well-capitalized strategic entity could make a significant investment or acquire Mint and become a substantial competitor to Intuit. There was also a risk to Intuit that Mint would raise more capital at a high value, creating a more robust competitor that could then attack several of its profit sanctuaries through superior execution. Once in this position, it would be harder to buy Mint at a reasonable price.

Along with all of this, there was a set of critical financial model assumptions that included Mint's management projections for 2010 extrapolated out to 2013. These focused on registered and active user growth, revenue per active user, gross profit projections, and EBITDA margins. To be sure, there were some large numbers in there, and to achieve them would require continued innovation and excellent execution from the Mint team.

As we debated, Bill Gurley from Benchmark came by our offices for a chat on deal valuation. Gurley spent four years on Wall Street as a research analyst, including three years at CSFB. He was considered one of the Street's premier technology analysts and was the lead analyst on the Amazon IPO. Gurley, known for his towering height at 6'9," cut an imposing figure in Mint's offices. He left us with one clear takeaway: we could justify a significant premium on this deal, not through any financial model but because it was strategic for Intuit. It was by integrating Mint with TurboTax and funneling our dynamic user growth and associated data model into that tax money-making machine that would be game-changing.

This theme echoed one that came up when the legendary Bill Campbell, who was chairman of the board at Intuit, called Goines to ask if Aaron would fit into Intuit's culture and structure. According to Campbell, the deal would fail if Aaron wouldn't. Goines responded that he could, but only if Intuit's leadership were to support and embrace him. Campbell also wanted to know what was different with this new PFM product. Goines raised the strategic stakes and declared that anything new was a matter of opinion. Still, at a minimum, by adding Mint users to TurboTax, the acquisition would pay for itself. With this, Campbell had done all the diligence he needed to, and he was not going to stand in the way of the deal.

The Mint board made their banker choice, with Boutros and CSFB winning the day after being heavily promoted by Benchmark. Allen & Co. fell by the wayside, just as Bessemer Ventures had in Mint's Series B funding. Everything now pointed towards the acquisition moving forward. From my perspective, there was nothing I could do to prevent it. If the board was willing to sanction the deal and manage it professionally, then that was that. It was time to accept the reality that Mint's future was about to change dramatically. We would not be masters of our destiny before the year was out. The only question now was, at what price?

CHAPTER 32

INTO THE ARMS OF STRANGERS

"There are no strangers here; only friends you haven't met yet."
WILLIAM BUTLER YEATS

At the commencement of the acquisition negotiations, Mint had arrived as America's number one online personal finance service, providing over 1.5 million users a fresh, easy, and intelligent way to manage their money for free. Launched only two years earlier, Mint had quickly grown to track $200 billion in transactions and $50 billion in assets and had identified more than $300 million in potential savings. Mint was so useful that more than 90 percent of its users said they changed their financial habits from using the service. How much would that be worth?

We still paled in comparison to Intuit, which had annual revenues of $3.2 billion and close to eight thousand employees with offices in the United States, Canada, the United Kingdom, India, and other locations. Intuit's revenues were now primarily derived via Quickbooks and TurboTax. Quicken was the original high-flying, but since-fading, personal finance brand. Nevertheless, Intuit was not about to cede the personal finance market, which fed into the consumer tax and small business markets, to some new kid on the block. If Intuit couldn't best us with Quicken, they could undoubtedly swallow us with the cash they accumulated each year from their small business accounting and consumer tax franchises.

It was deal time. Intuit's Smith knew that we'd set a price floor with the post-money valuation of Mint's Series C financing of $125 million, plus $14 million in new cash added to total $140 million. For outright control of the company, Intuit would need to pay a premium. Smith's original whisper number of $100 million was dead in the water. But Smith knew that he had a willing entrepreneur in Aaron. If Intuit could go 25-30 percent higher than our valuation, the deal might be there for the taking.

That's when Kagle stepped in. Unbeknownst to Aaron, Kagle placed a call to Scott Cook, who he knew as a Woodside neighbor, and from being on the board of directors together at eBay. Kagle told Cook that the numbers tossed around for Mint's acquisition were not in the ballpark, and the price needed to be $400 million. Kagle also let Cook know that if Intuit didn't pay up, Mint would be coming after their other businesses within two years. Kagle politely ended the conversation and left Cook to dwell on the staggering price he tabled for Mint.

When Aaron heard from Kagle about what he'd done, he was upset. First of all, Kagle had gone behind his back to talk to Cook directly. Secondly, there was no way in Aaron's mind that Mint was worth $400 million. Aaron thought that he could pull off the deal for $150 million at most. Throwing out crazy numbers in the hundreds of millions was counterproductive and would only serve to blow up the deal, just as Intuit's CFO had earlier come close to doing with a lowball offer. But here was a lesson in Valleythink for Aaron. While he was still stuck in his midwestern thinking, clinging to traditional financial models based on profitability and other rational valuation criteria, Kagle understood the hype's psychological impact and the war for market dominance in strategic technology franchises. He knew that Intuit wanted to acquire Mint and that by hyping its value, this would put additional pressure on them to close the deal faster at a higher valuation, lest their prized asset slip away. And Kagle's bold move was about to pay dividends.

With all the strategic reasons laid out by Boutros and Kagle as to why it made perfect sense to acquire Mint, and with Intuit being flush with cash and having just paid a similar amount for PaySafe, Intuit skipped the theatrics. It tabled $170 million as the new acquisition price. Intuit also agreed to pick up the tab on Mint's banker and attorney fees in the deal, up to another $5 million. With the price in the proper range, it was game on, and the deal became real.

A non-binding term sheet was drawn up and signed. It was to be an all-cash deal, which meant we'd receive a specified amount in cash for each share of Mint stock held.

The term sheet also contained an exclusivity provision prohibiting us from shopping the deal around for a certain period to allow time for due diligence and negotiation of the definitive and binding acquisition agreement that would replace the non-binding term sheet.

Intuit considered Mint's management team to be a vital part of the acquisition since we were the brain trust that built Mint and the best placed to take it forward at Intuit and inject native web and mobile thought leadership into Intuit. Intuit was not just buying the company; they were also buying the team. Campbell's call to Goines vetting Aaron and his assertion that the deal centered on his fit came into focus.

The ultimate prize for Intuit was Aaron, and they were playing hardball by requiring him to commit to staying on after the acquisition for at least three years. This was about the time it took him to start, build, and sell Mint. It was a long time to be tied up in the Valley, especially for someone of his resourcefulness. I wondered if he knew what he was letting himself in for. The Valley was full of stories of founders not being able to last even a year after larger corporations acquired their startups. Intuit also imposed a non-compete clause on Aaron, which meant that if and when he left Intuit, he would never be able to start another company in the personal finance space. It was a severe prohibition.

Following the term sheet's signature, the lawyers on both sides got to work on drafting the acquisition agreement. Now that Intuit had settled the price, one of the remaining hotly negotiated items was the scope and quality of the representations, warranties, and indemnities given by Mint to Intuit, as set out at length in the agreement. Mint's representations and warranties regarding financial statements, intellectual property, contracts, and liabilities would merit particular attention—especially considering our history with Intuit on growth numbers. Our attorneys, led by Rob Claassen, worked diligently to prepare a schedule of exceptions to Mint's representations and warranties, commonly referred to as the "Disclosure Schedule." If accurate and complete, the Disclosure Schedule would protect Mint and its shareholders from indemnification liability for any breach of our representations and warranties. A similar negotiation took place around the closing conditions and the terms of indemnification.

There followed an intense period of due diligence for which we needed to turn over every material document we had regarding Mint's financials, technology roadmap, customers, employee agreements, and other commercial agreements.

During this, one of the young finance guys on the Intuit diligence team, Matt Lowe, let me in on a little secret: Once Intuit saw the vast product roadmap Aaron had laid down, they knew they'd never be able to catch us. The acquisition was their only real option.

As part of the diligence process, I had to spend time over at the Intuit campus, and the day soon came for my interviews. I hopped in my car and drove the short distance from downtown Mountain View over to Intuit. Turning left on Charleston Road, I entered Google territory with the sprawling Googleplex on my right. Googlers on colorful yellow Google bikes with green wheel guards and red seats were everywhere as if children with backpacks strapped on were making their way to school in the morning.

I finally arrived in Intuit territory, a sprawling campus of more than twenty acres on the southern edge of the San Francisco Bay. Intuit had set up shop here more than twenty years earlier and grown gradually, building by building.

The Intuit campus seemed more isolated and less animated than Google's. No bikes were coming and going; the architecture was a series of low-lying, two-story office buildings in off-white concrete framed by Intuit blue concrete pillars. There was no scrappy fight for a parking spot as in the backstreets of downtown Mountain View. As I got out of my car, I noticed an outside basketball court where a handful of Intuit employees were jostling. This was part of the feel-good on-campus vibe the company was no doubt trying to maintain. As I walked past Building #7, I knew this was where Smith and Cook kept their offices. This building was noticeable for the three flags on long masts fluttering high in the light breeze coming off the Bay. One flag represented California, another the United States, and the third was in Intuit blue with the company's white logo. On the other side of the walkway was the campus cafeteria, where Intuit employees lined up every day at lunchtime to sample the various meals prepared for them that day. There would be no more exploring the small cafes, delis, and restaurants that had popped up along Castro Street and its offshoots after we moved over here. A little way further ahead, I arrived at Building #8, which sat on the edge of the Shoreline golf links and the Shoreline lake—the very place where Aaron capsized Rebecca into the turgid brown water several months earlier.

I entered the lobby, and a receptionist greeted me. I asked for Aaron Patzer of Mint as I completed the requisite NDA. I took a seat and waited. I observed a handful of people coming and going through the lobby, dressed in Valley business-casual clothing. Everyone had a corporate electronic badge card hanging off some part of their clothing that they would wave over a door to go through it. A young lady came out and brought me back through the building where Aaron and Dan Maurer were waiting for me.

Intuit had a large acquisition war room set up there to parse through all the diligence files and conduct a series of interviews with Mint's management team about our technology and business. Dan Maurer, senior vice president, and general manager of Intuit's Consumer Group (a position formerly held by our own Mark Goines), which included TurboTax and Quicken, was camped out there with his acquisition team.

Maurer was up from San Diego, where the TurboTax group had its main office. He was a classic Intuit corporate man, tall with fair skin, sharp blue eyes, and neat, thinning sandy hair on a receding hairline. I placed him in his early fifties and as someone who was professionally friendly with a natural smile, accompanied by senior gravitas. He wore a button-down, collared blue shirt and dark khaki pants. If his navy blazer jacket was not on, it was not too far from his side.

Like many Intuit executives, Maurer cut his teeth in general and senior management positions at Fortune 500 companies before leveraging his experience into a technology company. In Maurer's case, it was twenty-two years at Procter & Gamble. In 2006, he joined Intuit as its chief marketing officer, and by 2008, he moved up to run the Consumer Group. Maurer knew that it would depend on his leadership to conduct due diligence and make the integration work post-acquisition. If it didn't, he'd be held responsible. He was ready to exercise all the charm he possessed to win over Mint's management team without leaving any stone unturned in the diligence process.

I went over a range of business affairs with him in a session facilitated by Aaron and answered all of his questions. Then he wanted to meet with me privately. We went into a small office at the back of the building, and both sat down for our first one-on-one chat. I knew this was where Maurer would try to get a sense of who I would be as a future member of his team. Mint's team was personal capital to be appraised; we would, as part of the acquisition, be moving into management roles at Intuit after all.

Maurer was upbeat about the acquisition and keen to gauge my enthusiasm. He was fascinated with all the partnerships and deals we'd secured at Mint, including a recent agreement with Google to include our data in local merchant searches as part of our "real-world pricing" data set. This determined, for example, how much people paid for a local gym membership at a specified gym and then included that in the local search result for gyms in a given city. Throughout the conversation, Maurer would sprinkle mentions of Intuit's culture, clearly trying to motivate me about the company I was about to join. I listened politely and displayed genuine curiosity to my future boss, though careful not to betray that I was less than thrilled about the acquisition and about being sucked into corporate life.

After my interview with Maurer, I spent time with another gentleman who was head of human resources for the Consumer Group.

He was energetic and enthusiastic about Intuit's acquisition of Mint. He spent time explaining to me how strong the learning culture was at Intuit—how the senior people at the company went out of their way to educate and nurture their colleagues and to share the benefit of their experience. He thought that there was an excellent opportunity for Mint's management team to carry this tradition forward now that we were about to become part of the family.

The diligence process continued to move quickly, and eventually, the agreement was ready for signature. As the lawyers say, all the i's were dotted, and the t's crossed. There was nothing left to haggle over.

As part of the closing process, Intuit had to work out compensation packages for the Mint management team. Aaron told me what mine would be, and I was pleasantly surprised. They were rolling out the red carpet for us, and it was clear that big companies had money to splash around when they needed to. My new salary was significantly higher than it had been at Mint, with an annual bonus on top. Also, Intuit was offering us director-level positions and throwing in even more equity in the form of Restricted Stock Units (RSUs), as well as more stock options.

We learned that we would also be joining one of the best corporate healthcare plans available in the country. It was a lot to digest, with many benefits piled on top of the acquisition windfall we were about to receive. Maybe corporate life was not going to be so bad, after all.

The Mint board of directors met for a final time to ceremoniously approve the acquisition so that the agreement could be signed. Leading up to this climax, we had to conceal the deal from the rest of the Mint team for confidentiality reasons. Intuit was a public company, and there could be no leaks associated with its prospective market moves. One of the trickiest situations involved our pending deal with H&R Block. Carrie Cronkey from my team and Barb Chang from the product team were both working intensively on this project and partnership to be ready for the upcoming tax season. We couldn't back out of the agreement with H&R Block with no explanation as it would create suspicion and might mean a leak of our pending acquisition by Intuit. Nor could we assign Carrie and Barb to another project without giving the game away. I found it very difficult to act as if nothing was happening and to standby and allow my team to pour their resources into a project that I knew was going off a cliff. But I had no choice.

Finally, the waiting game was over, and Aaron got the call from Claassen that all the documents were ready for his signature. Aaron drove over to Wilson Sonsini's offices in Palo Alto and entered a large conference room laid out with all the closing documents for his signature. Upon entering the room, Aaron paused to take a deep breath to absorb the significance of what he was about to do. He sat down at the table as one of Claassen's junior attorneys systematically handed him a series of acquisition documents to sign. Then it was over. Aaron had just handed over control of Mint to Intuit.

Now it was up to the marketing and PR folks to scramble and get ready for a public announcement the next morning before the market opened. But things never quite go as planned.

On the eve of the official announcement, someone warned us that an unknown source had leaked the information to Arrington and *TechCrunch* and that he was going with the story that evening. There was nothing we could do about it at that point, and it was late enough in the game that it was not going to change the deal. It was part of the edge *TechCrunch* had as always being first to a Valley inside story and not being afraid to publish.

Arrington posted late in the evening of September 13, 2009, that Intuit would acquire the free online personal finance service Mint and that he had confirmed from a source close to the deal that the price would be around $170 million.[22] The next morning, we announced the deal over the wire, and our phones started buzzing like crazy, and our email inboxes filled up with congratulations.

In its press release, Intuit led with the caption, "Tried and True Combines with Fresh and New." It contained the obligatory CEO quotes, the first from Brad Smith:[23]

---

22 Michael Arrington. "Intuit to Acquire (Former TechCrunch 50 Winner) Mint for $170 Million." *TechCrunch*. September 14, 2009.

23 "Tried and True Combines with Fresh and New." *MintLife*. September 14, 2009.

"With this transaction, Intuit will gain another fast-growing consumer brand and a highly successful Software as a Service (SaaS) offering that helps people save and make money. This move will enhance Intuit's position as a leading provider of consumer SaaS offerings that connect customers across desktop, online, and mobile."

Then Aaron chimed in:

"Joining Intuit enables us to bring our vision of helping consumers understand and do more with their money to millions of Intuit customers. This is a compelling combination of our innovative product, technology, and user interface design with one of the most trusted brands in software."

Finally, Maurer remarked, "Mint.com's employees are proven inventors and pioneers in developing innovative SaaS offerings with their unique 'Ways-to save' engine, data analytics, and popular UI to their credit."

The press release continued to the effect that Mint's innovative capabilities could be applied broadly to millions of Intuit consumers and small business customers. Intuit declared that Mint's acquisition would also offer Intuit's financial institution clients the ability to strengthen their online offerings and deliver more value to their customers. They recognized that Mint's unique Ways-to-save engine generates a revenue stream while keeping the product free to end-users, and Intuit intended to integrate this capability across its businesses.

Then came the kicker—Intuit intended to keep both the Mint and Quicken Online offerings, with each serving separate and equally important purposes. Mint would become the first online personal finance management service that is offered directly to consumers by Intuit. But Quicken Online would connect Quicken customers across desktop, online, and mobile to deliver easy, anytime-anywhere access. Not only was Intuit keeping Quicken alive, but they were also going to make us manage it.

The next morning, the entire team gathered early at Mint's headquarters in Mountain View, where Aaron stood up and explained what just happened to anyone who didn't already know. He'd agreed to sell the company to Intuit. A strange mix of confused excitement and stunned gloom filled the room. Some folks felt the adrenaline rush of being part of something big, and they knew it would line their bank accounts. I glanced at my team, Carrie, Sid, Bentley, Ksenia, and others who were eagerly trying to process what would come next for them. Others seemed shocked and deeply disappointed that we had sold out, and we were going to a company that many of them considered a corporate dinosaur. Jason and Justin looked particularly unimpressed. I caught sight of Matt, whose body language, as usual, wasn't giving much away. He was Mint's first employee and must have just realized that Aaron climbed this tree independently. But there was no going back now. We'd all need to adapt and learn to live with the consequences, for better or worse. We were about to begin a new chapter in Mint's journey, one in which we would now be under Intuit's control.

PART V

CHAPTER 33

THE AFTERMATH

"What's done cannot be undone."

WILLIAM SHAKESPEARE

After the acquisition announcement, the press poured in with its verdict on the future of personal finance software. The *New York Times* concluded that "Quicken seems like something your dad uses. Younger, web-savvy users aren't likely to sit down nightly and enter a bunch of financial information online. These sites [Mint] appeal to the iPhone audience."[24]

TIME magazine pitched in with, "We all wish we were better at our personal finances, but it's just too confusing—and boring! Secretly, we wish someone else would do it for us. This is the key factor behind the success of Mint.com. Mint's rapid growth was something Quicken had to either kill or get in on. Buying the site means it can do either."[25]

Aaron was not about to be denied his opinion and the opportunity to take a bow either. Writing a guest post in *TechCrunch*,[26] he pointed

---

[24] Jenna Wortham. "Intuit Buys Mint, a Web-Based Finance Competitor." *New York Times*. September 15, 2009.

[25] Belinda Luscomb. "Intuit Buys Mint.com: The Future of Personal Finance?" *TIME*. September 15, 2009.

[26] Aaron Patzer. "The Value of TechCrunch 50: Mint Acquired by Intuit for $170m Two Years After Winning TC40." *TechCrunch*. September 15, 2009.

out that what Mint achieved was done in no more than three years—one year to build and two years in operation. "I doubt this could have happened anywhere but Silicon Valley," he declared.

Aaron explained how the company started in his apartment with Matt Snider and Poornima Vijayashankar as the first engineers. How David Michaels, a professional vice president of engineering candidate, was first interviewed in his kitchen. He laid out the modern-day technology stack that enables young entrepreneurs to build a website for next to nothing. Mint's technology was mostly open-source and free: MySQL as the foundation, Hibernate to avoid the need to hire a database administrator, Tomcat on Apache, and Yahoo's YUI as the base for Mint's AJAX goodness.

Aaron couldn't afford a lawyer, yet three offered to help set up the company for $25,000 in deferred legal fees and a sliver of company equity. Mint shared office space in a type of incubator, renting by the cube to avoid a long-term lease. There was no money for advertising, so Mint started a blog to attract users, and because it couldn't afford writers, most of the early content was original, supplemented by guest posts from other personal finance blogs. Mint also used these blogs as a content network to post its badges for free advertising while building SEO juice through links back to the site. Even the decision to launch at *TechCrunch* 40 came free instead of paying $20,000 to do the same thing at DEMO. It didn't hurt to walk away with a $50,000 check for taking the conference first prize in the process. Mint decided not to spend money on search engine marketing (SEM), as it was too expensive. Instead, Aaron would give up about 20 percent of his time to get free press and drive traffic to Mint.com. The net result was millions of visitors and 1.5 million users, primarily for free. Mint was never going to be inherently viral like a social network, but all good things are viral by word of mouth, and the Mint service was excellent for this.

Aaron proclaimed, "So that's the Mint story. $0 to $170 million in three years flat. While everyone else was doing social media, music, video, or the startup de jour, we tried to ground ourselves in what any business should be doing: solve a real problem for people." He concluded proudly, "Here's to the Mint team, from New Zealand, France, Tunisia, Armenia, Ukraine, Russia, Canada, Greece, and all over the US. I'm proud of you all today and very happy to live in this Valley."

Aaron was the man of the hour. He was the latest installment of the Silicon Valley wunderkind who made it after starting with nothing but a vision, raw intelligence, an ability to learn and adapt rapidly, and iron-clad determination. Provided he could overcome all those initial rejections, he was the type of person the Valley embraced and then rallied behind: a young, Ivy-league educated engineer with a will to change the world. He'd even dropped out of an engineering Ph.D. program at Princeton, adding to the myth of the go-it-alone entrepreneur, impatient with academia and eager to blaze a trail of self-determined innovation instead.

Arrington decided he'd chime back in and stir up the pot with a broader perspective. "Mint is Yodlee's Youtube," was his new headline.[27] Arrington invoked the Adobe and YouTube relationship and proclaimed that YouTube was just a pretty front end to the core Flash web video technology created by Adobe. We all know how that one ended—Google acquired YouTube for $1.65 billion in 2006, and as Arrington reminded all, "YouTube got rich. Adobe got peanuts." Mint ran on Yodlee's account aggregation technology, which was ten years in the making, and with more than $100 million of venture money burned through along the way. Mint's success was partly due to its leveraging Yodlee's technology, yet Yodlee would see no windfall.

Arrington turned the screw by questioning Yodlee for not even asking for some equity in Mint early on. He contrasted this with Hite Capital, which got a piece of the stock action by trading in a Mint.com name that Arrington claimed to be worth about $2 million. If all that weren't bad enough, Yodlee would no longer be collecting its fees from Mint since Intuit had its own aggregation technology, and Mint would be switching to it within months.

All of this woke up the bear over at Yodlee. Joe Polverari stepped

---

27 Michael Arrington. "Mint is Yodlee's YouTube." *TechCrunch*. September 18, 2009.

into the debate in an interview with *VentureBeat* and conveyed how unimpressed he was with the acquisition.[28] Polverari could have taken the high road and congratulated a customer for achieving a successful exit and building a meaningful audience with Yodlee's aggregation platform. Instead, he chose to characterize Mint as a Yodlee service with a pretty user interface layered on top. He declared that the natural place for people to go for online personal financial management was the banks. Polverari claimed that Mint had done an outstanding job attracting "a niche of early adopters and tech-savvy people," but that Mint had now woken the sleeping giants (the banks). Polverari was skeptical that Mint was worth $170 million, especially since its data isn't particularly valuable to big banks, which already have access to substantially identical databases through their financial management systems. The value of Yodlee, he said, is "exponentially greater than whatever the valuation of Mint should be."

Polverari did acknowledge that the banks now realized they needed to provide users with better data about hidden fees; otherwise, people will just go elsewhere. "Banks recognize they're going to have to behave their way out of this situation," Polverari said. My view was that if Mint's legacy were nothing more or less than that we'd elevated the levels of transparency and user experience in the online financial services world, we could walk away satisfied.

While the media machine whirred outside, the Mint team tried to get back to work and continue building the service for our users while returning to some form of normalcy. However, there was much trepidation about all the changes that were about to occur over the next few months as we waited for the acquisition to close. Aaron began to give company standups about how the team would be kept intact and that Intuit was putting us in charge of the service. How, with him as general manager of the Personal Finance Group, we'd be able to continue working on Mint and keep it "Minty." Aaron was doing his best to keep the troops motivated, but the reactions were mixed. Some people were

---

28 Anthony Ha. "Finance startup Yodlee: We weren't screwed by Mint's acquisition." *Venturebeat*. September 28, 2009.

hostile to the very notion of the acquisition and had already made up their minds they'd have nothing to do with it. They'd say nothing at these standups, and that was the point. You could tell by the looks on their faces and their body language that they were antagonistic.

Jason Putorti was among those not endeared to this new environment. Aaron relayed to me that he felt aggrieved that he wasn't consulted or, at the very least, informed about the acquisition before reading about it in the press. Justin Maxwell spotted the TechCrunch leak the evening before the official announcement and had immediately sent a "WTF?" text to Jason. Both were incredulous. From Jason's perspective, he was one of the first handful of employees at Mint and had contributed so much to Mint's success through his luminary design skills. Jason didn't rate Intuit as a design-centric organization and didn't think his skills would be appreciated or rewarded there. At some level, I admired the fact that he was unwilling to compromise. He stood to leave a significant amount of money on the table in letting his unvested options implode by refusing to do time at Intuit.

When the dust settled, Aaron circled back to check in with me. We sat down at a small round table across from each other in a tight meeting room on the second floor of our offices. We'd done this many times before, but this time it was different. He'd just sold the company, with me in it.

"So, what are you going to do?" Aaron started. I looked at him and said nothing. "Would you like me to fire you?"

Aaron was trying to be helpful. He knew I disliked the acquisition, and he was trying to mitigate things for me. I recalled before the deal closed how Aaron tried to promote it to me. There was a small whiteboard on the back wall of my cube just across from his. He came over, and as he discussed the potential acquisition, he picked up a marker and discreetly wrote a number on the whiteboard. "That would be your take," he said. I looked at the number in the low seven figures and could not immediately reconcile it with the reality of having that amount of money in the bank and how it would change my life. Aaron had gone through this analysis for himself and was much further along than me.

I looked again at the number on the whiteboard. It could have been bigger or smaller, but it didn't matter to me. I was at the most fulfilling point in my career, enjoying my work, and excited at the prospect of building a market leader and transformational company. I wasn't looking to change the balance I'd found. The financial rewards could wait for another day.

As for firing me, Aaron knew there was a provision in my stock option agreement that would accelerate one-half of my unvested options if Mint terminated me without cause following an acquisition. I thought about the temptation of making this move for a moment. But there was no point in dwelling on it; there was still too much money left on the table from unvested shares if I didn't go over to Intuit. Besides, I'd resigned myself to give the big company experience a go. I reasoned that I might learn one or two useful things while I was there serving time. So I told Aaron thanks, but no thanks, and we said nothing more of it.

As part of Intuit's charm offensive, Aaron announced that Scott Cook would pay a visit to our offices. That day came, and he was brought in by Aaron to be the guest speaker in a company standup meeting at our headquarters. Cook had charisma infused with a type of vibrant, boy-wonder energy. The Mint team fell to a hush as Aaron introduced Cook, who said a few words about how Intuit got started and then complimented Mint on its success.

Cook then called for a team-building exercise that was novel to me. He was going to go around the entire room, and each Mint team member would call out something about themselves that almost no-one else knew about them. It was an excellent move. Here he was, an outsider helping the Mint team discover more about each other even after working shoulder to shoulder in an open office space environment. The team relaxed and enjoyed the moment as different Minters revealed something strange and unusual about themselves. Bentley Rubinstein on my team revealed that he and his sister, as teens, were members of a tap-dancing group called "The Caravan Project," a global association of dancers. The entire team looked amazed as he sheepishly revealed this to Cook. When completed, Cook said a few more words of congratulations and conveyed his excitement at the prospect of us joining the family before departing back to the Intuit campus.

A week or so later, Dan Maurer joined us for one of our lunch events. When the weather was glorious outside, we'd occasionally stroll across downtown to the Pioneer Memorial Park behind the Mountain View Performing Art Center for "burritos in the park." It was a Mint tradition. It was a familial atmosphere with a long history and a challenging situation for an outsider. Maurer stood up amongst the Mint team and turned on his charm by sharing his excitement at the prospect of us joining Intuit. Nevertheless, he seemed noticeably stiff and corporate relative to the young Mint crowd now looking up at him or choosing to ignore him in favor of their burritos. His presence reminded us that this was happening. It was not a dream. In just a few weeks at the turn of the new year, we'd be commuting to the Intuit campus as Intuit employees, and people like Maurer would be our new colleagues.

Aaron and Maurer announced that Intuit selected a particular building and an entire floor for us. It was undergoing an overhaul to modernize the working environment to be more Minty. A few members of the Mint team were consulting on the layout and color schema for the new space. Intuit was trying to make us feel welcome. They really were.

Soon, meetings began between Mint and the TurboTax team in San Diego in anticipation of the upcoming tax season. It was too late to do anything significant, but some low-hanging, co-marketing initiatives were being explored to introduce Mint users to TurboTax. I attended the first couple of meetings. There were so many people on these calls that I couldn't fathom what the real agenda was. All that seemed to come of these meetings was an agreement to meet again—a meeting to decide upon the next meeting. I stopped attending. There were just too many cooks in the kitchen, and I felt I could be more productive elsewhere. As I suspected, no-one seemed to notice.

On November 2, 2009, as the year was drawing to a close, Intuit delivered a press release announcing that it had completed its acquisition of Mint.com.[29] Aaron was upbeat:

"As the leader of Intuit's new personal finance group, I'm looking

---

29 "Intuit Completes Acquisition of Mint.com." *MintLIfe*. November 2, 2009.

forward to bringing together the best of Quicken and all we've learned at Mint.com to help people save and do more with their money. We have an opportunity to leverage new technologies and new user-interface design principles to impact more than ten million Quicken users. Together with Intuit's expertise in tax, bill-pay, and banking, we can build powerful new online services that will make it easier for people to manage their money."

With this quote, Aaron was beginning to sound like a corporate man. He wouldn't be the only one. We prepared to move to Intuit's campus in January 2010.

CHAPTER 34

DON'T PULL A PATZER

"He who knows that enough is enough will always have enough."
LAO TZU

We built Mint for long-term value. We were not looking to be acquired; we were too busy trying to grow as fast as possible while continuing to innovate for our users and solve real-world money problems. The more things went right for us, the more we relentlessly focused on innovation and execution to stay ahead of the game. We quickly discarded the failures and doubled down on our successes while taking risks to explore new avenues of innovation. It was an impressive run during exciting times, and every day at work was an adventure. I counted my blessings.

Nevertheless, if an entrepreneur is a rational person that stops to think about how things might end in terms of a viable exit, then an acquisition, as opposed to an IPO, is the most likely outcome by far. In a 2017 *TechCrunch* article, Jason Rowley observed that of the companies that don't close down or achieve financial sustainability, more than sixteen times as many companies were acquired as went public across a data set spanning 2003–2013.[30] Around 92 percent of these companies raised funding through Series C, as did Mint before purchase.

---

30 Jason Rowley. "Here's how likely your startup is to get acquired at any stage." *TechCrunch*. May 18, 2017.

When Donna Fenn of *Inc. m*agazine interviewed Aaron, she asked whether an acquisition was always at the back of his mind.[31] His response: "Honestly, I didn't even think about it. I just wanted to create something that I wanted to use." But he was forced to confront the question when Brad Smith asked him if he would consider selling in their first meeting. Aaron explained that all of Mint's early investors said, "If you want to make us a billion-dollar company, we'll support you because we believe in you, but if you'd like to sell, we understand—it's your call." Aaron had to think about what he loves to do, and that is to build things and make them practical and real. He convinced himself that with Intuit, all of a sudden, Mint would have a way to reach fifty million people globally, which would be challenging to do alone.

Aaron omitted that he came to have doubts about Mint's business model and, consequently, its long-term viability. I subsequently learned that Aaron was studying the conversion data regarding Mint users acting on smart savings offers and did not like what he saw. While new users would invariably act on an offer soon after joining Mint (and we'd receive a commission), the data appeared to indicate that they did not regularly act on subsequent offers, which meant that we wouldn't be able to drive ARPU high enough.

Was this a fear of failure creeping in? These doubts seemed to run counter to the story of a brilliant young entrepreneur's compelling vision for the service and unyielding belief in his abilities. They also ran counter to Valleythink, which indicates that so long as you're building an audience rapidly, you can always find ways to monetize them. Aaron may have also forgotten an early Valley lesson he learned from Jeremy Stoppelman, Yelp's CEO. When Aaron was first introduced to Stoppelman as he was trying to get Mint off the ground, he shared that he didn't quite know how he was supposed to take on Microsoft to succeed with his proposed new venture. Stoppelman confided in Aaron that founding a startup is always going to be an emotional rollercoaster and that doubt is an integral part of the journey.

---

31 Donna Fenn. "The Kid Behind a $170 Million Website." *Inc.* date unknown.

Fenn questioned Aaron's intentions, remembering that he had once complained to her about working for IBM because "you can't do anything interesting until you're forty." So she had to ask how he thought he was going to like working for a big company. Aaron coyly responded that he'd be there for three years and that he imagined the transition would be "interesting." Whether or not the integration with Intuit would be successful, Aaron knew that after three years, he'd have enough money to start companies and to invent and build anything he wanted for the rest of his life. The only question that remained was whether he would still be young, crazy, and hungry enough to catch another technology trend and apply his entrepreneurial, product, and team-building skills to pull off the magic all over again.

Whatever the future held, Mint's success was borne of the Valley, and it was inevitable that Aaron would be judged by the Valley, including his entrepreneur peers, the investor community, and the tech press. Fellow entrepreneur Jason Fried, a cofounder of Basecamp, kicked off a spirited discussion on his blog by making it clear that he was less than impressed with Aaron's decision to sell out. Fried penned a blog post days after the Mint acquisition announcement, titled, "The next generation bends over."[32] Fried declared, "Mint's sale to Intuit really pissed me off." He went on to castigate the "VC-induced cancer" that was metastasizing in Silicon Valley, and he bet the sale was encouraged by a Mint investor. Fried believed that Mint had Intuit on the ropes and that it was wasteful to sell:

"Here's a fresh new company that was gunning for an aging incumbent. And not only gunning but gaining. They had a great product, great design, and great potential. They were growing rapidly and figured out the revenue game. They were on their way to redefining an industry—one that was left for dead by the current custodians…And now it's the property of Intuit—the poster-child for the last generation. What a loss. Is that the best the next generation can do? Become part of the old generation? How about kicking the shit out of the old guys? Whatever happened to that? ….They can issue press releases saying how

---

32 Jason Fried. "The next generation bends over." *Signal v. Noise.* December 18, 2009.

excited they are to bring their product to a whole new world of customers, and how their new suitor will bring enormous resources to bear, but we know that's usually not really what happens. Development slows, products stall, the staff that built the great stuff leaves, and mediocrity creeps in. Not always, but usually."

The comment stream on this post was robust and representative of the broader debate around Aaron's decision. Some took a more personal tack, decrying the sale as Mint betraying its users' trust and loyalty, which Mint worked hard to earn. Others took the sale as a possible admission that Mint wasn't so revolutionary at all and an acknowledgment that the challenge of evolving from a good product to a dominant brand in the PFM space was daunting, if not unlikely. A minority took a more rational approach, considering Intuit's right to progress and Aaron's right to kick on with more resources; it was the circle of life in the Valley, after all.

The post even drew commentary from the investor community. None other than Fred Wilson of Union Square Ventures offered:

"I agree with you that the objective should be to build a great independent company…but I would bet the VCs did not push this. I am a VC, and I've been one for twenty-six years now. I have never forced an entrepreneur to sell their company if it was succeeding, and clearly, Mint was. This smells to me of a young founder facing the prospect of making enough money at an early age that their life will be changed forever and not being able to resist it. That's why Joshua Schachter sold Delicious (bad move) and why Stuart and Caterina sold Flickr (another bad move). I can go on and on, but you get the point."

Aaron didn't respond directly to this blog post in the comment stream but did take up the theme in a subsequent *Newsweek* article and scoffed at the criticism leveled at him for selling out to Intuit. "I don't think that I owe it to the world to take down the old guard," he remarked. "My purpose in life is to build and invent and create things that are useful."

The debate and angst over the Mint sale continued into early 2010 with the publication of a guest post in *TechCrunch* with the title, "Don't

'Pull A Patzer' And Other Lessons Learned On Our Trip Down Sand Hill Road."[33] The author was Tod Sacerdoti, CEO of BrightRoll, a video ad network that raised a $10 million Series B round. The article's purpose was to share some of the lessons he learned in raising money over a six-week journey. The first highlight was that the Mint.com acquisition left anything but a Minty aftertaste in many on Sand Hill Road's mouths. As recounted by Sacerdoti:

"By most accounts, Mint.com's rapid rise to prominence and ultimate acquisition is the quintessential Silicon Valley success story. Yet, the Mint.com acquisition brought to light an interesting phenomenon, one I've coined the 'Patzer Problem.' Before submitting offers to invest, three separate VCs wanted to confirm that we had no intention of 'Pulling a Patzer,' modern-day Sand Hill Road parlance for selling too early."

Dave McClure, Mint's first senior marketing consultant, now established as part of the Valley's angel and seed funding infrastructure at *500 Startups* (thanks in part to the impressive win he got from investing early in Mint), was not to be left on the sidelines. He chimed in with his customary colorful language and a wake-up call to the old guard of Valley VCs:

"It's becoming 'cool' to pile on the 'Mint sold too soon' bandwagon by many VCs and others who couldn't find their ass with both hands, and really have no clue why Mint was so successful. And they can all go suck eggs. Smart VCs better start thinking about how to design and align fund structures where $170 million exits are 'homers' to go ring the bell about, not 'singles' to wring their hands over. Unfortunately, most of them would rather bury Mint than have it in their portfolio. Their loss, our gain."

For Mint's investors, life would go on, though to varying degrees. Kagle's reputation was already established, and he was nearing emeritus status at Benchmark. His short ride with Mint was full of promise,

---

33 Tod Sacerdoti. "Don't 'Pull a Patzer' And Other Lessons Learned On Our Trip Down Sand Hill Road. *TechCrunch.* March 1, 2010.

even if ultimately unfulfilled. He'd been around long enough to know not to dwell on what might have been. Surely, across his lengthy career, there were instances in which he was on the sell side of the board of directors where the entrepreneur resisted, and the company went on to have more success and rewards than ever anticipated. In this case, it was the opposite. So be it. He was looking forward to playing golf and spending more time with his wife in his golden years.

For Tod Francis of Shasta, Mint's sale was bittersweet. Tod was a true believer that Aaron and Mint were exceptional. Francis made an early bet on both before many on Sand Hill Road would have, and he worked hard to bring in Kagle from Benchmark to help take the company to the next level. Francis was also there to help us clinch the Mint.com domain name from Hite Capital in a decisive moment, along with many others where he stepped in to help and guide the company. Although Mint would not be the home run of Shasta's first fund, Shasta was emerging as one of the stronger venture firms in the Valley, and Mint's breakout success could only be good for boosting its brand.

As for First Round Capital, Mint was one of its first breakout wins. Our success validated Kopelman's contrarian approach and further pushed the firm into the limelight as the leader in seed-stage technology investing.

The other angel investors each benefited from the Mint win in their own ways. Aydin Senkut was able to attract institutional investors to his next Felicis fund, and he's been an early investor in Shopify, Adyen, Credit Karma, and other breakout successes. Paul Buchiet went on to be a managing partner at Y Combinator. And Ron Conway continued to be Ron Conway, the Silicon Valley Angel that has a hand in every deal worth doing in the Valley.

Mark Goines became a go-to investor for any emerging FinTech, including Personal Capital, which he invested in and became vice-chairman of. The company, which used Yodlee aggregation technology to build a Mint.com for personal finance, wealth management, and retirement planning, was acquired in June 2020 by Empower Retirement in a deal worth up to $1 billion.

For the Series C investors, including Peter Thiel, they understood that the acquisition might still happen when investing. They invested their money in the hopes of tremendous upside if Mint remained independent, but with a hedge that if the acquisition did move forward, they'd make an ultra-fast clip of smaller upside on their money. They got the latter.

We had one last hurrah to share success with our investors at the Village Pub in Woodside for the acquisition closing dinner. This was the bookend to our seed funding closing dinner with investors at Tamarine in Palo Alto just over two years earlier. Most of our investors were there that night to celebrate Mint's success and the executive team's performance. After the cocktail hour, during which we mixed and mingled, the wait staff summoned us to sit at our strategically combined tables.

Aaron was the man of the hour. Following dinner, several of the investors stood and toasted him. Rob Hayes joked about how much smarter Aaron was than him but referenced the one time he figured something out before Aaron—when Brad Smith wanted to meet with Aaron about personal finance education, Hayes knew it was a pretext for acquisition. Kagle, too, stood to toast our success and referenced that Mint was the second fastest and biggest return in Benchmark's history (no doubt eBay was the first). This surprised me coming from a man who thought we shouldn't have sold so early. Donna then took over proceedings and talked up each of her colleagues' qualities on Mint's executive team, which was a nice departing gesture from her as she would not be joining us at Intuit. As the evening wound down, we all knew that this would be a natural point of separation. Once a portfolio company is acquired, its investors close the chapter as they look to invest in new ventures and prop up their existing portfolios.

For the Mint team and me, the time for acquisition debates and celebrations was over. We were getting ready to move out of our friendly little headquarters in downtown Mountain View over to Intuit's corporate campus. The end of the year was upon us, and 2010 was going to be very different as we donned our Intuit badges and adapted to becoming citizens of a big corporation.

CHAPTER 35

LIFE IN THE SLOW LANE

*"It's not what happens to you,
but how you react to it that matters."*

EPICTETUS

After we packed our belongings in boxes on a Friday afternoon in early 2010, with most everyone left for home, I took one last lingering look around the empty office. Our boxes would be shipped to Intuit's campus over the weekend, ready for arrival at our new corporate offices the following Monday morning. This small, somewhat raggedy, two-story building at 280 Hope Street in downtown Mountain View had been our home since we first moved in and occupied three cubes more than two and a half years earlier. I saw Mint's evolution flash before my eyes. The board room on the ground floor, where Aaron first asked Shasta why he should take their money for Mint. My first cube on the first floor near the kitchen, where I did my interview for the Mint blog. The small meeting room on the second floor, where I told Aaron we had to build our own aggregation system to control our destiny. The small meeting room on the ground floor, where we kept all our trophies and where I first laid out a prototype sketch of a Mint free credit score and monitoring service for Mark Goines on the whiteboard. The large recreation room where we battled away at table tennis, and then all met together to share Friday free lunches before wrapping up the workweek. The shower room, hidden away upstairs, where we'd clean up after a Friday afternoon group run through the back streets of Mountain View. There were many memories of good people and good times flooding in.

We were leaving all of this behind. It felt strange and bittersweet—the end of an era.

The following Monday morning came, and I got up to get ready for work. It seemed like so long ago that I got up on another morning for my dawn round of golf with Rob Claassen that kicked off this journey. I finally had success under my belt in the Valley. The next two years, at least, would be spent at Intuit as a director-level executive. The next level up was vice president. Should I set about striving for that title and learn to get better at the game of big corporations and office politics to get there? Or should I put my head down and go with the flow until it was time to venture back into the high-risk world of startups to disrupt another industry and its incumbent dinosaur? I wondered what they'd expect of me. I'd still be responsible for monetization of the Mint service and any partnerships that enhanced our service or provided us with distribution.

Most was unknown. The only thing I knew was that my commute from Menlo Park would be shorter. That was good.

I exited the 101 freeway at Rengstorff Ave and wound my way into the parking lot of Building #3 at Intuit. Tree-lined, low-level office buildings sprawled as far as the eye could see; no neighborhood, shops, restaurants, or local businesses in sight. It felt odd to pull into a campus parking lot that was isolated from any sense of community. For the first days, weeks, months, and possibly years, I would not know who most people were.

I walked up to our new building and pulled my badge out of my pocket and held it up to a sensor. With a beep and a click, I was part of Intuit. And no longer was I free to come and go as I chose; I'd need that badge everywhere I went from here on in. Such was the corporate world I now inhabited.

I entered the building where Mint had its floor on the ground level and found my small corner office. Aaron, who used to be one desk away from me at the old Mint headquarters, was now in his own corner office on the other side of the building; David Michaels and Aaron Forth each got the other two corner offices. I should have been happy, I guess. There were only four offices for our team, and one was mine. But I felt like this office isolated me from the rest of the team, even though they were just outside my door, sprawled out in their cubes—the same type of cubes that we tore down at Mint so we could work more openly and collaboratively.

Feeling a bit sluggish, I decided to grab some coffee at the on-campus Starbucks in the building opposite ours. I followed a brick path across manicured lawns framed by bright flower beds with a large water fountain in the middle. Tables and chairs with sun umbrellas surrounded the fountain, where employees could lounge over lunch. As I entered the next building using my badge, I ordered a coffee and then walked back to our office to check in with my team and the rest of the Mint folks, now Intuit employees. People now flippantly referred to the combined company as Mintuit. It was almost as though we'd taken over the place, not the other way around. There they were: Carrie, Ksenia, Sid, and Bentley, camped right outside my office, the same people in a foreign environment. They seemed happy enough for now, perhaps buoyed by the novelty of their new surroundings and how they might further their careers. Maybe it was just me who felt alienated.

I walked the office's length, noting who was a Minter and who were original Intuit employees on the Quicken team interspersed in our midst. I didn't look for Donna, Jason, or Poornima, who had left. I popped my head into A4's office, but he was on the phone. I wandered across to the courtyard side to David's office, but he was not in yet. I was relieved to see Atish and Justin, who'd both decided to give this corporate thing a go. If they could stick this out, then maybe I could too. I walked back towards Aaron's office, but his door was closed. Perched right outside was Matt Lowe, the young financial controller involved in the Mint acquisition. He left his more junior role at TurboTax to join us as head of finance and business operations, but also, I suspected, to keep an eye on us for the benefit of Dan Maurer back in San Diego.

In an hour or so, I'd need to duck into our first staff meeting in our new large conference room. The rest of the team was already there: Aaron, A4, David, Mitch Bayersdorfer (director of engineering for Quicken), and Jean Sini, who could now join us officially. Untangly was no longer a stealth operation. Aaron seemed a bit awkward in this new environment, no doubt making his own adjustments. There was no board of directors to report to, and he could no longer officially call on Goines as a mentor or Kopelman and Hayes for moral entrepreneurial support. They'd done their jobs up through the acquisition. Now Aaron was taking input and direction from Smith, Cook, and Maurer.

Aaron began discussing many peripheral issues, such as the new interface he was designing for Quicken and a new Mac version. He wanted me to look at some deals the Quicken team had cut to place Chase credit cards exclusively in the product. This was precisely the thing the Mint service would never do, and I was not looking forward to going down that path. We discussed migrating from Yodlee to Intuit's aggregation platform and repositioning Jean to head up front-end engineering for the personal finance group. On and on it went. It was mostly Intuit business on the agenda, with minimal discussion of Mint's product roadmap, as though this would take care of itself. I could see these meetings were going to be a challenge for me to stay engaged.

As lunchtime came round, it was time to head over to the corporate cafeteria. It was strategically located near Building #7, the home of Smith and Cook, though these were the last people you'd expect to bump into in there. The cafeteria was different from the many local restaurants and food choices we had in downtown Mountain View. Yet, it was convenient, and there was a decent range of food, though nothing to write home about. As I started to find my way around the campus, I rediscovered the basketball court and also a full gym for use at any time of the day. We were also right next to the Bay with many trails for hikes and runs along the waterfront. Campus life could be comfortable, that was for sure.

On the less positive side, as I signed up for all the Intuit health plans, intranets, human resources, payments, and training systems, I marveled at how ugly and clunky business software systems could be. While these systems were functional, they were unfriendly and challenging for the average employee to use, resulting in many hours of frustration. Whenever issues arose, these were typically made worse by the support systems in place. Support calls were routed to India, where the thick accents of the support agents were difficult to understand, though assuredly less costly to maintain than local agents. And based on the support staff's low skill level, it turned out that it was faster to resolve the issue yourself with the helpful hack of a colleague who somehow managed to crack the code. I couldn't help but contrast this type of clunky, unfriendly software with Mint's focus on beautiful and seamless interface design and user experience that needed little support. I had to wonder why developers of business software seemed to pay so little attention to the user experience, which for us had meant everything. Perhaps it was hard to make complicated things simple, as we had done.

CHAPTER 36

IDENTITY STRUGGLES

"A frog in a well cannot conceive of the ocean."
ZHUANGZI

After a week or two of getting settled on campus, it was time to think about how we were going to take the business forward as Mintuit employees. Soon after the acquisition, Scott Cook had written a guest post on our blog about how Intuit was not out to change Mint.com.[34]

"For many of you, Quicken is a twentieth-century product in a twenty-first-century world. It's like the car your parents had growing up. So you turned to Mint.com. Because it wasn't Quicken. Mint brings a fresh, unique approach to managing money, creating new ways to help you save or get out of debt. I so admire what Aaron and the team have done and how they have done it. I can recognize great innovators and innovation when I see it.... On a personal level, Mint's leaders have earned the chance to re-invent personal finance on the broadest canvas possible. I will give them that chance. Will you?"

Would we take that chance? I have to say that our welcome at Intuit was fantastic. They did everything one could imagine to make us feel at home. While they were eager to talk with us, work with us, and learn

---

34 Scott Cook. "Intuit Not Out to Change Mint Says Founder." *MintLife*. September 18, 2009.

from us, there was also an implicit top-down directive that they should go slowly and not love us to death. What struck me as their greatest fascination with Mint was how we managed to offer our users a free service. They had a strange expression for this called "beyond user pays." This concept came up in just about every conversation about Mint on campus and at their leadership events. When they moved a new version of Quicken online reluctantly to a free service to defend their turf, they must have had no idea how to monetize it in the long run.

But rather than seizing on that fascination and broad canvas, we Minters began to struggle with our own identity and mandate in this new ecosystem. Instead of taking advantage of the newfound resources and support to execute ideas we couldn't afford before, such as expanding internationally, we got pulled in many different directions. We had to fix Quicken, which was losing about 7 percent of its users and revenue per year. Yes, it was still a significant part of Intuit's brand and worth nearly $100 million annually (which was far more than Mint would be generating any time soon). And there was a segment of the population that was never going to engage with an online service like Mint. Still, it seemed like a fool's errand that was distracting us from real progress.

We were also supposed to integrate with TurboTax, and discussions were underway to see where we could add value to Intuit's online banking platform. I don't know why, but Aaron seemed to relish this challenge. Perhaps it was the designer and developer in him that saw a clear path to streamlining something new without the burden of contemplating the consequences of that distraction from the core Mint service.

We didn't even know what to call ourselves. Aaron was thinking about Mint's much lower brand awareness ranking than Quicken. He wanted to brand our service as "Mint by Intuit" or, as he preferred, "Mint from the makers of Quicken." Aaron relied on published awareness data and thought he was perfectly rational.

I was opposed to this and felt Mint was on track to be a far superior brand to Quicken over time. I thought the Quicken brand, with its stodgy nature, would tarnish Mint rather than enhance it. At first, Aaron was having none of my pushback, and I wondered why I seemed more passionate about preserving Mint's brand integrity than him. Mint was his baby more than mine, after all.

I came up with the Toyota example in an attempt to turn him around. At the time, the Prius was the first attractive, well-priced hybrid electric vehicle on the market. Toyota also had the Camry, which was one of America's most popular vehicles and far outsold the Prius. However, by comparison, the Camry was viewed more for its fundamental value than its stylistic features, technological advancements, and environmental sustainability. I put it to Aaron that Toyota would never in a million years run advertising that proclaimed, "Prius from the makers of Camry." He got it and dropped the idea of Mint associated Quicken branding. But it left me wondering where Aaron's head was these days. He seemed overwhelmed by the enormous new task of trying to play corporate vice president at Intuit while simultaneously overhauling Quicken, and holding the Mintuit team together as best he could.

Our product identity, or lack thereof, followed suit, starting with the proposition of a Mint debit card. I challenged it with all the passion I could muster. What problem were we solving for our users by offering the world another debit card when there were thousands of cards already available to consumers? The last straw for me was that, because we would make interchange fees every time a user spent money on their card, it would be in our interest to encourage spending, rather than saving money, which was antithetical to our brand.

Part of the problem was that some on the Mint team began peeling off politically and ingratiating themselves with other Intuit business groups and their leaders and supporting initiatives like this that were against Mint's identity and ethos. They were in new territory and making moves to build their reputations and manoeuver career advancement. I understood that was part of the corporate game of thrones, but team cohesiveness seemed to be fraying at the edges.

There were now two camps within the Mint team: those that cared deeply about Mint's reputation and were embarrassed by our falling quality standards, and those that didn't care. I stepped back to try and take all this in. I'd heard multiple times that when a big corporation acquires a startup, it stifles innovation, and it's hard to get anything done. Yet, here we were, mostly left to our own devices, albeit distracted by Intuit on other initiatives, with all the resources we could ever dream of, and we were choosing not to move fast and maintain quality.

It became clear that the Mint team had distracted leadership and was making political decisions, but there was also a festering sense of entitlement and complacency that surprised me. I wanted to keep innovating on behalf of Mint users and grow the business for the company that had paid so handsomely to acquire us. But product releases slowed to a crawl, and the migration from Yodlee to Intuit's account aggregation platform was taking forever. No-one seemed too worried about it. The bugs started to pile up in our product, and the user complaints began rolling in. Our lumbering support systems largely ignored these as they fell on deaf ears.

A few months into the new Intuit gig, I sat down to have lunch one day with Sid Bhatt. He told me confidentially he was planning to leave and start his own company. I wasn't surprised; his exit was inevitable as he was entrepreneurial by nature. But he also indicated politely that he and the others were tired of watching the Mint management team play Intuit VIPs. I asked him to explain. In this case, VIP stood for "vesting in peace," he said. The indictment was clear. Others saw us as just hanging out, biding our time and waiting for the remainder of the cash from the acquisition to roll in over the next couple of years. If that was the perception of the Mint management team from other Minters, it was hardly conducive to high grassroots morale and exciting future product development.

As a result, a new wave of departures swept through our ranks, including Sid and other early Mint employees like Val Agostino, who was unable to tolerate further the decline in user experience, and Atish Mehta, who was finally joining his friends at Facebook. It was sad to see them go, but I admired their courage in searching out a new adventure, even as they were leaving behind so much unvested money in the process. I wanted to follow them out the door, but I had a family to support and couldn't justify the financial absurdity of doing so for the time being.

At the same time, Mint was hiring in a slew of new staff to fill various positions. Thankfully, our brand still had a halo, and we were able to attract some top people. Yet, as they mixed in with native minters and a sprinkling of Intuit employees in our group, it was inevitable that the culture would change. I found myself retreating to my office more. There, I spent time dealing with multiple outreach efforts from wealth managers who offered their services to me in every way, shape, and form. I was not interested. There were also numerous calls from startup founders, looking for advice, connections, and Angel money for their new ventures. They wanted to pick my brain and my wallet. However, I could only offer ad hoc occasional advice as Intuit frowned on any of us becoming advisors to startups.

CHAPTER 37

MINT 2.0

"Creativity is intelligence having fun."
ALBERT EINSTEIN

As life at Intuit bore down upon the remaining Mint employees, many struggled to find motivation in the corporate malaise. Inspiration would come from a concept that was inherent in Mint's mission, but a potential product build that had fallen by the wayside: "Goals." It was a last-ditch attempt to regain some Minty-ness—and since I spearheaded it, potentially my last fling at finding a fit within the four corners of corporate life.

The original idea for Mint was a life and goal planning system Aaron called "Carpe Viva" or "seize the life." Aaron figured that all of life's goals, including getting a college degree, learning Spanish, or buying a house, could be quantified in time and money. When I first met him, there was no hint of this. It was only later, after Aaron showed me his broader vision for Mint in a futuristic product roadmap presentation that I caught a glimpse of the power of Goals.

Aaron sketched one of the original car-buying goals—in his case, a vintage red sports car. The concept was emotive, aspirational stuff, and personalized to the user. How much would a user have to save, and for how long, before they could buy the car of their dreams? Mint could map all of this and help users achieve what they wanted, faster. Money could be a means to this end.

So why hadn't Aaron unleashed this powerful service on the world already? Aaron was young in years but still wise enough to test this concept with consumers to validate whether it resonated. Before Mint took conceptual shape, Aaron would stop people at train stations and coffee shops and ask for a few minutes of feedback as they were lingering. As he gathered their thoughts and reactions to his proposed goals service, Aaron realized that consumers could relate, but they would need first to get their financial house in order. Until then, these goals would always be on the back burner, more aspirational than realistic. The research data meant that what the world needed first and foremost was a better money management service. That's the reason Mint took shape as a personal finance service.

So Goals was not on the radar in Mint's initial run-up to success. There was no catalyst. However, after the acquisition, but before we'd moved over and officially joined Intuit, the Mint management team came together at the end of 2009 in search of a new year's initiative. Everyone listened as Aaron announced his vision that every Mint user would be able to save at least $1,000 over a year thanks to an optimized Mint.com. I felt that we could do a lot more. By offering Goals as a service, we could give people a real purpose for managing their money, and we could attract a broader audience. Intuit's resources could help us implement it.

Aaron asked me to present a Goals plan to the entire Mint team over the coming weeks at the next all-hands meeting. I did just that as I explained that Mint users would be able to plan and track their progress toward one or more specific goals from among eight initial categories or customize their own. Goals might focus on financial health objectives, such as getting out of debt or saving for an emergency fund. They might involve a life stage, such as buying or improving a home, saving for college, or retiring by a certain age. Mint would also cater to lifestyle goals, such as taking a major vacation or buying a car. The Goals service would provide a roadmap to help users determine the amount needed, and a step by step financial guide toward reaching the goal. We'd include a calculator to determine how long it would take to achieve a goal depending on the user's income and savings rate. For example, people planning to retire early could simply enter the expected retirement age and anticipated expenses, and Mint would do the rest. Mint would be able to link the goal to existing retirement accounts and show progress.

Goals would also provide a broader context for our existing financial partners. For example, a travel rewards credit card might be more meaningful to a Mint user with a vacation goal. And Goals would also allow us to bring in a new set of advertising partners, particularly around lifestyle goals, such as taking a vacation. Finally, we'd expand the content on our blog to include essential guidance for goal seekers.

However, as we moved over to Intuit's campus at the beginning of 2010, there were too many initial distractions for Goals to get off the ground. It wasn't until well into our first year at Intuit that Aaron decided the time was right to launch Goals. I was delighted. We'd be innovating on behalf of our users once again.

As we kicked off the project, A4 and Barb Chang defined the requirements for each goal and the design team worked on the UI and UX for the new service, with Justin overseeing quality control. The engineering team, led by David and Daryl Puryear, wrote the code based on the product specifications they received, while the marketing team prepared for a full launch and press tour. My team focused on shuffling the savings offers we had in our existing inventory to place them as and where relevant to a particular goal, while sourcing new partnerships with offers relevant to goal achievement. Aaron focused on overall product guidance, alignment, and motivation to keep everyone on track. Weekly team meetings tracked progress, during which there were many debates and decisions made to keep the first release of Goals as intuitive and compelling as possible. Things were Minty again.

After months of work, we finally made it, and by the end of June 2010, we put out a press release entitled, "Money Is for Living: Tie

Daily Spending to Achieving Goals With Mint.com. New Goals Feature Helps People Plan for What They Want in Life."[35]

Aaron's quote read: "Ultimately, money is not about the numbers. It's about having enough to do what you want with the people you love. Money is for living, and Mint Goals will help consumers set and achieve their life goals more quickly and easily than ever before, whether buying a car or house, paying off debt, taking a vacation, or saving for retirement."

Soon the results started to come in, and most of our users were signing up for at least one goal, with others setting multiple goals. Our goal-driven users were more engaged than our other users. Moreover, the range of savings offers associated with Goals, fired up our revenue engine beyond our Ways-to-save marketplace.

Now on a roll, I conceived another dynamic project to turn Mint into a financial advice engine. Once again, I felt the need to throw off corporate life's shackles and get creative on a new Minty project.

I rejected the proposal that Mint should turn our users' data over to their financial advisers, which Aaron was exploring. Instead, I believed Mint could be the adviser, and it was time for my thesis to take shape. Our Ways-to-save marketplace was an innovation, but the data showed that many users ignored this section of the site because they thought "it's where Mint advertises to you." I questioned why our savings offers were all combined under a single Ways-to-save tab, except for Goals. Wasn't the whole point of presenting a savings offer to do so with as much personalization and relevance as possible? Why weren't we doing this throughout the site where and when it was most relevant? In fact, why couldn't the site and service become a complete financial advisor? That's when it struck me: advice could be the next major innovation for the service and, on top of Goals, would culminate in Mint 2.0. And this would be my purpose at Intuit for the next several months—to see this built out and become an industry success.

---

35 "Money Is for Living: Tie Daily Spending to Achieving Goals With Mint.com." *Businesswire.* June 30, 2010.

I imagined that if a user were to entrust his or her money to Mint, our service would find ways to optimize every aspect of that person's financial life, automatically, and for free. It occurred to me that we were already on this path. Our first IRA center was conceptually beyond our Ways-to-save marketplace. We designed it to help our users realize the benefits of an IRA and choose the right provider. The Goals service was another step in the direction of providing advice to our users around their money-related life objectives. Now, I imagined that every piece of data we collected would get fed into an advice graph, and we could then offer advice-as-a-service, or "Advice". I had to get Aaron on board.

But a gap had opened between us. Whatever Aaron's mind was preoccupied with after several months at Intuit, it was not generating more revenue. One day, Aaron was in my office, and (with the door closed, I let him have it with both barrels. "What the hell do you think this is?" I demanded. "If we're not serious about making money, then we're not a business. We're more like a charity." He reeled and looked stunned, and that's when I rubbed salt into the wound. "We should rename the site to Mint.org," I said scathingly.

I didn't understand all the things going on in his new world of managing a much larger team and several new projects at a Fortune 500 giant. It must have been a daunting experience for him to try and conform. Notwithstanding his high-powered intellect, it was only four years ago that he was a fresh-faced kid who didn't know much about the Valley. Since then, he took hold of the reins and galloped his way through the startup world. But this corporate game of thrones was another world altogether, and Aaron was still trying to sketch his playbook for it.

Some time passed since our blow up on revenue, and things ran a little calmer between us. I knew that if I approached Aaron with the Advice concept, getting him onside was less about revenue and more about the product and user experience. I pitched him on the design aspects of Advice, what problem it would solve for our users, how they would benefit from the service, and how it would be an essential use of the data we were aggregating. And it worked! As an innovative extension of the core Mint product he'd conceived, he couldn't resist the rationale behind it. It was like bringing a second new powerful engine to someone who built a race car and letting him imagine how the car could now fly. Aaron asked me to pitch it to the entire group at the next all-hands meeting. It was deja vu. He admitted that my reference to renaming the site Mint.org had hit home, which was rare for Aaron. Typically, you could throw just about anything at him, and he would pull down that stoic mask of his, and you would not see any reaction other than a look of curiosity as to why you might be getting so worked up about something.

With the Advice project green-lighted, I felt energized again. It felt like being back in a startup, albeit within the four corners of a big company. For a while, I could forget the politics, strategic planning, endless meetings, corporate values, and just indulge myself in work—pure innovation work. By July 2010, my deck was ready to pitch the entire Personal Finance Group on how we would transform Mint into a personal savings advisor. I showed them how Mint could now provide free, actionable advice, personalized to help our users save money and achieve their goals. I envisioned a savings graph with the Savings Advisor as an engine that could understand the relationship between a user's profile, income stream, asset base, spending patterns, goals, and the savings offers from any provider in the market. The Savings Advisor would present advice to users at multiple touchpoints throughout the Mint service, always in a context where it was most relevant, personalized, and quantified.

I pitched that Advice would set us apart from several other consumer websites that were springing up to mimic our Ways-to-save service, like BillShrink, Offermatic, HelloWallet, and Credit Karma. Advice would take Mint from the number one personal finance service to the best free savings advisor. The audience was rapt. As I scanned the room, I realized we'd grown as a group far more in number than when we left the Mint headquarters in Mountain View. We'd added the small Quicken team to our midst and hired up a storm after the acquisition. It looked like a different team than the one I'd helped build initially.

Soon after, we began to build the new Advice section of the service. We designed a stack of approximately sixty pieces of financial advice to be embedded and triggered under specific rules. Small digital cards contained advice with a title, a nifty image, and a sentence or two of headline text. There was a button on each card that, if clicked, expanded to provide more information to complete the advice. Once launched, Advice became a resounding success. While there was a 7 percent engagement rate with our Ways-to-save marketplace, there was now a 25 percent engagement rate with our Advice offers. The Savings Advisor accounted for 30 percent of Mint's revenue within a matter of months.

Then the call for applications for the annual Scott Cook Innovation awards for 2011 came. Someone on the team suggested we apply with Advice, so I wrote the Mint personal savings advisor's submission. By this time, there were approximately one hundred pieces of advice live in the Mint system and growing daily. I submitted our application feeling that it was worthy, but I had no idea what else was coming in from other teams across the company. I didn't give the matter too much more thought. My intention was not to win awards. I just needed to spend the remainder of my time at Intuit with some creative purpose.

CHAPTER 38

CULTIVATING CORPORATE CULTURE

"I think culture is a big word for corporate character."
JENSEN HUANG

In contrast to Mint's wandering, Intuit was hyperfocused on its own identity and culture. I needed to learn more about the methods of its two leading culture developers: cofounder and chairman Scott Cook, and CEO Brad Smith.

Cook was a product marketing guy first. He was a vocal disciple of the lean startup movement and pushed the "trust behaviors, not surveys" mantra to Intuit teams. But he was humble enough to admit that "success and scale make you dumb", hence the acquisition of innovative companies like Mint.

Cook certainly hit all the right notes when discussing innovation and freeing up Intuit's people to be creative. I found he practiced what he preached. Cook was liable to drop into product meetings at any time, and he was constantly re-engineering his teams around lean experimentation. He hosted a stream of innovation leaders to speak and teach on campus.

Smith was a charismatic CEO who was orchestrating Intuit's transformation from an aging desktop company to a "Social, Mobile,

Global" company, as he termed it. He was a natural speaker and motivator, and a star at leadership offsites and company keynotes. But as a veteran of a long career in corporate America, and with his own multi-million-dollar failures to show for it, Smith also understood the value of a culture that valued mistakes as a learning opportunity.

Cook and Smith seemed like corporate leaders I could admire and align with. The opportunity to work for and learn from these leaders was a privilege. Add the chance to continue to work with a visionary entrepreneur like Aaron, mixed in with an overflowing compensation package, and it should have been enough to satisfy anyone. So why did I have my doubts?

One thing I struggled with was the company's values statement and its obsession with communicating those values to us. Like most start-ups, for the first ten years of Intuit, its values were implicit. At a certain point, Cook shut down the company for a few days as he took his executives offsite to come up with a written statement of the values, akin to an Intuit constitution. In the original form, there were ten values articulated. In the era of Intuit's need to transform, and with Smith taking over the reins, it was time to re-evaluate, streamline, and confirm these values. The Mint team was caught right in the middle of this refresh process, and I struggled with so much corporate navel-gazing. At an executive retreat at a luxury resort in Southern California, Intuit submitted us to half a day of indoctrination of the values—how Intuit initially conceived them and how they were revised and reaffirmed. The values had at least shrunk from ten to six in the new incarnation.

Intuit had two overarching values and then a set of six sub-values. The first core value was "Integrity without compromise." The subtext for this was: "We speak the truth and assume the best intent. We value trust, above all else. We hold ourselves and others accountable to the highest standards in all we do and say." The second core value was, "We care and give back." The subtext for this was, "we are stewards of the future and will do our part to make the world a better place."

Was this the corporate, elongated version of Google's "Don't be evil" refrain or Mint's unspoken code of being "Minty?" Why were they being promulgated like a constitution or the six commandments? What inspired a company to invest so much time in a set of values and ensure that all its employees understood and lived those values? And could the company's management and people live up to these standards in the cut and thrust of daily corporate career ambitions and the relentless drive to satisfy Wall Street's insatiable desire for more corporate profits?

Intuit gave everyone at the retreat a windbreaker jacket to mark the occasion. They must have spent a pretty penny on them. I would have been happy enough to wear it around on the weekend until I noticed that the jacket's inner lining was covered in the text of Intuit's values. It was not doublespeak, but it felt oppressive to me. Over the next weeks, as I passed by certain areas on campus on my way to meetings, I noticed framed plaques placed in strategic locations containing a statement of the company's values. I'd never seen worship like this before. It was strange.

Intuit's culture cult held many interesting moments for me. I received an invitation to one strategic offsite where the Small Business Group was to evaluate offering loans to its small business customers. This seemed self-evident to me. Businesses need software for their accounting, but you can only charge so much for this as an automation tool. What companies need more than anything for their growth is access to capital. Intuit was well positioned to move into this market with more than five million small businesses in Intuit's Quickbooks franchise and amazing financial data on every one of them.

The offsite was a day-long session, and some design thinking activities took place in the workshop. At one point, we went outside into the courtyard of the building as a group, and two of the younger members of the team led us through some kind of collective creative exercise that was supposed to fire up our imagination. The leaders told us to look up to the sky and imagine the stars dancing and then imagine we were some intergalactic space creatures. People crouched down and jumped up and threw their arms to the air as they circled in a group. I couldn't take it. It was like a weird religious exercise to me, and I quietly stepped to the side and observed, trying not to stick out like a sore thumb as the guy who wasn't joining in. I was relieved when it ended, and we were able to go back inside. I don't remember the team arriving at any breakthrough that day. At Mint, we'd never have the luxury of a group think tank without coming out of it with actionable items.

Aaron was having similar trouble adopting the new rules. Dan Maurer invited him to San Diego to participate in a TurboTax product and executive team offsite to explore proposed changes for the next tax season. When he returned, he recounted to me, with a nervous chuckle, how he'd blown up the meeting. It seemed he'd become quickly bored and frustrated with Maurer leading the meeting with the rest of the execs blindly following along. Aaron was a product guy, and as he listened to their product innovation exercises, Aaron couldn't resist ridiculing them. In particular, Aaron called out Maurer, who was not a product guy, as not knowing what he was talking about. I doubt whether Maurer had ever been challenged this directly in his entire career by a subordinate, though I'm sure he managed through it with his usual diplomatic aplomb. But Maurer's lieutenants were left stunned by Aaron's audacity and muttered among themselves whether what they'd witnessed was even believable. Aaron's bluntness violated so many corporate norms that they were left incredulous. But what were they going to do, fire the kid who personified the company they'd just paid nearly $200 million for? Not likely.

Aside from the pageantry, I mingled and continued to meet fellow Intuit colleagues on campus and discovered that many were genuinely nice people. This was not a cutthroat corporate culture with a toxic environment where you couldn't trust anyone. There was politics for sure, but they were more about playing the corporate game, living the values, and showing up in all the right places to get ahead. The cynic would argue that this had very little to do with serving customer-driven innovation or designing for delight but there you have it.

The other thing that struck me was how long some people had been at Intuit. Many had been there for over ten years, and some for almost twice that. It felt so different to startup life where a run of three to four years might be considered a marathon—such was the turbulence involved in flying on the startup jetstream.

Change was right, I thought. How could one stay fresh and not become fossilized by spending multiple years with one company? I also wondered how much seniority ranked in importance or whether the company could achieve a meritocracy. Indeed, the incentives to stay were impressive, and the longer one remained, the more they grew. There were handsome compensation packages with bonuses in the good years, fantastic health benefits, RSUs, stock options, and even deferred compensation plans for executives. I kept getting an enrollment form to join the latter but resisted in fear that if I got on that gravy train, I might never be able to get off.

The worst of all of it—the complacency, the theatrics, and the cultural navel-gazing—came to a head in what should have been our first signature moment at Intuit: strategic planning in early 2011 for the upcoming 2011-2012 fiscal year.

At Mint, we did this with a simple one day offsite at the end of the year. We decided objectives for the following year and put some quantifiable metrics against these as best we could. It was more or less a continuous process throughout the year that we gave some extra attention as one fiscal year transitioned to the next. We came together in moments of crisis and moments of opportunity, always looking to survive and thrive. We developed our lean process of a light business model case to make decisions on new initiatives quickly. The emphasis was on growth through continual product strategy and innovation rather than incremental planning and tactical execution.

When it came time for strategic planning at Intuit in February of each year, the various business groups would scramble to pull together a coherent view of the results from the prior year and an ambitious plan for growth in the upcoming years. The business group leaders would be called in front of Brad Smith and his executive staff to present their plans for approval in a formal meeting. I felt like a good deal of time was spent papering over the cracks in the last period and promising things that were unlikely to eventuate in the next performance period.

The day arrived for the Personal Finance Group to pitch its strategic plan for the upcoming fiscal year in an executive operations review. We were ready with a forty-one-slide PowerPoint presentation that Matt Lowe helped us prepare, full of numbers, charts, and graphs signifying something or other. Some slides declared that specific metrics were flat to downward because of x, y, or z, while other areas of the business showed signs of opportunity and growth. Employee engagement was up, while declining year over year sales of Quicken had slowed. It was full of corporate-speak, and after reviewing the slide set, I had difficulty seeing the forest for the trees.

We arrived and congregated in the lobby of Building #7, waiting until the moment we'd take elevators to the top floor to meet Smith and his executive staff. The stakes were high; this was our first meaningful evaluation by our new bosses, and a chance to justify our reputation and price tag—or risk revealing the complacency I'd started to notice. We headed for the conference room used for meetings of Intuit's board of directors. As we filed into the room, Brad Smith greeted us with Neil Williams, the chief financial officer who tried to lowball us on the acquisition price, and several others on Smith's executive team. They sat down on the side of a massive long conference table facing the windows, and we sat opposite. Dan Maurer took up his position on our side but distanced himself from us by moving further down the table. Smith opened the session with his usual boyish charm, and it seemed that there was a novelty interest from the other side in what the new web and mobile kids had to say.

Aaron kicked off the presentation from our team. His comfort level amongst this executive crowd seemed natural. But he had first to declare that revenues would be down, mainly driven by flat year over year Mint revenue per user. If it were not for the innovations from developing Mint 2.0, revenues would have been substantially down as focus slipped from the Mint business. But Quicken was doing better due to a slowing rate of decline from 9 percent to 4 percent. We had successfully launched Mint in Canada, but it wouldn't be a significant source of revenue for this year. Aaron then delineated the initiatives to drive revenue back up, which included monetizing mobile, introducing a premium paid Mint offering, and ramping up our synergies with TurboTax, whatever that meant. Both monetizing mobile and offering a paid premium Mint service would be firsts for us. And as Aaron pointed out, the key to meeting these challenges was to build a strong organization. While employee engagement was up twelve points year over year, he noted that Mint employee engagement was well below the Intuit average.

All of this felt sluggish to me. There was nothing to be proud of in what Aaron was presenting. I thought it was further evidence of our growing disarray and complacency. I felt a sting of irony because to get to our revenue goal, we'd need to introduce a Mint paid premium offering, the very thing we'd scoffed at upon the launch of Quicken Online. How had we gone from being the great disruptors offering a "beyond user pays" business model so admired by Intuit to now falling back on trying to have some of our users pay for the service?

I caught a glance at Williams, who seemed mildly bored with the proceedings. He was interested primarily in the numbers that might move Wall Street, and we did not fit into that category. Both Maurer and Aaron chimed in on occasion to speak for our side and qualify or underscore something one of us had said, with Maurer particularly eager to make our best showing and to refine what we'd said in a more Intuit corporate tone.

The Intuit executive team seemed satisfied, if unexcited, by what we'd presented, perhaps because we represented such a small fraction of their overall business. Smith, possibly picking up on the low Mint employee engagement numbers, seemed more interested in learning how we felt about joining Intuit's ranks and what they could improve about work-life on campus. We fed him a few polite suggestions for good measure, and the meeting ended.

Had we passed the test? I couldn't tell from anyone's faces. I thought we'd have a much more dynamic discussion about the scope of the personal-finance market and the strategy for maintaining Intuit's lead in it. I thought we'd be questioned, if not challenged, on a whole range of issues across our proposed initiatives and that there would be some moments of intense debate to liven things up. But there was nothing of the sort. It felt anti-climatic and rote to me. I left wondering why we'd taken up so much time preparing for this session—time that we could have spent making the Mint service better for our users.

CHAPTER 39

TIME TO CHOOSE

*"Live as if you were to die tomorrow.
Learn as if you were to live forever."*
MAHATMA GANDHI

As I stepped back from work on Mint 2.0 and reflected on the meaning of the corporate day-to-day, there was no escape from what I'd been feeling in the months preceding: corporate culture was not a home for me. In the early summer of 2011, my main stock vesting period would be up. The first two years of financial incentives from the acquisition that prohibited me from leaving would begin to slow to the point where I might consider a departure. However, due to additional performance-based shares I'd received while still at Mint, and due to all that Intuit had given us as incentives coming in, money would still be flowing well above my standard paycheck for the next couple of years after that. Even then, my standard Intuit compensation would be hard to beat in the Valley and certainly could not be matched by any startup. But it would no longer be enough to prohibit me from leaving if I wanted. Ultimately, the time would approach to choose. As it did, I continued to watch other core Mint team members depart, including Justin Maxwell and Stew Langille.

I wrestled with whether or not to make a go of it at Intuit. I realized that I was still deeply connected with Mint and that it meant something important in my life—something that I didn't want to let go of lightly. After the successes of Goals and Advice, I joined Aaron for a restaurant dinner and discussed the possibility of staying around to run Mint from within the Personal Finance Group. With the work I'd done on Mint 2.0, I felt refreshed and optimistic about Mint's future. Although it was no longer independent, Mint could still represent an excellent product and brand for consumers. To my surprise, Aaron warmed to the idea. But ultimately, there was a problem: I didn't want to take on the baggage of running Quicken and some of the other peripheral products that Intuit had left to us. I didn't want to run the Personal Finance Group so that I could run Mint. Once Aaron realized this, he came clean with me: he was working on his own exit strategy. Aaron was going to stick it out for the required three years that he had agreed to, but he wasn't necessarily staying in Mountain View. Nor was he going to be full time. The Intuit leadership admired Aaron for his product vision. Yet, over time, Intuit realized that Aaron was never going to be part of their cultural identity and play the long corporate game. He had too many politically incorrect run-ins with Intuit leaders in other groups.

I could only imagine what arrangement Intuit had reached with Aaron to keep him on the Intuit payroll and take advantage of his exceptional skill—product visioning and design. Whatever it was, they'd traded allowing him significant latitude to come and go as he pleased and relocate if desired. With Rebecca's acceptance into a prestigious college on the East Coast, the corporate cube culture at Intuit could no longer contain Aaron. Then I realized that for Aaron to serve out the remainder of his term at Intuit in this flexible way, he'd need to find a suitable replacement as general manager of the Personal Finance Group. That must have been part of his new arrangement with Intuit. He'd need someone comfortable in their own skin to mix and mingle in the Intuit political environment and cultural swirl. Someone competent who wouldn't rock the boat. That role did not suit me, and Aaron and I both knew it. I was no longer useful to him in his quest to free himself from corporate life at Intuit and become more of a product leader who could fashion the redesign of Quickbooks and strengthen its online offering. But that role fit Aaron Forth perfectly, and he was keen to embrace the opportunity.

All of this could only mean one thing: I could look for a role in another Intuit group or leave.

My goal in coming to Intuit was to be open and see what I could learn about life in corporate America in Silicon Valley. I had the feeling that it could serve me well in the future, and I believed I'd achieved that goal. I'd seen both good and bad. Intuit impressed me with its hiring practices, as did the company's deep understanding of its business lines at scale. Intuit's ability to provide predictable guidance to Wall Street on earnings was remarkable.

On the other side, there were too many meetings that were much ado about nothing, too much cultural navel-gazing, and constant requests for employees to complete surveys reviewing Intuit as one of the best places to work in the country. From where I stood, the most underwhelming aspect was that there was more talk about innovation and the customer experience than there was work carried out in furtherance of these objectives.

I could also relate to Aaron's product perspective that, unlike Apple, Intuit was yet to develop a cohesive vision for its suite of products. Intuit was not developing network effects in its businesses when, for example, they could have easily made Quickbooks invoices viral. And despite overseeing more small business data than perhaps any other company, there was still no strong integration with TurboTax. Finally, the company had yet to seize on its ability to develop a small business credit scoring system or a marketplace for loans.

At a macro level, I'd seen the enormous resources and discipline required to keep a giant corporation moving forward, albeit slowly, and the relentless pressure from Wall Street to keep the results up to expectations. This ebbed and flowed against a backdrop of internal corporate reorganizations and a steady drumbeat of acquisitions and dispositions. This replenished my faith in the future of startups and the Valley's infrastructure that supported them. I thought of the startup as a small team intensely focused on solving a single, hard problem in a new or changing market. This permitted the startup to think deeper, differently, and go faster than a large corporation that would be distracted and burdened by its core monopoly businesses. The startup was like a speed boat with just a handful of people on board, whizzing about at high speeds with a remarkable ability to make sharp turns. Meanwhile, the large incumbent corporation was like the aircraft carrier that plowed through the water slowly but relentlessly, towering over the startups zipping about it, but with limited maneuvering and speed.

I had to decide whether to graze in place or to seek pastures anew. It seemed to me that I'd faced this existential question before. It occurred when faced with leaving my lucrative legal career behind in search of startup adventures. It arose again when challenged by Rob Claasen on the golf course about going sideways on repeat with my pre-Mint startup. Each time the transition and change were hard but led to accelerated learning and personal growth. Yet, at some point, isn't it time to settle and give up the struggle? Isn't it right to reap the rewards of what you've sewn? One option was safe, secure, and lucrative; the other option was anything but. I had to think about my family and their future. This made it not just about my desires but also my responsibilities.

The ultimate factor in that first decision was whether I could see myself as a Silicon Valley lawyer for the next ten plus years. I looked at some of the most successful partners above me and discovered that I didn't aspire to their work life. They'd fallen into a routine, and I didn't think there was much left to learn or be excited about other than raking in more money. Now the question was whether I could see myself as an Intuit VP in a couple of years. And my feelings were the same.

If learning and growth are essential in a startup, they are equally so in your career and life. If you stop growing, you'll be left behind quickly, only to feel regret more than fulfillment. This was my rationale for leaving Wilson Sonsini, and my time at Mint had only strengthened my belief that it was true. Was I prepared to settle in and become an Intuit lifer like many other executives I'd met on campus at the risk of stagnating my personal growth?

I believe I always knew the answer. It was just all that money that gave me pause.

So it was time to leave. I didn't know what I'd do next; that would take some time to sort out. It was more important to get out, make a clean break, and find space to think about my future. It came as no surprise to anyone that I was leaving, and within a couple of weeks, things were in place for my exit. My team organized drinks and a departure dinner at a restaurant in downtown Palo Alto. At the dinner, they presented me with a bottle of wine with the inscription "48 months of delivering at or above revenue targets—Countless hours of e-Staff discussions—Millions of clicks to find savings for users." Everyone signed, and I was touched by it. At the end of the evening, we all stepped out on the curb to head home, and it was time to say goodbye. I hugged each of Carrie and Ksenia and shook hands with Sid (who returned for the occasion), Bentley, David, and A4. Last was Aaron, who initially shook my hand but then put his arm around me, and there was a man-hug moment. "We truly made a mark on the industry," he said, "and we've been through a life-changing event together."

I knew he was right. I also knew that most things have a beginning and an end. I headed back to my car and drove home. Tomorrow would be the first day of a new era without Mint being a part of my daily life. As with the others who had left, I would always be a Minter, but now I'd also have the chance to do something else, perhaps even more rewarding—that was the promise of the Valley for someone prepared for risk and adventure. And I knew that whatever the something else was, I'd do my best to keep it Minty.

PART VI:
AFTERTHOUGHTS

*"Logic will get you from A to B.
Imagination will take you everywhere."*

ALBERT EINSTEIN

CHAPTER 40

HOW?

"You've got to start with the customer experience and work backward toward the technology—not the other way around."

STEVE JOBS

What helped Mint defy the odds and grow out of a geek's apartment to reach millions of people and redefine an industry? How did Mint beat Intuit's Quicken, where even the mighty Microsoft once tried and failed? And how did Mint survive the Darwinian Valley startup culture where more than 95% of companies fail? That's the $170 million question, which in today's valuation climate would be nothing less than a multi-billion dollar question.

Tod Francis believes that Mint was the first true innovator in personal finance management. In particular, Mint's ability to integrate account aggregation technology and make it work simply for most users at scale was a tremendous accomplishment.

Matt Snider reflects on Mint as the zeitgeist of the era. Every VC pitch for the next four or five years talked about being the Mint of this or that. Even when Matt interviewed at AirBnB, they pitched the company to him as the Mint of Couchsurfing.

Josh Kopelman believes that Mint was first to showcase an online service programmatically acting upon financial data for its users' benefit.

For David Michaels, Mint proved that consumers could overcome privacy and security concerns and remain comfortable online concerning their money under the right circumstances. Mint also gave consumers more confidence regarding their finances; before Mint, most people weren't doing anything out of either ignorance, complacency or fear.

For Noah Kagan, it was Mint's business model that was a breakthrough. The ability to get banks and other businesses to pay for being a part of the service and keep the service free for the users was a precursor to freemium models on the web.

Echoing a modern theme of artificial intelligence, Rob Claassen thought of today's quest for the self-driving car as analogous to Mint being the first to come closest to achieving managing personal finances on auto-pilot.

Martha Shaughnessy boiled it down to Mint being the first to make something boring seem quite cool. She also thinks of three Mint breakthroughs that are now table stakes for online companies: data aggregation, data visualization, and content marketing.

Mark Goines put it all down to the Mint service providing ease of use and ease of insights. And Mint was at the forefront of matching people to better products and services, which was no small feat as machine learning was nascent back then.

For Jason Putorti, Mint represented bringing things together and making them simple.

Aaron would agree with everything said here, but he also enjoyed Mint providing him with a trail and record of his life. The places he visited, the experiences he had, and the stores, restaurants, and coffee shops he frequented were all laid out in Mint's spending transactions and timestamped.

Mark Hedlund, a cofounder of early Mint competitor, Wesabe, which launched almost a year earlier than Mint, shared his thoughts on why Wesabe lost to Mint after Wesabe closed down: "Mint used Yodlee to automatically get user's data from bank sites and import them into Mint, and as a result had a *much* easier user experience getting bank data imported.... That one mistake (not using or replacing Yodlee before Mint had a chance to launch on Yodlee) was probably enough to kill Wesabe alone....Mint focused on making the user do almost no work at all, by automatically editing and categorizing their data, reducing the number of fields in their signup form, and giving them immediate gratification as soon as they possibly could; we completely sucked at all of that."[36]

Hedlund concluded that, in the end, "it was far easier to have a good experience on Mint, and that good experience came far more quickly."

I think three things stood out.

Algorithms

Mint started with the algorithms Aaron wrote in the earliest days at his apartment in Sunnyvale. They would perfectly compliment an aggregated data set. Aaron designed them to automate the categorization of transactions and to find savings for users while optimizing these processes with machine learning and artificial intelligence. Beyond ingesting financial data efficiently into the service, if Mint users had to waste time recategorizing transactions, they would have dumped the service quickly. Just as Google made its breakthrough with an algorithm that focused on search relevance above all else, Aaron knew that one of the keys to personal finance was categorization accuracy.

Aaron designed the Ways-to-save algorithm to attract a new class of users to a personal finance service and to lay the foundation for Mint's business model. Again, if our customers had to do the work to dig out and calculate these savings, it would never happen. But our users were always one click away from signing up to get a new product or service that would improve their financial lives.

People

The Valley culture focuses so much on the founders and the founding team in the earliest days of a company. But the America's Cup in sailing is won out on the waters by the boat with the fastest design. Sure

---

36 "Why Wesabe Lost to Mint." *Marc Hedlund's Blog.* October 1, 2010.

enough, the crew has to be first-class to manage such a cutting edge boat, but you get the sense that if you swapped the crew from the leading competitor boat, they'd win by being on the faster boat. Why then is so much emphasis placed on teams in the entrepreneurial world? Wouldn't a better product or service generate that edge the way the fastest boat does? The answer lies somewhere in the fact that in a startup, the founding team has to design the boat, then crew and sail it while they're still building and improving it. Moreover, the entrepreneurial race they'll be competing in isn't just about speed and balance; it's also about strategic navigation, tactical execution, and psychological resilience. One day the seas may be quiet and calm as the team builds its boat. The next day, the winds may be high as the team races as fast as possible. And the next day, the stormy seas may be brutal with towering waves and lashing winds as the team hangs on for dear life and thinks only of survival. The team needs to thrive through all of these conditions and to set a course for sailing, yet know when to tack in search of fresh winds to win the race.

One of the things Aaron was most proud of was the team he assembled at Mint. He thought the team had fantastic strength at all levels. To this day, across the various teams he's assembled in other ventures, Aaron's ended up with one or two A+ players but has yet to replicate the bench strength he achieved at Mint. To bring out the best in the people he hired, Aaron had three principles of leadership. The first was to provide autonomy. The second was to reward star players immediately and not wait until they tell you they're about to leave before you recognize their value. And the last was to have everyone on the team focused on design and the customer experience.

Designing the Customer Experience

Mint was a product-first company with a design-driven ethos and an obsession with the customer experience. This aesthetic and philosophy included passionate consumer advocacy to build trust with our audience and to do everything for the benefit and delight of the Mint user. Anything less was not "Minty," and the team would not tolerate it.

Aaron's design philosophy had three core components: visual beauty and clarity, reliable information architecture, and pragmatism. Aesthetics was the first and most essential requirement; the consumer must enjoy using the service. An accessible and consistent information architecture that organized, structured and labeled content effectively was the backbone of the service, both in functionality and reducing friction. To cap it off, Aaron used his engineering knowledge to know what was possible to build and the resources and time required. There was no point in coming up with a design that was impractical or too resource-intensive. Design needed to be pragmatic.

The Mint design team set out to make something that was autoplay. "Turn it on and forget about it" was the guiding principle. Simplicity was a fundamental tenet for Mint. Customers were continuously asking for more features that would have risked making the product more complex. We ignored many of these requests to keep it simple for the majority of our users.

The Mint team also understood that the beautiful and emotional experience of Mint's design was crucial for the user. Countless hours were spent airbrushing design elements and choosing the right color scheme to get the feel of the service precisely right. The team emphasized the iconography for logins, which reinforced the secure nature of the page. This helped to convince users who might otherwise be skeptical of giving away their bank information for free to feel comfortable.

This is how Mint created a customer experience and community beyond the core functionality of the service: it was beautifully designed—from aesthetic, ease-of-use, a time-to-results perspectives—and it worked like no other. This was what Polverari and his ilk missed when they scoffed that Mint was just a pretty paint job on top of Yodlee. It was precisely because the banks that implemented Yodlee paid no attention to designing the user experience and making their service entirely for the user's benefit. Their aggregated personal finance offerings never held muster with consumers. Design was not in their DNA.

In their 2016 book *Org Design for Design Orgs*, Peter Merholz and Kristin Skinner start their first chapter with the title, "Why Design?

Why Now?"[37] The authors recount how 2009 was an uncertain time for both the economy and the technology sector after the global financial collapse. "That month [November 2009], a corporate acquisition occurred that has ripple effects to this day, though not in any way predicted at the time." They're talking about when Intuit paid $170 million to acquire Mint. According to the authors:

"Mint's innovation was a smooth and delightful experience on top of that technology, which created a passionate, active, and growing user base. In large part, Mint was acquired for its design, as that was the primary factor contributing to its desirable metrics."

The authors considered this to be a "lightbulb moment in Silicon Valley, along with the resurrection of Apple at the time." They noted that mergers and acquisitions for design firms and designer-led companies picked up the pace after 2010. That's when "every startup and tech company realized they needed a design competency to stay competitive." The Valley's design centricity then spread to more traditional tech stalwarts such as GE, which established the UX Center of Excellence, and IBM announced plans to hire one thousand designers over the next five years. Banks, too, jumped on the bandwagon, with Capital One and BBVA acquiring design firms. Management consultant firms swarmed in; Accenture acquired Fjord, and McKinsey acquired Lunar. All of this was preceded by the Valley's first-ever venture firm "designer in residence" role, when Bessemer Venture Partners announced it was bringing Jason Putorti, Mint's lead designer, in-house in December 2009.

And So What?

The proliferation of user-friendly design was far from Mint's only consequence. According to Mark Goines, Mint set off an avalanche in FinTech. There were no startup successes in financial technology for several years before Mint. The last was PayPal, acquired by eBay for $1.5 billion in August 2002, and everyone knew how tough it was for that company to achieve a breakthrough. Investors just didn't like the space.

---

37 Peter Merholz & Kristin Skinner. *Org Design for Design Orgs: Building and Managing In-House Design Teams*. O'Reilly. September 13. 2016.

Mint changed all that. Today, FinTech is ubiquitous, and the term is synonymous with innovation in financial services.

Ten years after Mint's launch, Matrix Partners created the Matrix FinTech Index in 2017. At the time, the top ten publicly traded US FinTech companies had just surpassed a total market capitalization of $100 billion. Twelve unicorns had emerged in the category, and the US VC industry had just poured in $6.7 billion—a record at the time. As we begin the new decade in 2020, this explosive growth has continued, with the total number of FinTech unicorns closing in on sixty and with VCs continuing to pour more than $16 billion into FinTech startups.

Among the more than ten thousand FinTech startups that have emerged, some among them, such as Stripe ($36 billion), Chime ($5.8 billion), and Robinhood ($8.3 billion), have blown past unicorn status. Everywhere you look, there is a disruption of traditional banking and financial services. For example, personal loans, a category popularized by FinTechs like GreenSky and Affirm, is now the fastest-growing form of debt in the US, according to Experian data. And Robinhood has sparked a movement toward free stock trading that has shaken the business models of the likes of Charles Schwab and E*Trade.

Not to be left out of the party, the hypergrowth monster tech companies—Facebook, Google, Apple, and Amazon—are all stepping up their FinTech ambitions. In 2019, Apple launched a credit card with Goldman Sachs, Alphabet announced a checking product with Citigroup, and Facebook attempted to make a new global currency.

Amazon, in particular, is offering many types of financial products and services, including Amazon Pay, Amazon Cash, Amazon Lending, and the Amazon prime card in partnership with Chase Bank. With these offerings and more in the pipeline, Amazon may be the new force in FinTech, perhaps more so than any other tech giant. Yet, Google, it seems, is not to be outdone. Towards the end of 2020, the company announced a massive relaunch of Google Pay, an all-encompassing money app. Google Pay will include tap to pay, peer-to-peer, personal finance aggregation, customizable deals, and even full banking services. Google's partnerships with retailers and its ability to offer its users targeted rewards based on their spending data is but one example of a new lucrative field of revenue Mint might have exploited by taking a clip of the retail spend that is driven from the reward incentive. For example, Mint could detect significant user spending on athleisure against which its partner Lululemon could offer future discounts to acquire a new user and increase its share of wallet. And it's easy to imagine Mint being first to implement that model at scale had it remained independent.

Where might Mint have ranked among these FinTech unicorns had we not sold to Intuit? Kopelman's view is that Mint was comparable to at least a combined version of Credit Karma, valued at more than $7 billion in February 2020, and Plaid, acquired by Visa for $5.3 billion in January 2020. Plaid is a modern-day account aggregation platform similar to Yodlee that links bank accounts to FinTech apps like Venmo, Robinhood, Coinbase, Betterment, and Acorns. Had Mint continued with Untangly, the world might never have heard of Plaid.

On February 24, 2020, *TechCrunch* ran a piece titled, "Intuit confirms that it is buying Credit Karma for $7.1 billion in cash and stock."[38] *TechCrunch* noted that Karma had more than 100 million registered users, 37 million were monthly active users and more than $1 billion in annual revenues. It was the largest acquisition in the company's history. At that time, Intuit had a market cap of over $77 billion, so they could afford the deal. Intuit's new CEO Sasan Goodarzi declared:

"We wake up every day trying to help consumers make ends meet. By joining forces with Credit Karma, we can create a personalized financial assistant that will help consumers find the right financial products, put more money in their pockets, and provide insights and advice, enabling them to buy the home they've always dreamed about, pay for education, and take the vacation they've always wanted."

Sound familiar?

It was as though Intuit didn't realize it already had this technology in-house from their Mint acquisition. But somehow, they'd squandered the opportunity to continue where Mint left off and build the audience and the revenue engine that Credit Karma was able to

---

38 Ingrid Lunden. "Intuit confirms that it is buying Credit Karma for $7.1B in cash and stock." *TechCrunch*. February 25, 2020.

develop independently over the years with the same business model as Mint developed based on lead generation. Intuit can now provide Credit Karma with TurboTax data and provide superior insight into a customer's income and ability to make loan payments—allowing it to improve its financial product recommendations. While Credit Karma could predict someone's eligibility for a personal loan using credit reports, credit worthiness is only 60 percent to 80 percent of the final approval decision. Other factors, like a customer's ability to repay the loan, are harder to estimate without more visibility into their personal finances—such as tax returns. Now with Intuit's TurboTax, Karma will be able to increase the loan qualification predictability to a much higher degree.

But in the end, might that be considered an $8 billion failure of execution by Intuit to deliver on its Mint acquisition? Should we add another $5 billion for Intuit's inability to turn its in-house account aggregation technology, since supplemented by integrating cutting edge Untangly technology, into a financial data services platform? Let history and the reader be the judge of that debate.

Tod Francis believed that Mint could have been at the forefront of most of what is happening in FinTech today. If he was right, might Mint have emerged to become a FinTech unicorn or even the Amazon for money? Perhaps this is what Kagle foresaw when he decided to check out of eBay and into Mint. But now we'll never know. Maybe, in the end, Mint will only be a footnote in the history of FinTech.

CHAPTER 41

THE VALLEY WAY

"There is freedom waiting for you, on the breezes of the sky, and you ask, what if I fall? Oh but darling what if you fly?"

ERIN HANSON

The Netscape IPO landed in August 1995 and announced a new era of technological innovation and wealth creation not seen since patent number 223,898 to Edison's electric lamp (the incandescent light bulb) was granted on January 27, 1880. Edison's invention set off another from one Nikola Tesla, a Serbian immigrant and former employee of Edison. Tesla was an engineer and scientist who designed the alternating-current (AC) electric system, which is the predominant electrical system used across the world today. Tesla went on to patent the Tesla coil, which laid the foundation for wireless technologies and is still used in radio technology. In 1926, Tesla predicted the internet and the smartphone in this way:

"When wireless is perfectly applied, the whole earth will be converted into a huge brain, which in fact, it is, all things being particles of a real and rhythmic whole. We shall be able to communicate with one another instantly, irrespective of distance. Not only this but through television and telephony, we shall see and hear one another as perfectly as though we were face to face, despite intervening distances of thousands of miles; and the instruments through which we shall be able to do this will be amazingly simple compared with our present telephone. A man will be able to carry one in his vest pocket."

Edison's laboratory, where Tesla first worked, was in Menlo Park, New Jersey. Fast forward over a century later to Menlo Park, California, and its Silicon Valley surroundings, where the venture capital industry has been busy over the last fifty plus years funding a new wave of hardware, software, and biotech inventors and visionaries.

But why here? What is it about Silicon Valley that incubates such technological innovation and wealth creation, the speed and scale of which is unprecedented in modern history? What is behind the gravitational pull and mystique that draws luminaries around the world away from their homes, secure careers, and well-laid plans to seek their fortunes in the San Francisco Bay area? That was the question I was pondering as I packed my life away and left a leading law firm in one of Paris's most stylish neighborhoods to join the fray in 1996.

What was the fuel and force behind the relentless cycle of industry-changing companies springing up, either failing or growing, then scaling rapidly and being acquired or going public, only to be disrupted by the next in line? What fostered the ingenuity, freedom, and access to capital needed for it all to happen so quickly? Those were the questions I tried to answer from the inside at Wilson Sonsini. The Valley's action, deals, and characters came streaming through our offices as I worked and observed with constant fascination. The answer to these questions was something I understood subconsciously, but I'm not sure I was fully aware of it until after the wake-up call at that round of dawn golf with Rob Claassen. What underlies the Valley's pull, the founding of revolutionary companies, the wheeling and dealing, the massive prices paid, and the even greater rewards reaped was one foundational concept: the appetite for risk and adventure. The need to break the status quo. The overwhelming desire to have an impact on an industry, and potentially to influence the way we work and live. This was no place to fear failure; indeed, failure was inevitable and something to embrace for the fantastic learning opportunity it provides. Failure was necessary for progress, advancement, innovation, and revolution. As Edison declared, "I have not failed. I've just found 10,000 ways that won't work."

Spend enough time watching the whirlwind machinations of the Valley up close, and you realize that this is what is different about this environment. The willingness to take a chance and fail, to be the 1 percent of startups that make it big is what drives bright minds like Aaron to risk their life savings to take a chance at revolutionizing an industry. The understanding that you cannot win big without swinging and missing most often is what drives the big venture capital bets—and exorbitant fortunes—like Kagle's win on eBay.

And if you spend enough time within it, you come to embody that appetite for risk and acceptance of failure yourself. It's why I left a secure, lucrative career in law to get in the startup game. It's why I left my pre-Mint startup in 2006 when I saw myself stagnating. It's why I worked hard for Aaron when I saw potential even though he couldn't pay me. And it's why I left a pile of money on the table to leave Intuit when I felt I was going through the corporate motions. From the outside, risks like those look crazy. But it's those with an inherent appetite for risk and a willingness to embrace failure that are drawn to the Valley, which fosters their appetite. Finding the edge is the only way forward. As basketball great Michael Jordan put it: "I've missed more than nine hundred shots in my career. I've lost almost three hundred games. Twenty-six times, I've been trusted to take the game-winning shot and missed. I've failed over and over again in my life. And that is why I succeed."

Ironically, it was that notion of risk that defined both the start and the end of Mint as an independent company. Did we let the fear of failure in going it alone overcome enormous potential? Should we have doubled down on the risk we took to start the company that led to our initial success and rejected Intuit's sweet deal? If we had kicked on, might Mint have become the first FinTech unicorn since PayPal, and possibly the Amazon of money?

These are good questions for endless debate. I know that we did have an impact on the financial services and broader technology industry that lingers to this day, and that the product is still being used by millions to improve their financial lives. And thanks to those millions of users who put trust in our service, to the investors who backed us to win that trust against the odds, and to the Mint crew who steered the ship at breakneck speeds through all kinds of seas and weather. The Mint journey was nothing short of an adventure, and my life is better for it. Mint was a once-in-a-lifetime journey where the stars aligned at the right time in the right place for the right people, the likes of which may never be repeated for those involved. That's an experience to seize and to cherish and not to let pass for fear of failure that can only lead to regret. I would encourage anyone anywhere in the world who is thinking of embarking on their own entrepreneurial adventure to think first, calculate the risk, fear not of failure, and then take the leap if it feels right for you. You'll never learn what you're capable of until you try. Ultimately, your rewards, both in terms of personal development and financial freedom, will be measured by the risks you take and the learning and skills you develop on your journey.

EPILOGUE

THE PLAYERS— WHERE ARE THEY NOW?

Several months after my farewell dinner, I learned that our submission of the Personal Finance Savings Advisor had won the Scott Cook Innovation Award. Each team member that I included would be heading off on an all-expenses-paid trip to somewhere exotic as the prize. I was delighted for them and proud of that achievement as my last hurrah and as the closing chapter on my time with Intuit.

The curtain had closed on my time at Intuit. I wasn't the first to leave, and I was far from the last.

The first to leave Mint after the Intuit acquisition was Donna. She spent time at Intuit earlier in her career and had no desire to return there. As Mint's CMO, responsible for record growth in customer acquisition and for orchestrating Mint's phenomenal PR run, Donna's reputation in the Valley was at its zenith. She became the CEO of Mindflash Technologies, an early leader in online training for businesses. She retired from that role in 2017. Donna now spends some time on a handful of boards and as a management lecturer at the Stanford University Graduate School of Business. She still lives in Portola Valley.

After leaving Intuit in July 2010, Matt Snider became cofounder and CTO of Votizen, a platform for connecting the social networks of registered voters to empower them to take back their government. Matt is now a husband and father of two. He lives with his family in Sunnyvale and works for none other than Google as a Staff Engineer—Tech Leadsenior engineer.

Poornima Vijayashanker left Mint in January 2010 to found Bizeebee, a CRM solution for small businesses in the fitness space. Poornima is also the founder of Femgineer, an organization focused on educating and empowering tech professionals to level-up in their careers while building products and companies. Poornima is a featured speaker and author on the tech circuit. She has published two books: *How to Transform Your Ideas into Software Products,* and *Present! A Techie's Guide to Public Speaking*. Poornima also hosts and co-produces a weekly web show called Build. She is married and lives in Palo Alto.

Noah Kagan paved his way with pure hustle and chutzpah to become Chief Sumo at the Sumo Group (Sumo.com/AppSumo.com), which, as only Noah could put it, "helps entrepreneurs kick more ass." Noah hosts a podcast for entrepreneurs called Noah Kagan Presents, where he interviews guests who are top performers in all industries. Noah still sports his Facebook profile photo sideways, lest he ever forgets the lessons of his failures.

Jason Putorti skipped Intuit to join Bessemer Ventures as a designer-in-residence, pioneering a new role at a venture firm. He then cofounded Votizen with Matt Snider and later cofounded Brigade.com, a civic technology platform. Eventually, Jason left the Valley for fresh pastures in Tampa St. Petersburg, Florida. He's now the executive director of Resistbot, an all-volunteer non-profit dedicated to civic engagement year-round and delivering the people's will to their elected officials. The Resistbot service enables people in the US to compose and send letters to elected officials from the messaging apps on their mobile phones. Resistbot is an all-volunteer non-profit dedicated to civic engagement year-round and delivering the people's will to their elected officials.

Atish Mehta's Linkedin profile declares that he's a former Silicon Valley engineer turned full-time DJ/producer/record label guy. He did quit his day job! Atish left Intuit for Facebook in August 2010, ahead of Facebook's IPO in 2012. He left Facebook in 2015. His timing was impeccable, with two superb exits in less than three years. These days Atish lives in New York and is married. He still does the clubs with his pulsating techno music as DJ Atish. He's also branched out as a co-owner of Manjusami, a San Francisco-based underground dance music label featuring artists from home and worldwide.

Sid Bhatt left Intuit in 2010 to cofound and lead Aarki, a mobile app marketing platform that's now a global and profitable business. Sid is married and lives close to his former apartment at Mint's offices in Mountain View. These days his Amazon packages are going to his real home.

Justin Maxwell left Intuit in early 2011 to become the director of user experience and game design at Smule. Justin was then lured to Google to create a Mint-like experience for Google Wallet, which became another one of many Google projects that fell by the wayside. These days Justin is the cofounder and chief design officer of Smith.ai, a company that helps businesses qualify leads and triage incoming phone and chat communications. Justin and his spouse Cynthia live in Portola Valley with their children.

David Michaels stayed at Intuit for another year after I left, completing Mint's behind-the-scenes transition from Yodlee to Intuit's account aggregation capability. David was the first vice president at Mint and the founder of Mint's security and scalability architecture. With the public recognition of having built a secure and popular Internet-scale application, I thought that David's resume would enable him to start his own VC-backed company, a typical Silicon Valley next-step. However, he took a different path. There has been public mention of only a few advisor positions and angel investments that he has made since leaving Intuit. Rumor has it that David engineered an algorithmic stock trading system and spends his days applying machine learning to different problems in finance.

Aaron Forth took over the reins from Aaron Patzer and became vice president and general manager of Mint and the Personal Finance Group at Intuit in June 2011. A4 lasted in this role for fifteen months before joining Strava as its chief growth officer. These days, A4 is the chief product officer at Newfront Insurance, a modern FinTech company whose mission is to build a better insurance brokerage. He lives in San Francisco with his wife and three children.

In 2012, Jean Sini left Intuit to join One Kings Lane, a home decor e-commerce business, as its chief product and technology officer. Jean later joined Aaron Patzer as a cofounder and the CTO of Fountain. This micro-consulting marketplace allowed users to ask questions to experts through mobile video, voice, and text. Home services company Porch.com acquired Fountain for an undisclosed price in October 2015. Jean became a steady angel investor over the years and now spends his time flitting between New York and San Francisco as a new partner at Partech, a global venture capital firm.

Martha Shaughnessy left her role as a Grayling PR managing director to found her own PR agency, The Key, in January 2017. The Key is a boutique shop on a mission to serve high-impact, low-bullshit communications services to clients. Now married with two kids, Martha remains politically active and is a core part of the leadership of the Women's March San Francisco.

Aaron Patzer transitioned out of the Personal Finance Group at Intuit. Aaron became the VP of product innovation at Intuit in June 2011, working part-time while remaining at large. Aaron's major accomplishment was the redesign of QuickBooks online, which has since seen accelerated growth worth hundreds of millions in revenue. Aaron, true to his word, tried his hand at his alternative transportation project under a company called Swift. After months of research and coding, he determined that the personal maglev system he envisioned was not economically viable. These days, Aaron is living in Auckland, New Zealand, and is back at the helm of a startup as a cofounder and CEO of Vital Software, which develops modern emergency department software for patients and providers. The company uses artificial intelligence to significantly reduce wait times, identify high-risk patients, and predict admit hours before they occur.

When Aaron founded Mint.com, the Great Recession struck the world, and Mint found its sweet spot. Now with Vital Software, at the time of writing, Aaron's new healthcare company is well-positioned for growth in the face of a global COVID-19 pandemic. Martha jokes with Aaron that he's mediocre in regular times, but in times of crisis (first financial and then in healthcare), he excels.

As for Aaron's relationship with Rebecca, it turned out to be real love, and they did stay together for more than ten years. They ended up choosing to go their separate ways with Aaron now leading his new healthcare venture and Rebecca focused on undoubtedly becoming a great architect as she completes a post-professional Master of Architecture degree at Yale University.

After leaving Intuit, I eventually founded Avencia to provide go-to-market consulting services to technology companies, focusing on foreign entrepreneurs who founded their startups outside the United States. My vision was that in the near future, world-class technology companies would be started more readily outside the Valley in almost any country as the Valley's culture was exported around the globe. I bet that these foreign founders would seek market entry in the U.S. and Valley know-how on their path to global expansion and that I could help them on this journey as they inevitably passed through the Valley. In this capacity, Apple chose me as an advisor to select international developer partners in Apple's Worldwide Mobility Partner Program as part of Apple's strategy to foster #iOSinBusiness. Similarly, the Australian Government's Innovation Program selected me to advise on launching technology startups in the U.S. I also became a regular mentor with Endeavor.org, the leading high-impact entrepreneurship movement around the world. I've traveled to Latin America, China, Europe, Australia, and many other countries to speak at technology events and advise local entrepreneurs on finding go-to-market fit and scaling. While continuing to enjoy occasional investing and advising in the startup world, these days, I'm more focused on exploring my creativity as a jazz composer, pianist, and vocalist. I've just released my first jazz album titled "On a Brighter Note." And there are many more albums to come in the years ahead. Oh, and I wrote a book along the way—this one that you're reading.

As for Mint, without its founding team at the helm, nothing much else has changed over the past decade. With so much potential as an expansive service, Goals did not progress, and Advice-as-a service seems to have practically disappeared, perhaps to make way for a paid premium service on the Mint app to get advice from live experts for $14.99 per month. So much for "beyond user pays." Mint became more of a mobile service than a web service, to be sure. Mint did go on to integrate a free credit score and freemium package to a credit monitoring service. This was significant, but by the time of implementation, so many other similar services were available online for free. Credit Karma led the pack of free credit score and monitoring sites, and Mint lost its early mover advantage in this arena. Mint also released a bill pay service in 2014 after Intuit acquired another of Mint's competitors, PageOnce, which then became Check, but was shuttered in 2018. I felt a tinge of validation at the news since I'd forcefully rejected the idea of bill pay in our early days.

Today, Intuit mentions Mint as a core product alongside it's other two leading products, Quickbooks and TurboTax, but its brand rank is undoubtedly higher than its business rank. Mint barely rates a question or a mention in Intuit's quarterly and annual earnings reports to Wall Street. We do know that more than twenty million consumers have used Mint since its launch in late 2007, which is more than ever used Quicken across its thirty-plus-year history. Mint remains the most recognized online brand in personal finance, though for how long remains to be seen.

In January of 2020, *Fast Company* ran an article titled, "What the hell happened to Mint?"[39] The report concluded that Intuit had let its $170 million acquisition wither on the vine. The author was frustrated because he couldn't access his investments on Mint. After all, Intuit had failed to wean itself off Adobe's Flash player, which was required for the investment graphs to render. According to the article, Mint was now "a fossilized financial tool" and an app that "exhibits severe symptoms of neglect." Many transactions were not cleansed of extraneous data from the raw bank feed, and categorization accuracy was in decline.

---

39 Rob Pegararo. "What the hell happened to Mint?" *Fastcompany*. January 23, 2020.

And perhaps the most significant missed opportunity was the inability to merge Mint and TurboTax accounts to avoid a problematic import/export ordeal for users every spring in tax season.

Aaron's quote mentioned that he thought Mint had been in maintenance mode for the last eight years. In its 2019 fiscal year, Intuit's Consumer Group (Mint and TurboTax) generated $2.775 billion in revenue versus $3.533 billion for its small business and self-employed division, which is dominated by its QuickBooks accounting software. But Mint has been left out of prepared remarks for the company's last several quarterly earnings calls. The article concludes that for all of Mint's failure to evolve and improve, its core functionality—putting your accounts in one free and easily scanned dashboard—continues to be fundamentally useful. It's not for lack of competition that Intuit remains stuck in apathy, but thus far, those competitive efforts, including such mobile apps as Albert and Charlie, have not broken through to disrupt the core Mint service. Perhaps a former Minter, Val Agostino, might have the secret formula with his new personal finance venture, Monarch Money.

Although Yodlee lost Mint's high-growth business after the Intuit acquisition, Mint proved to be a showcase to their technology platform such that in 2010, Yodlee partnered with Y Combinator, providing its financial services platform to all Y Combinator-funded companies. I was personally flooded by calls from various startups seeking my advice on how to get the best deal from Yodlee. On October 3, 2014, Yodlee went public on NASDAQ, trading under the symbol YDLE. In August 2015, Envestnet acquired Yodlee for a reported $660 million.

And what of Quicken? In the fall of 2015, Intuit announced that it would divest itself of Quicken to focus on its core tax and accounting businesses. Today, Quicken operates as a standalone company. You can buy their most popular plan, the Deluxe package, for only $29.99 per year. Notwithstanding the Valley's penchant for disruption, it seems some things never change.

www.ingramcontent.com/pod-product-compliance
Lightning Source LLC
Chambersburg PA
CBHW052341220526
45465CB00003BA/905